P9-BTN-838

Fifty Animals

that Changed the Course of

History

A Firefly Book

Published by Firefly Books Ltd. 2011

Publisher Cataloging-in-Publication Data (U.S.)

Chaline, Eric.
Fifty animals that changed the course of history / Eric Chaline.
[224] p. : col. ill., photos. ; cm.
Includes bibliographical references and index.
Summary: Guide to animals that have had the greatest impact on human
civilization; each is selected based upon its influence on agriculture, disease,
trade, transportation, or clothing.
ISBN-13: 978-1-55407-897-4
1. Animals and civilization. 2. Animals and history. I. Title.
590 dc22   QL85C546   2011

Library and Archives Canada Cataloguing in Publication

Chaline, Eric
Fifty animals that changed the course of history / Eric Chaline.
Includes index.
ISBN 978-1-55407-897-4
1. Animals and civilization. 2. Animals and history.
3. Human-animal relationships--History. I. Title.
QL85.C43 2011   590   C2011-902229-X

Published in the United States by
Firefly Books (U.S.) Inc.
P.O. Box 1338, Ellicott Station
Buffalo, New York 14205

Published in Canada by
Firefly Books Ltd.
66 Leek Crescent
Richmond Hill, Ontario L4B 1H1

Conceived, designed and produced by Quid Publishing
Level 4, Sheridan House
114 Western Road
Hove BN3 1DD
England

Designed by Lindsey Johns
Printed in China

Fifty Animals

that Changed the Course of

History

written by Eric Chaline

FIREFLY BOOKS

Contents

Introduction

Man is the only creature that consumes without producing. He does not give milk, he does not lay eggs, he is too weak to pull the plough, he cannot run fast enough to catch rabbits. Yet he is lord of all the animals.

George Orwell, Animal Farm *(1945)*

Humans have developed close relationships with many animal species in the past 20,000 years, changing both themselves and animals in the process. Once predators, humans became herdsmen and harvesters caring for and protecting the animals they once hunted.

DOMINION OVER EVERY LIVING THING

The traditional Judeo-Christian understanding of man's relationship with the animal kingdom is summed up by Genesis 1:28, when God, having created Adam and Eve, told them: "Be fruitful, and multiply, and replenish the earth, and subdue it: and have dominion over the fish of the sea, and over the fowl of the air, and over every living thing that moveth upon the earth." For millennia, this belief gave humans the god-given right to exploit, exterminate, or transform the animals around them at will without a thought to the consequences to the wider environment. For several species, like the American buffalo (pp. 22–5) or the dodo (pp. 182–3), this meant near or actual extinction, whereas others have thrived alongside humans, playing their part in the development of human civilization.

For tens of thousands of years, *Homo sapiens* (pp. 210–7) lived in small bands of hunter-gatherers, migrating with the seasons and following the animal species they predated in order to survive. In this they were not unlike wolves (pp. 44–7), which were the first animals to be domesticated, and who in turn gave rise, over generations of selective breeding, to the domestic dog (pp. 48–51). Once humans realized that animals could have just as much or more value to them alive than as mere ambulatory sources of meat and fur, the human–animal relationship changed forever: The predator became a herdsman. The herbivores humans had preyed on now provided humans with much more than meat. The cow (pp. 34–9) and goat (pp. 52–5)

EXTINCT
Although not the first species to be driven to extinction by humans, the dodo is their most iconic victim.

gave milk; the sheep (pp. 142–7) and llama (pp. 116–119), wool; the horse (pp. 76–81), donkey (pp. 72–5), and camel (pp. 40–43), their strength and endurance.

Status symbols

Liberated from the constant search for food, humans were able to establish permanent settlements that grew into the first cities, and with them appeared the refinements of civilization: art and ornamentation. Humans turned again to the animal kingdom to find

new materials, such as silk (see Silkworm, pp. 28–33), and dyes and pigments to bring color into their world (see Spiny Dye-Murex, pp. 26–7, and Cochineal, pp. 66–7). These products were used to set apart the rich and powerful from the ordinary citizens, and also became the basis for an international trade that brought distant cultures together for the first time. However, large concentrations of humans also attracted less welcome animal visitors, such as the rat (pp. 184–7) and the feral pigeon (pp. 62–3). Humans are not always the dominant species in the animal kingdom—some of its smallest members, such as the louse (pp. 158–161), can cause discomfort or illness, or, like the malarial mosquito (pp. 8–11) and the flea (pp. 204–209), have been the cause of worldwide pandemics.

In addition to their role in trade and agriculture, animals have contributed in several other ways to human culture and history. Certain animals, such as the lion (pp. 152–7), the scarab beetle (pp. 188–191), the cobra (pp. 134–7), and the bald eagle (pp. 100–103), have had a long history as religious and political symbols. In the fields of science and medicine, the study of animals, such as the fruit fly (pp. 68–71), the finch (pp. 96–9), and the iguanodon (pp. 110–5), has been instrumental in the development of our understanding of the evolution of the natural world.

Often taken for granted, the produce and work of animals have not only met our basic needs of food and clothing; they have relieved us of the burden of survival, allowing us to develop the rich succession of human civilizations. Without animals, human history would be much poorer and our future, as we may one day discover, may be much shorter.

CHANGED LANDSCAPE
Through the domestication of large herbivorous species, humans have transformed the natural landscape.

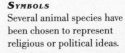

SYMBOLS
Several animal species have been chosen to represent religious or political ideas.

Mosquito

Anopheles gambiae

Native range: Sub-Saharan Africa

Class: Insect

Size: Up to 0.6 in (16 mm)

✦ Edible

✦ *MEDICINAL*

✦ Commercial

✦ Practical

For the people of the developed world, the mosquito is at worst an annoying summer pest, but for many in the developing countries of sub-Saharan Africa, *Anopheles gambiae* is a deadly harbinger of a disease that is responsible for the deaths of almost a million people every year.

TROPICAL VAMPIRE

Folklore is full of bloodsucking, flesh-eating monsters—vampires, ghouls, ogres, and werewolves—which feed on humans as they sleep. And though there are species of vampire bat in South America that will occasionally take human blood when animal blood is not available, the most common creatures that feed on humans are insects: fleas, ticks, midges, sandflies, lice, and the subject of this entry, mosquitoes. The English word "mosquito" is derived from a diminutive of the Spanish word for "fly," *mosca*, and translates as "little fly." There are some 3,500 species of mosquito distributed around the globe, spanning the equatorial, tropical, and temperate zones. The only places on Earth you're never likely to be troubled by the annoying nighttime buzz of this airborne pest are in the Arctic and Antarctic regions.

The mosquito is a prehistoric creature. It is a member of the huge insect class that evolved 400 million years ago, 100 million years before the reptiles and 200 million years before the mammals. The oldest specimen of a mosquito found that is anatomically similar to members of modern species was discovered preserved in Canadian amber dating back 79 million years ago. This means that until it came to its sticky end, our feisty friend was feasting on the blood of dinosaurs 75 million years before the earliest species of the genus *Homo*. An older but more primitive mosquitolike specimen, also found preserved in amber, dates back 100 million years.

The mosquito has a place in this book not because it can make the summer vacations of the unwary or unprepared a misery, but because it is a killer that has contributed to the deaths of millions of humans and animals over the centuries. Several species of mosquito are carriers of deadly diseases, including yellow fever, dengue fever, Chikungunya, and malaria. In 1900, mosquito-borne malaria killed three million people worldwide, including 80,000 in Europe and North America. In addition to the human and animal death toll, the disease had a huge socioeconomic impact in areas where it was endemic, stifling economic development, investment, and agriculture. Thankfully, the annual death toll from malaria has been reduced to less than one million, as the disease has now been eradicated from the developed world and many parts of Asia and Latin America. However, it remains endemic in sub-Saharan Africa, where malaria still claims some 850,000 victims, many of whom are children.

The *Anopheles* mosquito is responsible for the human and animal malarial infections in the regions where the disease remains endemic. The name *Anopheles* is a compound made up of two Greek words: *an*, meaning "without" or "not," and *opheles*, meaning "use" or "profit," the whole meaning "useless" or "profitless." There are 460 recognized species within the genus *Anopheles*, of which about 50 can transmit different forms of the malaria parasite. While several *Anopheles* species prefer animal hosts, others feed indiscriminately on both humans and animals. *Anopheles gambiae*, which carries the most dangerous and often fatal malaria parasite, *Plasmodium falciparum*, prefers to feed on human blood, and is thus one of the most efficient animal vectors of the disease.

DEADLIER THAN THE MALE

Like many other insects, *Anopheles gambiae* has a four-stage lifecycle consisting of egg, larva, pupa, and adult, which it completes in one-and-a-half to three weeks depending on humidity and temperature. The female lays a batch of 50–200 raft-shaped eggs on the surface of still, unpolluted water. In favorable conditions, the eggs hatch into larvae after two or three days, though hatching can take much longer in cooler climates. The larvae live on the surface of the water feeding on bacteria and algae and only submerge when disturbed. They do not have the ability to

FEVER PITCH
An ad for a malaria cure c. 1881—a reminder of the disease's impact in the U.S. in the past.

WATER BABY
The mosquito that spends its adult life living and feeding on land has a semi-aquatic larval stage.

extract oxygen from water like fish or true aquatic invertebrates so they spend most of their time on or close to the surface. Over a period of a week, the larvae shed their skins four times, growing in length from 0.04 in (1 mm) to between 0.2–0.3 in (5–8 mm) after the final molt. Once fully grown, the larva metamorphoses into an aquatic pupa, which splits open after two or three days to allow the emergence of the adult mosquito. The young adult *Anopheles* emerges at dusk and is capable of flight within minutes.

The body of the adult *Anopheles* is divided into the head, thorax, and abdomen. The head carries the eyes, a long pair of antennae with which it can detect food sources, breeding sites, and human hosts, the feeding tube known as the proboscis, and two long sensory feelers called palps; the thorax carries three pairs of legs and the wings; and the large, segmented abdominal region specializes in food digestion and reproduction. The adult *Anopheles* feeds on flower nectar and juice from fruit, and can survive perfectly well on this vegetarian diet. The male never takes a blood meal. It is only the female that requires blood, not to sustain her own life, but to acquire the necessary nutrients to grow eggs. Mating takes place when the males swarm at dusk and the females fly into their midst. Once she has mated, the *Anopheles* female will seek a blood meal from a human host. After feeding she will seek out a resting place where she will digest the blood, and begin to produce eggs. These will be ready for laying after about two or three days. Adult mosquitoes can survive up to two weeks in natural conditions, depending on the weather and the availability of food.

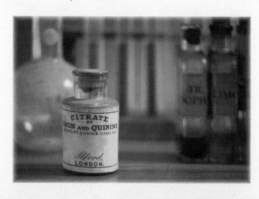

TREE OF LIFE
The first effective treatment for malaria, quinine (shown center right), was first isolated in the nineteenth century from the bark of the cinchona tree (shown far right).

FIRE IN THE BLOOD

The malaria parasite *Plasmodium falciparum* is the most common cause of the disease in sub-Saharan Africa, where it is responsible for about 80 percent of all malaria cases and about 90 percent of fatalities. The adult *Anopheles* will ingest the malaria parasite when it feeds on the blood of an infected human. The parasite, while it causes disease in a human host, does not harm its insect carrier. Once inside the mosquito, the parasite will complete the first stage of its lifecycle, producing sporozoites that migrate from the mosquito's gut to its salivary glands. The malaria parasites are injected into the skin of the human host along with the saliva, enter the bloodstream, and migrate to the liver. They infect the liver cells, where they multiply, rupture the cells, and escape into the bloodstream. There the parasites infect red blood cells, where they multiply and also produce gametocytes that will infect a mosquito taking a blood meal, and so continuing the cycle of infection from human to mosquito and back to human.

Mosquitoes are not indiscriminate in their choice of victims. They possess an extremely acute sense of smell through multiple receptors on their long antennae. They are more attracted to people with a certain type of sweat (anecdotally, it is believed that they are particularly attracted to smelly feet). Although all *Anopheles* species hunt at dusk or at night, their preferred resting and feeding place varies—some prefer the interiors of buildings, while other remain outside. Understanding where the mosquitoes can be found plays an important role in controlling malaria infections. Measures against those inside of houses include spraying with insecticides and sleeping in mosquito nets, while screening doors and windows prevents the entry of mosquitoes from outside. Effective prophylaxis and treatments for malaria have existed since the seventeenth century (see box), but these are not available in the poorest regions of sub-Saharan Africa, where children are at the greatest risk from the disease and among its most numerous victims. Despite strenuous efforts to eradicate malaria in sub-Saharan Africa, it remains one of the major avoidable causes of death in the world.

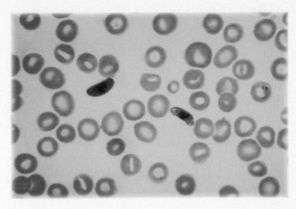

INFECTED
The darker sausage-shaped bodies among the rounded red blood cells are malarial parasites at the breeding stage.

The mosquito knows full well that he is small, he is a beast of prey.
D. H. Lawrence (1885–1930)

Honeybee

Apis mellifera

Native range: Europe, Near East, and Asia

Class: Insect

Size: 0.4–0.6 in (12–16 mm)

+ EDIBLE
+ *MEDICINAL*
+ *COMMERCIAL*
+ *PRACTICAL*

The importance of the honeybee is not only based on its production of honey and beeswax, but also because it plays a vital role in the pollination of many commercial plant species. The appearance of Colony Collapse Disorder has raised the specter of crop failures on a worldwide scale.

MODEL SOCIETY

Many insects are solitary and will not hesitate to predate on members of their own species, even sometimes eating their own young. But the honeybee lives in large, well-ordered colonies, which if taken to the human scale would be small- to medium-sized towns. A colony consists of between 40,000 and 100,000 individuals, divided into three castes: a single fertile queen, infertile female workers, and male drones, each devoted to the good of the colony in a way that would make the average Communist dictatorship green with envy. In folklore, the honeybee colony is an exemplar of perfect social order, cooperation, and hard work. But this ideal insect society is not an association of free individuals who have agreed to live and work together out of enlightened self-interest. From the queen down, the members of the colony are slaves whose lives are forfeited as soon as they are no longer able to fulfill their roles.

Morphologically, the honeybee is similar to other insects, with a head, thorax, and abdomen, but with added anatomical refinements that have evolved to enable it to exploit its ecological niche. The worker bee has a pollen basket, or corbicula, on the rear pair of its six legs. The corbicula is a smooth, hollow depression surrounded by a fringe of pinlike hairs. When the bee is foraging for food, it collects the dustlike pollen over its head and body. It uses its forelegs to brush the pollen toward its hind legs,

I'd like to be a busy little bee,
Being just as busy as a bee can be,
Flying around the garden
Brightest ever seen,
Taking back the honey
To the dear old queen.

The Bee Song (1938)

where it mixes the pollen with nectar to make it more malleable and compresses it into a ball that it spears onto one of the hairs around the corbicula. In this way, a bee can carry a large load of pollen safely back to the colony. The honeybee has a second stomach in which it transports nectar to the colony, where workers collect it to make honey or feed the brood. Several glands located on the abdomen secrete small clear wax scales, which are softened by chewing and used to build the wax cells for egg laying and for the storage of honey and pollen.

DRY STORES
Bees collect flower pollen, which is either made into honey or stored dry in the hive for future use.

Another bee-specific adaptation is the stinger, which bees use to defend themselves against intruders. For infertile female worker bees, the stinger is a modified ovipositor (egg-laying tube). The stinger is barbed and when the bee stings the thick, elastic skin of a mammal, the stinger and its attached poison sac and musculature is pulled out of the bee's body. This will kill the bee within minutes but will also ensure the delivery of the poison because the musculature continues to work even after it is detached. The larger male honeybees, or drones, do not have an ovipositor, and therefore cannot sting. The queen is the only bee in a colony with an unbarbed stinger, which means that she can sting repeatedly without sacrificing her own life.

What differentiates the honeybee from solitary bees and insects, however, are the social adaptations that the honeybee has evolved over several million years to enable thousands of individuals to function as a single unit. These include strict role differentiation and sophisticated methods of communication: between the queen and the workers through chemical signals; and between worker bees through the famous bee "dance," by which they can tell other workers the exact location of food sources. During warm weather, the workers will use their wings to cool the colony; in cooler periods, they will congregate to maintain a constant temperature around the queen and brood.

The only fertile female in a colony is the queen, whose lifelong role is to lay eggs in the individually

STINGERS
✦
Starting in 1990, the media warned that Africanized honeybees would swarm into the U.S. bringing death and destruction. Although more fierce than ordinary bees, "killer bees" account for only one or two deaths a year.

crafted wax cells built by the worker bees. She will only leave the colony on two occasions: in her nuptial flight, when she will mate with as many drones as possible, storing their sperm in an internal sac to be used during her reign to sire her thousands of offspring; or, if the colony becomes too large, the queen may form a swarm and leave the colony with half of the workers, leaving the original colony to a younger successor. This is the only occasion when there is a bloodless, uncontested succession. A healthy queen can live up to three or four years, but once she begins to weaken, her daughters will kill her and raise several princesses to succeed her. They feed the fledgling queens on a superfood known as "royal jelly" that accelerates their development from the typical 21 days to 15 and ensures that their sexual organs fully develop. The first queen to hatch will kill any unborn rivals, but if two queens hatch at the same time, they will fight to the death.

The winner will set off for her nuptial flight, and then return to the colony, where she will begin to lay eggs. After a few days, the eggs will

SINGLE USE
Early designs, such as these medieval straw hives, could be harvested only once.

hatch into larvae that are fed on royal jelly for the first three days. Unless they are destined to be queens, the larvae are then fed on a diet of honey, pollen, and nectar for another seven days, after which time they are sealed up in their cells, where the larvae will spend seven to eight days as pupae, undergoing the process of metamorphosis into an adult bee. They emerge as fully grown workers and immediately embark on a lifetime of service to the colony.

In the first three days of their lives, worker bees clean cells and keep the newly laid eggs warm; for the next three days, they will take care of and feed older larvae, before spending six to ten days as the nurses of newly hatched larvae. Days eight to 16 are spent receiving pollen and nectar from forager bees to store in honeycombs; during this time they will build

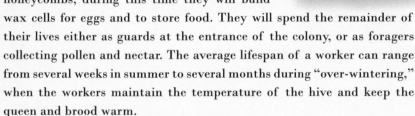

FOOD OF THE GODS
This representation of an ancient Greek bee goddess attests to the importance of honey to ancient cultures.

wax cells for eggs and to store food. They will spend the remainder of their lives either as guards at the entrance of the colony, or as foragers collecting pollen and nectar. The average lifespan of a worker can range from several weeks in summer to several months during "over-wintering," when the workers maintain the temperature of the hive and keep the queen and brood warm.

The male drones have the longest maturation of all honeybees— around 24 days from egg to its emergence as an adult. Drones do not look after larvae or forage for food; their only function is to mate with the queen. The effort of mating is so great that they will die immediately after their nuptial flight. Unmated drones that have outlived their usefulness will be expelled from the colony before the winter. As they cannot forage or feed themselves, they will quickly die of cold or starvation, or fall victim to predators against which they have no defense.

GOLDEN HARVEST

The honeybee has a long association with humans. Before refined sugar was introduced to Europe from the Near East during the Middle Ages, one of the few sweetening agents available to flavor food was honey. Since prehistoric times, hunter-gatherers have raided wild bee colonies to collect honey, and the large-scale keeping of domesticated bees, known as "apiculture," is evident in many ancient cultures, including Egypt, China, Greece, Crete, Israel, and the Roman Empire. Evidence from documents, frescoes, and bas-reliefs show that beekeeping was a high-status profession, reflecting the value of the products obtained from honeybees. Like today, honey was eaten in its natural unprocessed state

SMOKING

In modern beekeeping,
smoke is used to pacify the
bees, and hives with movable
frames allow harvesting
without damaging the
brood or colony.

and used for cooking. Honey was also fermented into an alcoholic beverage known as mead, particularly in colder areas where wine grapes could not be grown.

Honey has many medical uses. It is still found in many cough and cold remedies, and the antiseptic and antibacterial properties that have long made it useful as a dressing to prevent the infection of wounds has recently been applied to the treatment of hospital "superbugs" such as MRSA. Another much sought-after product of honeybee colonies is beeswax, which has had many important domestic and industrial uses since ancient times. Wax was made into candles, and beeswax candles are still preferred in the Greek Orthodox Church. In Roman times, a thin coat of wax was applied to wooden tablets, which was then used as a reusable writing surface. Molten-wax seals are still used in some countries on official documents, proving their authenticity. Beeswax also played a vital role in the development of early metallurgy, as it was used in the lost-wax casting process; it was also used as a waterproofing agent for clothing, and in building and shipbuilding.

**Obedience: for so work the honey-bees,
Creatures that by a rule in nature teach
The act of order to a peopled kingdom.**

Henry V *(1599) by William Shakespeare*

Until the late eighteenth century, domesticated bees were kept in straw hives know as "skeps," hollowed-out trees, or large ceramic jars. Because this type of hive could not be opened or dismantled when the honey and wax were harvested, they were broken apart, killing the eggs and larvae, and effectively destroying the colony. This was an extremely inefficient and wasteful form of apiculture, but it was only in the eighteenth and nineteenth centuries that naturalists and beekeepers produced new designs for hives that would obviate the need to destroy the colony to harvest wax and honey.

The American apiculturist Lorenzo Langstroth (1810–95) created the first modern beehive design. He understood the practical application of the earlier discovery of "bee space"—the specific gap between wax combs that bees retain as a free passage. Having determined this to be between 0.2 and 0.3 in (5–8 mm), Langstroth designed a rectangular wooden hive equipped with removable frames that he carefully separated to preserve the all-important bee space. He found that the bees would build parallel honeycombs in the hive without bonding them to each other or to the walls. This enabled the beekeeper to slide out the frames to inspect them without harming the bees or damaging the honeycombs, and protecting the eggs, larvae, and pupae. The major advantage was that the honey and wax could be harvested without destroying the colony.

In the present day, though honey remains an important cooking ingredient and comestible in its own right, the most important role for honeybees is as a pollinator for commercial food crops. The largest managed pollination takes place in the Californian almond orchards every spring, when around one million beehives are trucked to the state from all over the U.S. Other important fruit crops that require the large-scale use of honeybees for pollination include the New York apple and the Maine blueberry crops. Bees are also important copollinators for many other crops in Europe and North America, including cucumbers, melons, strawberries, and squash. The growing incidence of Colony Collapse Disorder (see box, right) has raised the specter of a major crisis in world agriculture, because a sudden decline in honeybee numbers would not be compensated for by other insect pollinators.

MARY CELESTE COLONIES

✦

The past few years have seen growing instances of Colony Collapse Disorder (CCD) worldwide. CCD's alternative name, the "Mary Celeste" phenomenon, named for the ship that was found adrift without its captain and crew, describes a situation in which the colony is found with very few or no worker bees, although there are unhatched brood sealed inside their wax cells, and the queen is still present. The disorder is still poorly understood, and several factors have been put forward to explain what prompts it. These include natural causes such as disease, parasites, and fungal infections, as well as manmade causes, such as the increased use of pesticides, antibiotics, climate change, electronic pollution, and the long-distance transport of hives for pollination. Given the importance of honeybees in pollinating important commercial crops, CCD presents a serious threat to the future of commercial agriculture.

SHARECROPPER
The commercial U.S. almond crop is entirely dependent on bee pollination.

Common Minke Whale

Balaenoptera acutorostrata

Native range: Worldwide

Class: Mammal

Size: Up to 30 ft (10 m)

✦ *EDIBLE*
✦ *MEDICINAL*
✦ *COMMERCIAL*
✦ *PRACTICAL*

No other species better exemplifies humanity's changing attitude to animals than the baleen whale. Until 1986, whales were ruthlessly harvested for their meat and oil until many were nearly extinct. Today, although whaling continues on a very limited scale in Japan and the Nordic countries, these gentle giants of the seas have become the emblems of the conservation movement, and whale-watching has replaced hunting as a major earner in many whaling areas.

MONSTER FROM THE DEEP

From the biblical story of Jonah and the whale to Melville's *Moby Dick* (1851; see quote opposite), the whale has been portrayed as a ravenous monster bent on the destruction of humanity. Whale sightings are probably the basis for the many stories of sea serpents and monsters reported by ancient and medieval explorers. With their gigantic size and sudden appearance from the depths, whales would have terrified sailors in their vulnerable wooden ships. However, the baleen whales, which include the fin, sei, blue, humpback, and minke whales, do not even have teeth—they filter food from the water as they swim. The only threat they could present to mariners would be if they accidentally rammed their craft, but since they are skilful navigators, this is unlikely to happen under normal circumstances.

What we all know about whales is that they are air-breathing mammals like ourselves. All life originated in the oceans and slowly migrated to the land, but some species reversed direction during their evolution, to escape predation or find new ecological niches to exploit. Paleontologists suggest that the baleen whale's earliest ancestors were land-living mammals, roughly the size of small deer, which started to return to the water some 53 million years ago. By around 40 million years ago they had evolved into several species of fully aquatic animals,

FILTER FEEDER
The largest creatures now living on the planet, the baleen whales feed on some of the smallest.

He piled upon the whale's white hump the sum of all
the general rage and hate felt by his whole race from
Adam down; and then, as if his chest had been a mortar,
he burst his hot heart's shell upon it.

Moby Dick *(1851) by Herman Melville (1819–91)*

" Both jaws, like enormous shears, bit the craft completely in twain."

—Page 510.

including the giant *Basilosaurus*—long thought to be a dinosaur, but which was in fact a carnivorous toothed whale
measuring 60 ft (18 m) in length, and thought to be the largest
living creature of its time. The first baleen whales appeared
some 12–13 million years ago.

The minke whale is one of the smallest of the baleen whales,
reaching no more than 30 ft (10 m) in length, and is dwarfed by
its giant cousin, the blue whale, which can be over 100 ft (30 m)
long. They have a black or gray dorsal region with a single
dorsal fin and a white underside. They use two flippers and a large tail for
locomotion. They undulate their whole body to propel themselves
through the water and can reach speeds of 24 mph (38 km/h). They
breathe through two blowholes on their heads and can stay underwater
for up to 20 minutes before needing to surface again for air. They are
known as "conscious breathers" because they risk drowning if they fall
asleep. It is thought that only one half of their brains sleeps at any one
time so that they do not breathe while underwater.

They eat by swallowing small marine animals along with large volumes
of water, which they sift through the hundreds of comblike baleen plates
that line the sides of their mouths. Like all other cetaceans, the minke
has a large, well-developed brain. It communicates with other members
of its species through sounds known as "whale song" that carry for many
miles underwater. Like other mammals, minke give birth to live offspring
after a gestation of ten months. The minke mother will nurse her calves
for five months, feeding it on a thick toothpastelike milk. Minke can live
up to 60 years, but unlike other animals they do not establish lifelong
partnerships.

Ahab's bane
Melville's murderous Moby
Dick helped form the
popular image of the whale
in the nineteenth century.

Small fish, big pond

Humans have been hunting whales since prehistoric times. At first this
consisted of the hunting of smaller species that came into inshore coastal
waters. The whales would be herded toward shallow water, where they
could be speared or netted. This type of whaling continued well into the
modern period in coastal areas of Japan, the Pacific Northwest, and the

Arctic, by peoples who depended on whale meat and blubber for their
survival. The number of whales taken was relatively small, and did not
threaten the survival of the species. These cultures did not have the
ability to hunt the larger baleen whales that spend most of their lives in
the deep oceans.

Modern large-scale industrial whaling began in the early seventeenth
century, when the British, French, Spanish, Dutch, and Danes sent
whaling fleets to the Svalbord archipelago between Scandinavia and
Iceland. Whales were hunted in the bays and fjords of the archipelago in
small boats and then towed ashore to temporary whaling stations so that
their blubber could be processed into whale oil. For the next century, the
various European powers constantly squabbled and skirmished over the
best whaling bays, sparking several minor "whaling wars." Gradually, as
ships got larger, whaling expanded into the open ocean, and land stations
were abandoned in favor of processing the blubber when the fleet returned
to its home port.

PRACTICAL USE
Before the discovery of
petroleum, whale oil was
used for lighting, cooking,
and lubricating machinery.

While the whalers of the Arctic, coastal Japan, and the
Pacific Northwest hunted whales for their meat, which was a
staple of their diets, the industrial whaling fleets harvested whales
for their blubber, to be converted into whale oil. Until the end of
the nineteenth century, when it was replaced by petroleum products, whale oil was a major source of lamp oil for domestic
lighting. The baleen, also known as "whalebone" (although it is
much more flexible than bone), was used for a number of applications

such as collar stiffeners, parasol and umbrella ribs, and most famously for whalebone corset stays.

The late nineteenth century saw another huge change in the intensification of whaling. The much bigger ships, many now steam-powered, could hunt much larger baleen whales, including the largest of them all, the blue whale, which yielded huge quantities of meat and oil. While the oil was no longer in demand for lighting, it was now made into margarine. Whale meat, which is not particularly appetizing and was not eaten widely, was made into pet food. The new scale of whaling meant a respite for the smaller minke whale. However, over-hunting of the larger whale species meant that minke whales were once again on the menu from about the 1970s until the whaling moratorium of 1986. Since the moratorium, a few countries, including Japan, Norway, Iceland, and Korea, have taken small number of minke whales for "scientific research," although most of the meat ends up on dinner tables in Tokyo, Oslo, Reykjavik, and Seoul.

With the end of large-scale whaling, baleen whale populations have recovered worldwide. The new growth industry in many former whaling areas such as Iceland, Greenland, the Pacific Northwest, Australia, and South Africa is whale-watching. Minke whales are often seen because of their relatively large numbers, their proximity to coasts at certain times of year, and also their natural inquisitiveness that makes them "human watch" just as they are being watched. The minke is not the most popular of baleen whales, however; unlike other species that breach vertically out of the water before diving, the minke is fairly unspectacular in its movements, and its ability to dive for 20 minutes at a time also means that it can appear and then vanish from sight for the rest of a whale-watching cruise.

A timely ban on hunting and the development of new ways of commercializing baleen whales has saved these gentle marine giants for future generations to enjoy and maybe one day communicate with. Once feared and butchered, the whale is now the symbol of humanity's new relationship with the natural environment and the species it shares it with. For our own survival as well as theirs, we must learn to be protectors and exploiters of the earth's rich biological diversity.

LOST

✦

Whales occasionally get lost and swim into estuaries and rivers, where they often become stranded and die. Among the most famous was Humphrey the humpback whale, who twice swam into San Francisco Bay, the first time in 1985 and then again in 1990. In 2006, a bottlenose whale swam up the Thames as far as central London, where it unfortunately died of stress. But perhaps the most extraordinary lost whale story occurred in 2007, when an 18-ft (5.5-m) minke was found beached on a sandbar near Santarém, Brazil, in the middle of the Amazon jungle—almost 1,000 miles (1,600 km) from the sea.

American Buffalo

Bison bison

Native range: North America

Class: Mammals

Size: Up to 6.6 ft (2 m) at the shoulder

+ *EDIBLE*
+ *MEDICINAL*
+ *COMMERCIAL*
+ *PRACTICAL*

The fate of the American buffalo symbolizes the conquest and settlement of the Great Plains during the nineteenth century. Once the mainstay of the Native American tribes, the buffalo's near extinction signaled the tribes' defeat and the destruction of their traditional way of life.

MONARCH OF THE GREAT PLAINS

The common name for *Bison bison*, "buffalo," is a misnomer caused by the sloppy naming practices of early European explorers. In biological terms, the American buffalo is much more closely related to the wisent, the European bison, than to either the Asiatic or African buffalo. The largest living creature native to North America, the fully grown adult buffalo stands some 6.6 ft (2 m) tall, measures 7–11 ft (2.1–3.5 m) in length, and weighs 770–2,200 lb (350–1,000 kg). Although the male, or bull, is slightly larger than the female, or cow, there is little physical differentiation in buffaloes. Both sexes are powerfully built, with solid heads and necks that are covered with a shaggy mane of brown fur. The shoulders are markedly humped. Their long tails have a furry tuft at the end. Despite its size and its relatively short legs compared to its massive body and head, the buffalo can hit a top speed of 34 mph (55 km/h). Apart from their speed, weight, and strength, which they use against predators, they also have a pair of sharp, curved horns that extend from the sides of their heads to defend themselves. Bulls also use their horns during the rutting season to fight rival males.

Although now limited to commercial ranches and national parks, the buffalo's original range stretched from northern Mexico to Canada and as far east as the Appalachians. They are divided into two species: the slightly larger woodland bison and the plains bison. Like other bovines, buffaloes are herbivores, feeding on a large range of plants, including grasses, rushes, willow, aspen, ash, mistletoe, mushrooms, ferns, lichens, mosses, acorns, and blackberries. They graze at dusk and nighttime, and rest during the day. Buffalo herds quickly overgraze an area and have to constantly

migrate in order to find fresh pastures. In winter, they use their heads and necks to clear the snow from the ground, and so have little difficulty finding food.

Buffaloes live in single-sex herds that only come together during the annual breeding season, which takes place in August and September. Bulls compete with one another for females during the rutting season by ramming and head-butting one another. The dominant males mate first, gathering a small harem of females,

FREE-RANGE
The American West just prior to intensive European settlement was home to a huge herd of buffalo. This painting depicts Missouri in 1833.

which they protect for a few days after mating. Once they have mated, the females separate from the males to form their own herds. Calves are born after a gestation of nine months. The lighter-colored calves develop their distinctive shoulder humps and horns after about two months. The cows will nurse their young for about one year, during which time the calves will become socialized in herding behavior. In the wild, buffaloes live for about 20 years, but they can live twice as long in captivity. Apart from man, the buffalo's main predators are the wolf and the grizzly bear. Like other herding animals, buffaloes have evolved collective defensive strategies against predators.

SIGHTING THE MEXICAN BULL

The first sighting of an American buffalo by a European did not take place on the Great Plains of North America, but many hundreds of miles away from the bison's native range in the Aztec capital of Tenochtitlan in 1520. Among the many treasures amassed by the Aztec ruler Moctezuma II (1466–1520) was a menagerie of rare beasts collected from all over the Americas. A later historian gave the following description of the animal the conquistadors called the "Mexican Bull":

Among which the greatest Rarity was the Mexican Bull; a wonderful composition of divers Animals. It has crooked Shoulders, with a Bunch on its Back like a Camel; its Flanks dry, its Tail large, and its Neck cover'd with Hair like a Lion. It is cloven footed, its Head armed like that of a Bull, which it resembles in Fierceness, with no less strength and Agility.

This first encounter with the conquistadors, who were soon to annihilate the Aztecs, was a presage of much worse treatment to come from later European settlers. The first recorded sighting in North America dates to almost a century later in 1612, when a British explorer somewhere near the future site of Washington DC described seeing and eating buffalo: "I found great store of Cattle as big as Kine, of which the Indians that were my guides killed a couple, which we found to be very good and wholesome meate, and are very easie to be killed, in regard they are heavy, slow, and not so wild as other beasts of the wildernesse." Apart from these occasional meetings with Europeans, the buffalo's main human predators were the Native American tribes.

Before the reintroduction of the horse to the Americas by Europeans in the sixteenth century, Native Americans hunted on foot with bows and arrows and spears, picking off individual animals from a herd, stampeding a herd over a cliff, or trapping it in a closed canyon. They used every part of the buffalo, from the horns to the hooves. They butchered and ate the best cuts of meat fresh, and preserved the surplus as jerky or pemmican, a mixture of dried meat and fat that is flavored with berries or cherries. The hides were used for tipis, shields, bags, clothing, and drums, and the sinews were used for bowstrings. The arrival of the horse made hunting easier, and Native Americans living on the plains evolved a migratory lifestyle dependent on the buffalo herds. In comparison to the total size of the herd, Native Americans took a sustainable number of animals, helping to maintain the balance of the Great Plains ecosystem.

HUNTER TURNED CONSERVATIONIST

✦

Soldier and buffalo hunter turned Wild West showman, "Buffalo Bill" Cody (1846–1917) earned his nickname for killing over 4,000 head of buffalo during a single hunting season in 1867–68, while he was working for the Kansas Pacific Railroad. By the early 1870s, when the great herds had been slaughtered, Cody realized that the pressure on the buffalo was too great, and he supported measures to protect the species. A coalition of ranchers, the military, and the railroads ensured that the law was never passed, and by the 1880s, the buffalo was close to extinct in the Great Plains.

KILLING FIELDS

The situation began to change in the nineteenth century with the arrival of Europeans. At first the newcomers came as traders, purchasing buffalo hides and meat from Native American hunters, and bringing firearms in exchange. In certain areas, native commercial hunting began to make serious inroads into buffalo populations as early as the 1830s. As the pace of settlement increased, so did the pressure on the buffalo and the Native American peoples who depended on them. A range of factors, both human and natural, combined to cause the near extinction of the species by the last decades of the century. A serious drought between the 1840s and 1860s led to a collapse of the buffalo population, from which it was just recovering when it faced its greatest human onslaught.

The buffalo was an obstacle in the relentless westward expansion of European settlers: they competed with cattle for grazing; they damaged or delayed railroad trains; and they sustained the Native American plains tribes, who fought the settlers to protect their ancestral lands. A coalition of ranchers, the military, and the railroads had a common interest in the eradication of the buffalo. Additionally, buffalo hides were a valuable commodity for use back east and for export. During the 1860s and 1870s, professional hunters like "Buffalo Bill" Cody (see box, opposite) were employed to exterminate the buffalo from its native range. The slaughter was immense, with thousands of animals killed in one day. The animals were skinned for their hides but the carcasses were left to rot. There were so many bones piled along the side of the railroad tracks that there emerged a secondary industry of bone collecting to make fertilizer. By the 1880s, the policy of extermination was so successful that the plains tribes were forced into submission through starvation, and their way of life was destroyed forever.

WILD WEST
"Buffalo Bill" Cody and Sitting Bull both unsuccessfully lobbied against the Federal government to protect the American buffalo.

Only seven years ago we made a treaty by which we were assured that the buffalo country should be left to us forever. Now they threaten to take that from us also.

Sitting Bull (1831–90)

Spiny Dye-Murex
Bolinus brandaris

Native range: Western Mediterranean

Class: Mollusk

Size: Up to 1.5 in (3.9 cm) in length

+ ***EDIBLE***
+ *MEDICINAL*
+ ***COMMERCIAL***
+ *PRACTICAL*

O ne of the most precious substances of antiquity was the secretion of a humble rock snail that was used to make the rich blue and indigo dye known as Tyrian purple. The dye was so expensive to produce that for centuries it was reserved for imperial use.

THE COLOR PURPLE

As we shall see with the source of another traditional colorant, cochineal (pp. 66–7), ancient dyestuffs sometimes have the most unlikely sources. According to an ancient Greek legend, we have Hercules' dog to thank for the discovery that the spiny dye-murex snail contained a strong purple colorant. When the hero was walking along a beach in the Near East, his dog ate some of the snails, instantly staining his mouth a deep purple. Like many ancient myths, the story may contain a kernel of truth about how the colorant was first discovered. The snail is also eaten, and it is possible that the dye was discovered as a result of a cooking accident. The dye, also known as Tyrian purple, was produced in the ancient Phoenician city of Tyre (now in Lebanon), and exported to the rest of the ancient world. However, more recent archaeological investigations indicate that the Minoan civilization of Crete also cultivated the snail to extract the precious dye.

The spiny dye-murex snail lives on rocks in shallow water and tidal pools in the western Mediterranean. The shell has a long protruding siphonal canal at the base of a rounded body showing several whorls, topped by a low pointed spire. The shell is covered in short spines that indicate the age of the animal. The spiny dye-murex has a two-stage lifecycle: egg and adult. The female lays eggs within a hard protective capsule to protect them from predators. The juveniles hatch as miniature adults and take around three years to mature. The spiny dye-murex is something of a mollusk Hannibal Lector, being both a carnivore, preying on other shellfish, as well as a cannibal not averse to predating its own kind. The snail will first soften the shell of its prey with a chemical secretion and then pierce it with its radula, a hard tonguelike structure, to get to the soft inner tissue.

Said to be worth its weight in gold, the murex-dye was one of the foundations of the wealth of the Phoenicians. In addition to being collected from the seashore, the snail was bred in captivity in large tanks. The colorant, found in the snail's hypobranchial gland, was removed and boiled down with sea salt and potash to produce a dye that was not only extremely vibrant but also resistant to fading. The yarn to be dyed was then immersed in the solution for varying amounts of time, once or twice, until the desired color was obtained. The colors obtained ranged from blue and indigo to dark purple. Production of Tyrian purple declined in the Middle Ages, especially after the conquest of the Byzantine Empire by crusaders in the early thirteenth century. Although production of the dye continued in the Muslim Levant, Western Europe turned to other dyes until, like all natural colorants, their use was diminished by synthetic chemical dyes in the mid-nineteenth century.

BORN TO THE PURPLE

✦

Color has been used to denote rank since ancient times. In China, yellow was the prerogative of the imperial family, and in the Roman Empire, the color denoting imperial rank was purple. This latter association was so close during the Byzantine period that members of the imperial house were referred to as "porphyrogenitos," literally "born to the purple." In the Byzantine context, however, this had a dual meaning. In addition to the wearing of purple clothing, it also referred to the color of the imperial birthing chamber, which was clad from floor to ceiling in the purple stone porphyry.

"HERE, BOY!"
According to legend, Hercules' dog discovered Tyrian purp le when eating snails on a beach. However, it is more likely that the dye was discovered as a result of a cooking accident.

Silkworm

Bombyx mori

Native range: Northern China

Class: Insect

Size: 1.5–2.5 in (4–6 cm)

♦ EDIBLE
♦ MEDICINAL
♦ **COMMERCIAL**
♦ PRACTICAL

Silk was a fiercely guarded secret of the Chinese, who controlled its manufacture and sale for over 3,000 years. Trade in the precious fabric was the mainstay of the Silk Road that linked China with the Near East and the Roman Empire, which was an avid consumer of Chinese silk. In the sixth century CE, the Byzantines and Persians learned the secret of breeding silkworms, and from there the manufacture of silk spread gradually across the Old and the New Worlds.

THE EMPRESS' TEA

According to Chinese legend, the Empress Leizu (fl. 27th century BCE) invented the art of silk farming, or sericulture, while she was sitting under a mulberry tree in the palace gardens sipping tea. A cocoon fell into her cup and began to unravel in the hot liquid. One version of the story has it that the silk covered the whole garden before the cocoon was unwound to reveal the silkworm enclosed within it. She realized the role of the insect in the creation of the fibrous cocoon and asked permission from her husband, the Yellow Emperor, to breed the silkworm in a grove of mulberry trees and study its lifecycle. She discovered not only how to breed the insect for its cocoon, but also how to spin silk thread and how to weave it into cloth on a prototype silk loom. Leizu was deified for her great gift to China, becoming the goddess of silk.

Although charming, the legend is entirely fanciful. The Yellow Emperor is the mythical founder of Chinese civilization, therefore it is fitting that his consort should be credited with the invention of sericulture. However, like the discovery of many other preindustrial processes, the development of sericulture probably took many hundreds of years of trial and error in several different areas. What is known is that the breeding and harvesting of the silk moth's cocoon dates back more than five and half millennia to the very beginnings of Chinese civilization. The secret, fiercely guarded by the Chinese state, would not reach the West until the sixth century CE. In antiquity, the true nature of silk was not well understood outside Asia. Most Romans, who were great consumers of silk cloth, believed that it was a vegetable fiber like cotton, rather than the byproduct of the lifecycle of an insect.

WEAVER WORM
The secret of silk was so well guarded that most Westerners did not know that it was produced by the larval stage of an insect.

Like the other insects we have seen so far, the mosquito and the bee, the silkworm has a four-stage lifecycle consisting of egg, larva, pupa, and adult. The name "silkworm" refers to the larval stage of the silk moth, which is a member of the order Lepidoptera, which includes all moths and butterflies. The eggs are tiny in comparison to the fully grown adult and are about the size of poppy seeds. The eggs incubate for about two weeks and hatch into larvae. The silkworm larva is the only phase of the silk moth's lifecycle during which it feeds. It eats only the leaves of the white mulberry tree (*Morus alba*). The larva is covered with tiny black hairs and, when the head darkens, the larva is ready to molt. After molting, the silkworm emerges white, naked, and with little horns on its back.

MONOFILAMENT
A silkworm cocoon is made of a single thread up to 3,000 ft (900 m) long that is many times finer than a human hair.

After its fourth and final molt as a larva, the silkworm produces a silk filament from its salivary glands and weaves it into a cocoon around itself as protection from the weather and predators during the final stage of its metamorphosis. The cocoon is made of a single unbroken microfilament of raw silk 1,000–3,000 ft (300–900 m) long and 10 micrometers thick (a human hair is between 20 and 180 micrometers thick). After a final molt inside the cocoon, the larva develops into the brown, chitin-covered pupa. If the silkworm is allowed to survive and complete the pupal phase, it will release an enzyme to make a hole in the cocoon and emerge as an adult moth. The enzyme breaks down the silk filament and makes the cocoon useless for commercial silk production. The adult moth is covered in round, furry scales, which are usually white or light brown and, despite the large size of its wings, it is flightless. The mature moth has no functional mouthparts and cannot feed itself; its only function is to reproduce and lay eggs. The silk moth is unusual insofar as it is one of the few insects to have been fully domesticated, to the extent that it is now entirely dependent on humans for its reproduction and survival.

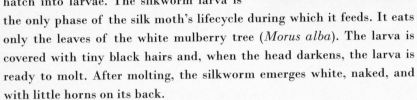

With time and patience the mulberry leaf becomes a silk gown.

Ancient Chinese proverb

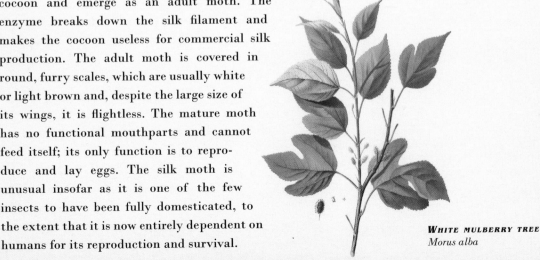

WHITE MULBERRY TREE
Morus alba

THE FIRST INFORMATION SUPERHIGHWAY

The earliest archaeological evidence for the manufacture of silk in China dates back to the fourth millennium BCE. By the third millennium, silk fabrics found in tombs show that the Chinese had developed sophisticated dyeing and weaving techniques. Silk's bright colors, and its fine luster and texture marked it as a luxury product. In ancient China it was reserved for use by the royal and noble elites, and was much coveted by China's barbarian neighbors to whom it was given as gifts or sometimes as bribes to prevent attacks. Silk cloth was so valuable in its own right that it was a recognized unit of exchange alongside silver and gold coinage.

The trade of silk to the West dates back to the second millennium BCE. Silk has been found in the pharaonic tombs of the Valley of Kings in Egypt. The great empires of antiquity, Persia, Hellenistic Greece, and Rome, were all addicted to silk, which they had to import at great cost from China. Silk was so important a product in East–West trade that it has given its name to the trade routes that linked China to the Near East and Europe. In fact, the "Silk Road" was not a single road but a network of overland and maritime trade routes. The most famous route crossed the deserts and mountains of Central Asia and Persia and reached the city of Antioch on the Syrian coast, but there were also a more northerly route through what would one day be Russia, and a southerly route through India. The maritime Silk Road skirted Southeast Asia and India, and then up along the Red Sea to the Egyptian port of Alexandria.

Silk was not the only product traded. Other Chinese manufactures such as paper and ceramics went westward, in exchange for the West's glass, amber, ivory, horses,

SUPERHIGHWAY
Silk was the mainstay of the ancient Silk Road that linked China with the civilizations of the Near East and Europe.

gold, and silver. Although trade was the *raison d'être* of the Silk Road, it played an extremely important role as a means of cultural and artistic exchange. It would not be an exaggeration to say that the Silk Road was the world's first information superhighway, a precursor to the Internet, that facilitated the exchange of industrial and military technologies, artistic styles, and religious and philosophical ideas between Asia, the Near East, and Europe. In the field of religion, for example, Christianity traveled east as far as China, where Christian communities were established in the first century CE. Buddhism traveled from its native India and established itself as the dominant religion in Asia until it was displaced by Islam in Central Asia and Daoism in China.

DRAGON ROBE
Ancient Chinese textile artists created complex pieces, such as this embroidered silk ritual garment from the fourth century BCE.

Women have played an important role—both real and legendary—in the manufacture and dissemination of silk. In keeping with the legend about its discovery (see above), sericulture was traditionally women's work. After the larvae had been raised on mulberry leaves they spun their cocoons in preparation for pupation. The cocoons were collected and immersed in boiling water to kill the pupa and to soften the hardened silk to allow the filaments to be reeled off by hand and spun into thread. The thread was then dyed and woven into cloth. The export from China of silkworm eggs was forbidden on pain of death, but another story tells how a Chinese princess, sent to marry the ruler of the central Asian kingdom of Khotan in the first century

And the merchants of the Earth shall weep and mourn[...]; for no man buyeth their merchandise any more:
The merchandise of gold, and silver, and precious stones, and of pearls, and fine linen, and purple, and silk [...]
Revelations 18:11

CE, smuggled silkworm eggs out of the country because she could not bear to live without her favorite fabric. Sericulture spread from Central Asia to India, where it was well established by the third century CE. China's near neighbor, Japan, learned the secret of sericulture in the early fourth century and developed a thriving silk industry that survives to the present day.

The secret of silk finally reached the West in 522 CE, when the Byzantine emperor Justinian (483–565 CE) obtained silkworm eggs from two monks he had sent on an undercover mission to Central Asia. The monks smuggled the eggs back to Constantinople hidden in bamboo rods. The Byzantine emperors established a monopoly of silk production, emulating their Chinese counterparts in their efforts to control the lucrative trade with Western Europe. Their rivals were the Arabs, who began their lightning conquest of the Near East, North Africa, and Southern Europe in the seventh century. They established sericulture in their conquests in Africa, Spain, and Sicily. Although the Chinese had lost their monopoly on silk, the trade in high-quality silks continued along the Silk Road.

The crusades of the twelfth and thirteenth centuries finally brought sericulture to Christian Europe. The crusaders, whose ostensible aim was the liberation of the Holy Land, conquered the Christian Byzantine Empire. Many silk workers left Constantinople and settled in southern France and Italy, which soon became major centers of silk production. In the fourteenth century, the disintegration of the Mongol Empire that spanned the entire length of the Silk Road signaled the end of the Chinese silk trade. Henceforth, the Italian city-states of Florence, Lucca, and Venice, would manufacture the highest-quality silks for the European market. The drain on the exchequers of France was such that in the sixteenth century King Francis I of France (1494–1547) established silk farming in the southern French town of Lyon, which remained a major

SHINE AND SHIMMER
Silk is the material of choice for evening wear from Western ball gowns to intricately ornamented Indian saris decorated with sequins and seed pearls.

center of silk production until the late nineteenth century. Similar efforts in England, where the climate was less favorable, weren't so successful. But in the seventeenth century, Protestant French and Flemish silk weavers escaping religious persecution in predominantly Catholic France and the Low Countries established themselves in the Spitalfields area of east London, which remained a center of silk cloth and clothing manufacture for the next century.

Silk vs. nylon

The Industrial Revolution of the eighteenth century was led by textiles manufacturers, in particular those of cotton in England. In France, there were improvements in silk production with the invention of the Jacquard loom in 1801. The loom was operated by punch cards like an old-style computer. The new machine was so effective that it caused riots among silk weavers who were afraid it would replace them. By the end of the century, however, European silk manufacture was in serious decline. Three factors contributed to the collapse: outbreaks of diseases that affected first the silkworm and then the mulberry tree it fed on; a change in fashion and the appearance of alternative fabrics; and the modernization of the Japanese silk industry that began to undercut its European competitors.

Until the World War Two, Japan was the world's largest exporter of silk yarn and finished products. However, the Pacific War interrupted the trade, and led to the development of cheap synthetic alternatives, such as nylon. After the war, silk was not able to regain its earlier preeminence. Currently the world's leading silk producer is the People's Republic of China, followed by India. Silk remains a luxury fabric used by the high-end fashion industry for shirts, blouses, men's ties, lingerie, suits, and dresses. In Japan and India it is used to make traditional dress—the kimono and sari respectively. Silk is also used in the home for upholstery, wallpaper, and curtains.

Fit for a princess

✦

Since antiquity, silk has been the preferred material of royalty. For centuries, it was used to make the court dress of European aristocrats, kings, and queens, and only made way for more practical fabrics in the Victorian age. However, silk is still the material of choice for special state occasions. On July 29, 1981, an expectant world awaited the arrival of Diana, Princess of Wales, at St Paul's Cathedral, where she was about to marry the heir to the British throne, Prince Charles. The buzz on the street and in the media was about what Diana would be wearing. The dress, designed by Elizabeth and David Emanuel, had been kept under wraps until the day of the wedding. Diana emerged from the glass coach in an enormous romantic extravaganza, with a full skirt, huge puffed sleeves, and a frilly neckline. The dress was made of ivory silk taffeta, decorated with lace, hand embroidery, sequins, and 10,000 pearls, and was finished by a 25 ft (7.6 m) train.

Cow

Bos taurus

Native range: Europe

Class: Mammal

Size: 4–5 ft (1.25–1.5 m) tall

+ **EDIBLE**
+ **MEDICINAL**
+ **COMMERCIAL**
+ **PRACTICAL**

The cow is probably the most important edible, practical, and commercial species featured in this book. The cow provides us with meat and milk—the source of all dairy products—and it would be difficult to imagine cooking without it. Cattle farming is the basis of cultures as diverse as ranching in the U.S., nomadic pastoralism among the Maasai of East Africa, and dairy farming in rural England.

MILCH COWS

If you asked readers to come up with one animal out of the 50 listed in this book as the one that has had the greatest influence on the course of human history, I bet that very few would think of the cow first off. The proverbially stolid cow is not the most exciting of animals. It does not trigger the same emotional response as the dog, cat, or horse; it stands placidly ruminating in the background of our thoughts—ever-present but largely taken for granted. Yet if you could magically make the cow disappear and surgically remove it from history, today's world would be a very different place—the diet, clothing, religious beliefs, and lifestyles of billions of people would be unrecognizable. The cow has shaped many cultures from prehistory to the present, and its influence on human civilization, as the world gets richer, is increasing, and not always in positive ways. Cattle farming is now firmly in the sights of environmentalists as a threat to biodiversity and human health, a waste of precious resources, and a contributory factor to global warming.

INDISPENSABLE
Although not the most exciting of animals, the cow is probably the single most significant edible species featured in this book.

The common ancestor of all domestic cows, including European taurine beef and dairy cattle, is the now extinct aurochs. The aurochs evolved in India around two million years BP (Before Present) and slowly migrated westward, reaching Europe around 250,000 years ago. Physically, the aurochs was much larger and more powerfully built than the modern domesticated cow, standing 6.6 ft (2 m) tall, and crowned with a pair of long lyre-shaped horns. In the Neolithic period, man hunted the aurochs, as is evidenced by its depiction in cave paintings in France and Spain. Between 8,000 and 6,000 years ago, the aurochs was domesticated. As with the development of agriculture and the domestication of other species, the domestication of the aurochs probably occurred in several places independently. It is likely that the first cattle farmers were nomadic pastoralists, who traveled with their herds constantly seeking out fresh pastures. The aurochs survived as a separate wild species until the early modern period. The last know specimen died in Poland in 1627.

The cow is part of the large group of ungulate mammals that have hooves on their feet, which also includes the horse, llama, goat, and sheep. Its other defining anatomical feature is that it is a "ruminant," having a stomach divided into four chambers: the rumen, reticulum, omasum, and abomasum. This complicated internal plumbing allows the cow to digest cellulose-rich plant material such as grass and leaves that humans cannot digest, and transform them into usable protein, fat, and carbohydrate. It does this by breaking down food by chewing, ingesting it into its rumen and reticulum, where it undergoes processing by microorganisms, regurgitating it to be rechewed (chewing the cud), and then redigesting it several times. The cow's true stomach, which matches our own in functionality, is the abomasum.

The ability of the cow to convert what is to humans indigestible material into edible protein and fat is what makes the cow one of nature's marvels, and has made it the basis of many cultures past and present. The cow can be raised for its meat, or kept for its milk to make dairy products; it can be used as a draft animal to transport goods and people, and to plow heavy soils, thereby increasing crop yields. Cattle are also the main

AMBUSH
The wild European ox, or aurochs, was a formidable adversary for predators such as wolves and early humans.

DAIRY COW
Humans first hunted and raised cattle for their meat, but soon realized the value of the animal as a milk producer.

SACRED COW
Although central to Indian life as a provider of milk, butter, and ghee (a specially prepared variation of butter), the cow was never deified or worshipped in Hindu India.

source of leather for the clothing and footwear industries, and cow leather also has its uses in home upholstery and car interiors. Historically very little of the animal was wasted, though today synthetic materials have replaced products once made from cow hides, horn, bones, sinews, and hooves.

HOLY SYMBOL

The practical importance of the cow to many ancient civilizations is evidenced by its use as a religious symbol. In ancient Mesopotamia (now Iraq), horns were symbols of divinity and royalty; in Egypt, two gods, Hathor, the goddess of love and motherhood, and the sacred bull Apis took the shape of cattle. Apis was worshipped in his own temple, the Serapeum, in the Egyptian capital of Memphis. When the Serapeum was excavated in the late nineteenth century, archaeologists discovered the ritual burials of 60 bulls entombed in their own sarcophagi. The cow is an important animal in Egyptian iconography and was reproduced in sculpture, painting, and the applied arts. The boy-pharaoh Tutankhamun (1341–23 BCE), for example, was buried with a state bed in the shape of the goddess Hathor in her cow form.

The cow played an important role in Cretan and ancient Greek religion and myth. Among the wall paintings discovered in the great Minoan palace of Knossos is a scene of a Cretan youth leaping acrobatically over the horns of a galloping bull. It is unclear whether this was a sporting pastime or a religious ritual, or a combination of both, but the bull played a central role in Minoan religion. Cretan bull-worship was probably the origin of the story of the monstrous half-man, half-bull Minotaur, who fed on the flesh of sacrificial victims sent from Greece. The ancient Greeks also held the cow in high regard. The bull was the sacrificial animal of choice at the great festivals dedicated to the Olympian gods. In Athens, hundreds of bulls were sacrificed every year to Zeus and Athena to protect the city from its enemies and from natural disasters. The Romans, who were the heirs of Greek civilization, also sacrificed bulls to the gods. The Roman games in which gladiators were pitched against bulls are probably the origin of the modern bullfighting traditions of Spain and southern France (see box, p. 38).

The culture perhaps most closely associated with cattle is India, the home of the "sacred cow." In contrast with Greece and the Near East, where cattle were both worshipped as gods, sacrificed, and eaten, the cow in India is not regarded as a divinity in its own right, and the Hindu religion forbids its killing and the consumption of its meat. In a country where food has until recently been at a premium, the cow is too precious a natural resource to waste. Dairy products form an important part of the diet of many Indians who otherwise would have no access to any other source of animal protein. In contemporary India, however, raising living standards in the cities has increased the demand for beef.

WHAT'S IN THE BEEF?

When the Spanish conquistadors arrived in Mexico in the early sixteenth century, they found no large domesticated animals. The American horse had become extinct many thousands of years earlier, and the only bovine in the Americas, the American buffalo, lived far to the north of the Aztec capital. Activities performed by oxen in Europe, such as transportation and plowing, were performed by humans in central America. The Europeans reintroduced the horse, which transformed the life of the Native Americans of the Great Plains, and they also brought European livestock, including sheep, goats, and cattle, which slowly began to change the ecology of the continent.

MINOTAUR
Cretan religion was centered around the cult of the bull.

The Spanish introduced ranching to the Americas, adapting practices brought from Europe, which North American settlers adopted as they moved westward. The vast open grasslands of the Great Plains were ideal for the "open range" method of livestock rearing. Cattle were allowed to roam free, like the buffalo that they would soon displace. In the fall, cowboys rounded up the stock, sorting the animals by the brands they had been marked with and driving the mature animals to market. Open-range ranching was largely responsible for the opening up and development of the Western frontier between the 1840s and 1860s.

As more settlers arrived, however, there was a greater demand for food crops to feed both humans and livestock. The Homestead

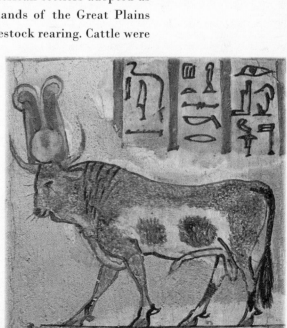

HOLY HORNS
The bull god Apis had his own temple in the Egyptian city of Memphis, where 60 sacred bulls were found entombed in their own stone sarcophagi.

Act of 1862 opened the way for the establishment of farms on the open-range lands, which farmers fenced off to prevent animals from eating the crops. This created conflict between farmers and ranchers that has been dramatized in hundreds of Westerns. The end of the open range did not come because of an increase in crop farming and the reduction of grazing land, but because of a combination of an extremely severe winter in 1886–7, when many thousands of cattle died, and catastrophic overgrazing. As a result, the ranchers themselves petitioned the government for land grants so that they could enclose the land and preserve the prairies for their own stock.

Although romantic images of the cowboy driving herds of cattle over the prairies and of the dairy farmer milking his dozen or so cows in his barn persist in the imagination of city-dwellers, the reality of modern beef and dairy farming is very different. Cows are now big business, and the global trade in beef and dairy was worth around $6 billion in 2000. In the developed world, supersized dairy farms housing thousands of animals and operating 24-hour milking in huge mechanized factories are becoming the norm in order to produce milk for the best return. Factory farming methods, cloning, and biotechnology have been applied to beef farming, especially in the U.S. where beef cattle are given antibiotics and growth hormones to maximize meat production and quality. In addition to raising animal-rights issues, critics of intensive farming warn of the possible adverse effects on human health of the chemicals used to promote

RED RAG TO A BULL

✦

The *corrida de toros*, the Spanish sport of bullfighting, has its origins in ancient Roman circus games when gladiators fought wild animals as a form of public entertainment. The modern *corrida* is performed in a circular arena modeled on the Roman circus. In the Spanish bullfighting style, the bull is first tested by a picador, who is mounted on a horse and is armed with a long lance, or *pica*, and by the *banderillero*, who stabs barbed flags into the bull's shoulders. The matador then uses two different capes, the large magenta or yellow *capote*, and the smaller red *muleta*, to make the bull charge repeatedly. The matador shows his skill and bravery by allowing the bull to approach before turning away at the last moment to avoid the bull's horns, and by judging when he can turn his back on the bull. In the final stages of the *corrida*, the matador will use the red *muleta* and a long curved sword to kill the bull by severing its spinal cord. A particularly skilled matador is awarded the ears of the bull as a prize.

BIOHAZARD
Once one of the foundations of civilization, cattle have now become a major ecological problem using up scarce land, water, and food resources.

growth and leanness in beef. Conservationists have also pointed out that cattle farming is an extremely wasteful way of producing food for the world's population. While in the past cattle turned useless plant matter into meat and milk, they are now fed on grain that reduces the supply available to the growing human population. Cattle are also a major source of the greenhouse gas methane, and therefore contribute to global climate change. As demand for beef increases in developing countries such as China and India, greater areas of the world are being deforested and converted into pastureland, thereby further reducing biodiversity and threatening sustainable ecology on the planet.

Historically, cattle have played a major role in the creation and development of human civilization by providing a dependable supply of high-quality meat, milk, and leather that freed humans from the need to hunt and forage. In many areas of the world, the raising of beef and dairy cattle encouraged permanent human settlement and land clearance and management. It would be one of the great ironies of human history if cattle were now responsible for the slow decline and ultimate destruction of human civilization through the degradation of the environment.

To my mind, the only possible pet is a cow. Cows love you [….] They will listen to your problems and never ask a thing in return. They will be your friends forever. And when you get tired of them, you can kill and eat them. Perfect."
Bill Bryson (b. 1946)

Camel

Camelus dromedarius

Native range: Arabian Peninsula

Class: Mammal

Size: 6–7 ft (1.8–2.1 m)

✦ ***EDIBLE***

✦ MEDICINAL

✦ COMMERCIAL

✦ ***PRACTICAL***

The dromedary camel is to the deserts of Arabia and North Africa what the horse and cow are to more temperate climes: beasts of burden, war mounts, milk producers, and meat animals. Despite its ungainly appearance, the camel is superbly adapted to arid environments, enabling humans to thrive in very challenging conditions.

ONE HUMP OR TWO?

What everyone knows about the camel is that they come in two varieties: with one hump or two. And like many people, I had a moment of doubt and had to make sure which was which. The Bactrian camel of central Asia is equipped with the double hump, while the Arabian camel, or dromedary— the subject of this entry—has a single hump. The camel, as Alec Issigonis pointed out (see quote opposite), is one of nature's most ungainly animals—not so much designed intelligently as assembled haphazardly from whatever parts the creator had left over: long, bandy, knock-kneed legs, a conical hump in the middle of the back, a small head with outsized bug-eyes—no wonder the camel has the reputation for being permanently bad-tempered.

Although the camel is firmly associated with the deserts of Arabia and North Africa, the camelid family is an early North American import, evolving in the New World around 45 million years BP. Between 2 to 3 million years BP, the camel's ancestors migrated across newly formed land bridges to South America and Eurasia. The North American camelids became extinct after the arrival of the first humans between 10000 and 8000 BP, probably because of hunting, leaving four species in South America: the humpless alpaca, llama, guanaco, and vicuña, which survived because they were domesticated, and two in the Old World: the dromedary and Bactrian camels.

Camels are ungulates, like cows and horses, but do not have hoofs. Instead they have two toes embedded in large leathery footpads that distribute their weight evenly on the ground and prevent them from sinking into sand. Another similarity with cattle is that camels are ruminants with multichambered stomachs that allow them to convert plant matter into protein- and fat-rich meat and milk. Although they also chew the cud (regurgitate their food to chew it several times before digesting it), they only have three stomachs, lacking the cow's omasum. What set the camel apart from other large mammal species, however, are the physical adaptations that make them ideally suited for arid desert environments.

DESERT LIFE
The camel's adaptations allow it to thrive in conditions that would prove fatal to other mammal species.

A commonly held fallacy is that the camel stores water in its hump, and that a thirsty camel will show a limp, deflated hump hanging limply to one side. The hump is actually a store of body fat, not water. The hump is a portable larder enabling the camel to go for days without food. In most mammals, including humans, fat is distributed evenly all over the body to act as insulation against the cold, which is not only unnecessary in a desert climate, but would also make it more difficult for the camel to dissipate body heat. The camel's light-colored coat is good at reflecting heat, but is also warm enough for cool desert nights. The camel has several adaptations to protect it from sandstorms: it can close its nostrils at will so that it doesn't inhale sand; and its eyes and ears are fringed with long hairs to protect them from sand. The eye has a thin extra eyelid that moves from side to side and front to back. These act as windshield wipers brushing away sand, or can close to protect the eye while still allowing the camel to see.

A camel is a horse designed by a committee.
Car designer Alec Issigonis (1906–88)

The camel is also superbly adapted to preserve water. The mammalian adaptation to deal with excessive heat is sweating. We lose water through our skins to cool ourselves down, but this could prove fatal for an animal whose habitat is the waterless desert. Instead of sweating, a camel can vary its body temperature by 14°F (11°C) from 93.2 to 107.6°F (34 to 41.7°C). The equivalent temperature change in a human would be a symptom of a violent and most probably fatal fever. Camels also conserve water by excreting highly concentrated urine, and dung pellets so dry that they are used as fuel for cooking and heating.

However, even with these adaptations there will be times when the camel runs short of water. It maintains the fluid level in its circulatory

WAR MOUNT
Used in war since antiquity,
the camel carried the soldiers
of Islam across the Near East
and North Africa.

system by taking fluid from its other tissues. The red blood cells of camelids are oval rather than round, which means they can circulate more easily in thicker blood. Camel blood is 94 percent water, like our own, but it can lose up to 40 percent of its water safely, while a human would die after losing 12 percent. To make up for this loss, a camel can drink 30 gallons (113.5 l) of water in ten minutes. A dehydrated human drinking so quickly would succumb to water intoxication. But in the camel the water is absorbed by the red blood cell, allowing them to swell to almost two and a half times their normal size and then quickly circulated around the body to rehydrate the body's tissues.

RIDERS OF ARABIA

Archaeologists believe that the camel was first domesticated in the coastal regions of the Arabian Peninsula in the third millennium BCE, around the same time as the horse in more temperate regions. Once hunted for its meat, the camel became a beast of burden, and a source of milk and later of wool for weaving. But the innovation that enabled the camel to reach its full potential as a riding animal for long-distance travel and warfare was the invention of a stable saddle. While the horse has a flat, broad back suitable for riding, and the Bactrian camel has a natural seat between its two humps, the dromedary camel presented a challenge for saddle designers. In some regions the saddle was placed in front of the hump, and in others behind it, but a new design, first seen in northern Arabia in the second century BCE, consisted of a wooden frame that surrounded the hump, giving the rider a secure seat for both riding and fighting.

Starting in the first millennium BCE, the domesticated camel spread to the Near East, Western Asia, and North Africa through trade and warfare. Camels were used as pack animals in the incense trade from Arabia to Egypt, and to carry goods along the Silk Road that

CAMELS DOWN UNDER

✦

The world's southernmost continent, Australia, is a vast desert fringed by a habitable coastal strip. There are no large native animals that can be used as pack or riding animals, so the camel was the natural choice for those wishing to explore Australia's arid interior. The first camel arrived in Australia from the Canary Islands in 1840, to be followed by an estimated 10,000 to 12,000 animals imported from the Indian subcontinent between 1860 and 1907. The first camel stud was established in Western Australia in 1866. Until they were replaced by motorized transport in the 1920s, camels were used in the construction of telegraph lines and water pipelines, to resupply central towns, mining camps, sheep and cattle stations, and aboriginal communities. When they were no longer needed, the camels were released into the wild, where they thrived and established the world's largest feral camel population, which is estimated to be between 150,000 and 200,000 animals, though some experts estimate it to be as large as one million.

linked the Roman Empire and China. The warlike Assyrians and Persians took camels with them when they invaded the Levant and Egypt, but the greatest dissemination of the camel came with the Arab invasions of the seventh century CE. Fired by their new faith, Islam, and mounted on their camels, the united tribes of Arabia conquered the Near East, Egypt, North Africa, Southern Europe, the Persian Empire, Central Asia, and Northern India.

After the fall of the Roman Empire in the fifth century CE, and the decay of its road network, the camel replaced wheeled transport throughout North Africa and the Near East. It remained the main form of overland transport for goods and people well into the modern period when it was replaced by motorized and rail transport. In the nineteenth century, camels played an important role in the opening up of Australia (see box opposite), and the U.S. Army had its own camel corps for transportation in the Southwest during its wars against the Native Americans of Florida. Although the camel has now been supplanted by the truck and motorcar, it remains an important source of milk, wool, and meat in the Arab world.

DESERT TRAIN
In desert areas where wheeled vehicles were unsuitable, the camel provided the main form of transportation for goods and humans.

Wolf
Canis lupus subsp.

Native range: North America and Eurasia

Class: Mammal

Size: 32–34 in (80–85 cm) tall at the shoulder

+ EDIBLE
+ MEDICINAL
+ **COMMERCIAL**
+ **PRACTICAL**

While the big cats inspire both the fear and admiration of humans, the wolf inspires only primal terror—the product of centuries of folk stories that feature the Big Bad Wolf. However, unless they are rabid or starving, wolves do not present a serious threat to adult humans. It is true that wolves have taken many thousands of human lives over the centuries, as well as a great deal of livestock, but this represents an insignificant number compared to the wholesale slaughter of humans by other humans. Despite this, the wolf has become the dark reflection of the domesticated species that live with us—feral, dangerous, and wild—the bloody incarnation of "nature red in tooth and claw."

LEADER OF THE PACK

"Who's afraid of the Big Bad Wolf?" asks the song. We are, of course. It's bred into us from childhood with the stories of "Little Red Riding Hood" and "The Three Little Pigs." But 20,000 years ago, humans and wolves were more likely to be allies than enemies: both species shared the harsh environment of the last ice age; both preyed on large wild ungulate herbivores; and both were social animals that lived in hierarchical family packs led by a dominant male. It is thought that it was around this time that wolf–human interactions began, to the mutual advantage of both species. The wolf was a cunning hunter, and humans had developed stone-tipped weapons with which they could bring down large prey, and their cooperation led to the evolution of the domestic dog. It is at this stage that our relationship with wolves changed. We were no longer allies in our fight for survival but increasingly rivals. The wolf had become the untamed, wild other—an intelligent, bloodthirsty, and ruthless killer. This shift in attitude led to the extermination of the wolf from much of its native range in later centuries. In the modern period, there have been attempts to reintroduce the wolf to certain parts of Europe, though in the UK these have so far been blocked by livestock owners.

Like the camel, the wolf's ancestors were a North American import that evolved in the present-day U.S. and Canada before migrating across land bridges to Asia. The wolf's native range in America never reached further south than northern Mexico and is now limited to Canada, in addition to a few protected populations in the continental U.S. In the Old World, the wolf had a very extensive range, covering all of Asia as far south as India, the Near East including the Arabian Peninsula, Europe, and North Africa. Today the wolf has been eliminated from a large part of Western Europe, with the exception of the mountainous areas of Spain, Italy, and the Balkans. The largest European populations survive in Eastern Europe, Turkey, and European Russia. Further east, wolves are still found in coastal Arabia, Central Asia, the Indian subcontinent, China, and the Russian Far East. With such a large range, the wolf has evolved into several subspecies, which are grouped into northern and southern gray wolves. These subspecies show several morphological differences in size, coloration, and thickness of fur.

Because of their close relationship, the wolf resembles the dog, particularly such breeds as the husky and the German shepherd. However, they are more powerfully built and have larger teeth than domesticated canines. The European gray wolf is the largest subspecies, followed by the American and Asian wolf. The wolf has a thick winter coat that allows it to survive comfortably in temperatures of 25°F (–4°C). It will shed most of its dense underfur in spring and regrow it in the fall. Wolves show much less color variation than dogs—they range from white through various shades of blond, cream, and ocher, to grays, browns, and blacks, although gray predominates. There are no major physical differences between the sexes, although the females are slightly smaller.

PUP FICTION
The ferocious wolf—either the animal or the mythical werewolf—has always been a popular bad guy in mass-market adventure fiction.

WOLFMAN

✦

Many cultures have stories of shape-shifters who can take on the appearance of wolves. In the Western tradition, immortalized in hundreds of "wolfman" movies, a human becomes infected by the bite of a werewolf. Then he or she changes into a monstrous wolf–human hybrid at full moon to prey on other humans. The belief that a werewolf can be killed with a silver weapon or bullet originated in nineteenth-century fiction, but was enthusiastically adopted by later writers and filmmakers. In wolf form, the werewolf displays much worse behavior than real wolves: it is a solitary creature with murder in its heart, which kills indiscriminately without mercy or sense. But rather than a fear of the wolf, the myth of the werewolf expresses our deep-seated fears about ourselves and our own capacity for mindless violence and cruelty toward fellow humans and other animals.

The wolf is a social animal living in family packs consisting of a dominant pair that have mated for life, along with their cubs and yearlings. It is unlikely that a strange adult wolf would be admitted into a pack, though it has been known for orphaned juveniles to be adopted. Wolves are fiercely territorial, marking their territories, and warning other wolves off by howling. Members of neighboring packs are careful not to stray into each others' territories, as this would entail a bloody confrontation ending in death. Wolves will hunt alone or in packs and have been known to use feints and ambush techniques to capture their prey. More experienced wolves do not attack larger prey head on but prefer to chase them down to exhaust them, and bite them on the body to kill them through loss of blood. The wolf is at the top of the food chain and has few predators apart from the tiger, the bear, and, of course, humans.

A wolf eats sheep but now and then, ten thousands are devoured by men.

Benjamin Franklin (1706–90)

"MY, GRANNY! WHAT BIG TEETH YOU HAVE!"

As will be seen in the next entry on the dog, humans have had a long and complex relationship with the wolf since prehistory. The wolf was the first animal to be domesticated by man, long before the cow or horse. Humans took advantage of the wolf's hunting skills, and the wolf learned that it could obtain food from the waste heaps of human settlements, much as feral dogs still do today in parts of the developing world. This symbiotic relationship continued until humans bred dogs of their own and began to domesticate the herbivores that had once been their, and the wolf's, prey. At this point the wolf turned from an ally into a dangerous pest that threatened the herds of sheep, goats, and cattle.

Although wolves have been attacking and killing humans for centuries, their victims worldwide can be counted in the thousands since the Middle Ages—a death toll dwarfed by the number of wolves killed by humans for sport, fur, or out of fear. Under normal circumstances, a wolf will stay away from humans and keep their dens out of sight of human habitation. However, a wolf suffering

PACK ANIMAL
The wolf's social nature made it an ideal candidate for domestication.

ONCE UPON A TIME

from rabies, or one that is starving, will attack and kill humans. Wolves predate domesticated animals and will also kill dogs. Apart from a very limited trade in their fur, wolves have little commercial value to humans. Like other species that are considered to be rivals, the wolf has been hunted to extinction in many countries. They now survive in isolated mountainous or densely forested regions, where they are unlikely to be disturbed by humans.

The main function of the wolf in the past several hundred years, it seems, is as a monster to frighten and entertain children, and to remind them that, outside the safety of the home and daytime, there lurk dangerous predators that prey on the unwary and the innocent. The wolf has become a metaphor for that part of human nature that remains untamed and dangerous— the criminal, the perverse (take the wolf in sheep's clothing, for example), and the uncivilized elements. The ultimate expression of this fear of ourselves is the legend of that sad monster, the part-man, part-wolf werewolf.

Fortunately for the wolf, its absence from many parts of the developed world during the past hundred years, and a new understanding fostered by conservationists and through nature documentaries, has enabled its rehabilitation in the eyes of humans. It has not only been protected but also reintroduced in several countries in its former range. Although not universally welcomed, especially by livestock farmers and dog owners, the wolf's return may one day renew our fellowship with humanity's oldest animal friend.

WOLF CHILDREN

✦

The most famous children said to have been raised by wolves were the brothers Romulus and Remus, the mythical founders of the city of Rome. The image of the brothers suckled by the she-wolf was one of the emblems of the Roman state.

Dog

Canis lupus familiaris

Native range: Worldwide

Class: Mammal

Size: 2.5–42 in (6–107 cm) tall at the shoulder

The wolf was the first animal to be domesticated by humans and also the first to be bred selectively for specific characteristics such as size, shape, coloration, and temperament. The result is hundreds of breeds of dogs that have played an important role in the economic development of civilization, assisting humans in transportation, hunting, and livestock rearing. Today, however, the dog's major role is as a domestic companion and family pet.

GENETICALLY UNMODIFIED ORGANISM

At first sight, it seems unlikely that the diminutive chihuahua, standing a few inches tall at the shoulder, is a direct descendant of the gray wolf, which is many times larger, and would probably regard it as a bite-sized snack. However, genetic research has now confirmed that all dogs, large, small, dopey, and ferocious, are all wolves. This link can be conclusively demonstrated by the ability of dogs to interbreed with wolves, though in the case of the chihuahua, this would require the use of a stepladder. The extraordinary variation that is seen in modern dog breeds was not achieved through the manipulation of wolf genes in the modern sense of the term, but by slow, patient breeding over hundreds of years to select the desired characteristics.

The questions of when, where, and how wolves became domesticated, and whether this occurred once or several times, are still the subject of fierce academic debate. The most widely accepted theory places the first instances of domestication sometime between 20,000 and 10,000 years BP, but some authorities claim that domestication and the differentiation of wolf from dog could have begun as early as 100,000 years BP. There are also arguments as to whether this took place in one area and gradually spread throughout the human population, or whether it happened several times at different periods and in different locations. Among the contenders as earliest sites for the beginnings of domestication are China and the Near East. Because of the poor communications between distant human populations during prehistory, and the multiple domestications of other species such as the cow and horse, it would seem logical

WOLF HOUND
Although physically very different, all dogs are genetically identical to wolves.

to conclude that wolf–human interactions led to domestication several times across different regions.

One intriguing theory is that the wolf domesticated itself by choosing to associate with early humans. Wolves that were less afraid of humans and more social, so the theory goes, would feed off the waste heaps of human settlements and so have a better chance of reproducing than wilder, more timid animals. They passed on these traits to their offspring, who became more and more at home in human company, until they became accepted as part of human communities. A third theory proposes that domestication began when wolf cubs were raised by humans to help them in hunting and to use them as beasts of burden. Native Americans used dogs as pack animals until the introduction of the horse, and the Inuit peoples of the Arctic still use dog teams to pull their sleds. Wolves have a keen sense of smell and good tracking abilities, so they would have been useful adjuncts in hunting, and the wolves themselves would have benefited from the arrangement by obtaining food from their human masters.

COMPANION
Dogs were our earliest animal companions and could have been domesticated as long as 100,000 years ago.

DNA evidence suggests that dogs and wolves began to diverge some 15,000 years BP, and archaeological finds in the Near and Far East demonstrate the existence of domesticated dogs around 12,000 years BP. By the 1st century CE, Roman noblemen kept packs of hunting dogs, and Roman ladies coddled small dogs on their laps, much like the canine fashion accessories of modern times. The roles and nature of dog breeds changed as civilizations rose and fell, but they have remained our constant companions. Although morphologically dogs show enormous variation in shape, size, color, and temperament, they are genetically indistinguishable from their wolf ancestors. They, too, are social pack animals, but because of their long interaction with humans, are more social than their wild cousins, and able to form large packs of unrelated individuals that exhibit complex hierarchical relationships.

Yesterday I was a dog. Today I'm a dog. Tomorrow I'll probably still be a dog. Sigh! There's so little hope for advancement.
Snoopy the dog *by Charles M. Schulz (1922–2000)*

MAN'S BEST FRIEND

It has been suggested that humanity's first relationship with the dog was a source of food and pelts. Although eating dogs is now unthinkable in our own pet-loving cultures, the practice is well attested historically, and continues to the present day in East Asia. In ancient Mesoamerica, which lacks large herbivores, the dog was a valuable source of meat. Currently dog is still eaten in Korea and in parts of China and Southeast Asia, although increasing affluence, the growing availability of alternative meat sources, and the adoption of the dog as a pet and companion will probably signal the demise of chow on the menu. In Europe and America, where there have always been alternatives, dogs have only been eaten in times of extreme need.

Until the modern period, most dogs kept by humans have been kept for their labor. We have already seen that they have been used as beasts of burden, especially in North America where the horse was only reintro-

TALLY HO!
Historically, one of the main functions for which dogs were bred was as hunters to stalk, chase down, or retrieve prey.

duced in the sixteenth century. But in Europe, where the horse and oxen did the heavy lifting, the traditional roles of the dog have been in hunting and in animal husbandry. Dog breeds have evolved with the changing styles of hunting. In hunting on horseback, which is still practiced by the "hunts" of England, a pack of "scenthounds," such as bloodhounds, foxhounds, or harriers, will track an animal prey and, when they catch it, will most likely kill it unless called off. The development of firearms was accompanied by the breeding of gun dogs, such as pointers, setters, retrievers, and span-iels, that will show the location of the prey to the hunter, but not attack it. When the prey is killed or wounded, they will retrieve it. A third group of diminutive hunting dogs, which include the terriers and the Jack Russell, are used to destroy vermin, such as rats and rabbits, which they can pursue into their burrows.

Even in these times of increasing mechanization and factory farming, dogs are still found on farms as herding animals. Breeds such as the border collie and German shepherd use modified hunting behavior to control and round up animals. Dogs also act as guards for livestock against predators such as wolves, coyotes, and foxes. A much less edifying use of dogs is in dog fighting, which although illegal in most of the developed world continues as an underground activity. More benign and socially beneficial uses for dogs include as rescue animals that can sniff out victims buried in buildings after earthquakes or under snow in avalanches; as police dogs that are used to find narcotics and explosives; and as seeing-eye dogs that guide the blind or partially sighted. Dogs have played an important part in scientific research, such as Laika

(c. 1954–57), the first animal to orbit the earth, though in her case it was a one-way trip; in medical research; and more controversially in the testing of cosmetics and other consumer products.

Today, the vast majority of dogs in the developed world are kept as domestic pets. Medical research has shown that dog owners experience reduced levels of stress and are therefore less likely to suffer from degenerative conditions such as heart disease and stroke. In the affluent regions of the world, the dog has been commoditized and turned into a profitable product. Pedigree breeds and new hybrids are the latest fashion accessory to be found at the side or in the handbags of the rich and famous. Dog-related merchandise and services are now a booming industry, as Westerners buy clothing, toys, grooming, and even the services of dog psychologists for their beloved pets. And when the grim reaper comes to fetch Rover for that final walk to doggy heaven, the cherished pet is laid to rest in its own plot in a canine cemetery.

ANTI-TANK DOGS

✦

Dogs have been used in warfare since antiquity. During World War Two, when the German Army invaded the USSR in 1941, the Russians were very short of anti-tank mines and weapons. They devised the hare-brained scheme of strapping explosive belts onto the back of dogs and training them to go under tanks, where the explosive would be detonated by a simple wooden trigger, thereby destroying the tank. There were several serious drawbacks to the plan. Dogs often panicked in battle and ran back to their own lines, and because the dogs had been trained with Soviet tanks, they were just as likely to run under their own tanks as the enemy's. Although the tactic claimed a few early successes, the Germans learned to pick off the dogs with machine guns or flamethrowers before they had a chance to get close to the tanks.

Goat

Capra hircus

Native range: Anatolia (eastern Turkey)

Class: Mammal

Size: 17–42 in (43–107 cm) tall at the shoulder

+ **EDIBLE**
+ MEDICINAL
+ **COMMERCIAL**
+ **PRACTICAL**

The goat is thought to be the first ruminant species to have been domesticated by early human farmers and pastoralists. Hardy and capable of surviving on varied rations in difficult environments, the goat is one of nature's generalists providing us with food and material for clothing.

THE ALL-PURPOSE ANIMAL

The goat was first domesticated around 10,000 years BP in Anatolia, eastern Turkey, where it was kept for its meat, milk, hide, and wool. Although it played an important role in the development of human civilization, providing a valuable addition to the human diet, it is now restricted to a niche market in the developed world's increasingly industrialized agribusiness. Unlike the cow, sheep, and pig, which have been selectively bred to provide ever-increasing yields, the goat remains a generalist among domesticated animals. It provides meat, but not in the same quantities as beef cattle or pigs; wool, which though of very high quality cannot match the sheep's in quantity; and milk, but not in the same quantities as dairy cattle. However, in the Near East, India, and the West Indies, where beef and pork are either less available or not eaten, goat is still a popular source of meat.

Goats have long furry coats, and both males, or "bucks," and females, or "does," have beards and pointed black horns. Like other ruminants, goats have no upper incisor or canine teeth. Instead they use a dental pad in front of the hard palate, lower incisor teeth, lips, and a tongue to take food into

GENERALISTS
The goat is a versatile animal, providing humans with meat, milk, and wool, as well as other services such as transportation.

their mouths. Adult goats have four stomachs that allow them to digest cellulose-rich plant material and convert it into valuable fat and protein. The rumen is the largest of the goat's four stomachs, with a capacity of three to six gallons (11–22 l). It contains microorganisms that break down the cellulose fiber into fatty acids that are absorbed through the rumen wall. The reticulum is located just below the entrance of the oesophagus into the stomach. It is considered the smaller half of the reticulorumen, the other half being the rumen, from which it is separated by an overflow connection known as the "ruminoreticular fold." The omasum consists of many folds or layers of tissue that grind up feed ingesta and remove some of the water. Finally, the abomasum, which is functionally similar to the human stomach, secretes acid and digestive enzymes that break down food before it enters the intestinal track.

CURIOUS FEEDERS
Goats are inquisitive and intelligent, and will test most things to see if they are edible.

Goats are browsers rather than grazers, preferring fibrous food to grass. They are very particular about what they eat and will not eat food that is dirty, of poor quality, or that has been trampled on. Goats will eat young thistles, brambles, twigs, and tree bark, as well as plants that are poisonous to other ruminants without any ill effects. Goats are intelligent and naturally inquisitive and will nibble and investigate almost any item, including discarded human refuse, such as cardboard boxes and tin cans, and even washing hung out to dry. They are also extremely sure-footed and

SURE-FOOTED
The agile goat is particularly
well suited to mountainous
terrain that would challenge
cattle and sheep.

excellent climbers. They will
either break down or climb
fences, and can climb into trees
to reach fresh shoots and leaves.

Dairy goats produce approximately two percent of the world's
milk production. In their prime,
they produce three to four U.S.
quarts (2.7 to 3.6 l) of milk per
day. Their milk contains an
average of 3.5 percent butterfat.
Goat's milk has small, well-emul-

sified fat globules, and the cream remains suspended in the milk, instead
of rising to the top, as in cow's milk. This means that the milk does not
need to be homogenized, which is an advantage if it is
intended to be made into cheese. The process of
homogenization alters the structure of milk, reducing
its ability to coagulate, and affects the quality and
yield of cheese. Goat's cheese is widely made in
Europe, and is a specialty of several French regions,
where it is known as *fromage de chèvre* or simply
chèvre, the French word for "goat."

In addition to its meat and milk, the goat is prized
for its fiber. Most goats have softer insulating hair
close to the skin and longer guard hairs on the surface.
The guard hairs are of little value as they are coarse
and difficult to spin and dye. The most sought-after
fiber for the textile industry is the down, which goes
by several names, the best know of which is "cashmere." The cashmere goat produces cashmere wool,
which is one of the most expensive natural fibers
available commercially. Cashmere fiber is harvested
once a year, and the average goat produces around
9 oz (200 g) of down. The other goat species kept for
its fiber is the Angora goat, which produces long,
curly, lustrous mohair. The entire body of the goat is
covered in mohair locks, and there are no coarse
guard hairs. The locks grow year round and can reach
four inches (10 cm) or more in length. The coat is
shorn twice a year, yielding an average of ten pounds
(4.5 kg) of wool.

FAINTING GOATS

✦

The "myotonic" or "fainting" goat is
an American breed whose muscles
freeze for about ten seconds when
the goat is startled. Although
painless, this generally results in the
animal collapsing on its side. The
characteristic is caused by a
hereditary genetic disorder called
myotonia congenita. When startled,
younger goats will stiffen and fall
over. Older goats learn to spread
their legs or lean against something,
and often they continue to run about
in an awkward, stiff-legged shuffle.
The goat does not actually black out
but remains conscious during its
brief paralysis. The condition has
been exploited by livestock farmers
who station fainting goats with their
herds of sheep to act as decoys in
case of attack by wolves or coyotes.
The unfortunate goat is paralyzed
and is eaten, giving the sheep the
opportunity to make good
their escape.

GOAT-HEADED GODS AND DEMONS

In ancient Greek and Roman mythology, the horned, forest-dwelling satyrs and the god Pan had a human upper body and the legs and horns of a goat. These human–animal hybrids lived outside of the rules of civilized conduct, wandering as they pleased, and giving themselves over to their sexual passions with the local nymphs and any passing human females. They represented the uncontrolled part of the libido that is enslaved to lust and passion. The goat features in Norse mythology as a symbol of plenty, and is associated with the pagan winter festival of Yule. In Judaism, the goat is considered to be a clean animal, and in biblical times, it was offered as a sacrifice along with sheep. During the Jewish festival of Yom Kippur, the Day of Atonement, the priests selected two goats: one was sacrificed, while the other—the "scapegoat"— was set free in the wilderness, taking with it the sins of the community. The goat features in the Chinese zodiac, as well as in Western astrology, in which it is the tenth sign, Capricorn.

> **Happiness isn't happiness unless there's a violin-playing goat.**
>
> *Julia Roberts (b. 1967)*

With the coming of Christianity, and its establishment as the official religion of the Roman Empire in the fourth century CE, many of the ancient pagan gods were transformed into demons. Pan, with his animal attributes and uncontrolled sexual appetites, was a particularly easy target for early Christians. In medieval folklore, he became associated with the Devil. Satan is often represented with goat's hooves, horns, and a pointed goatee beard. In Satanic rituals, both real and imagined, Satan was supposed to appear in the form of a black goat.

The goat is an animal that has one of the longest associations with humanity, but unlike other domesticated species, it has managed to maintain its independence. Along with the cat, the goat is one of the animals that will most readily return to the wild. When Europeans began to explore and colonize the wider world in the sixteenth century, they took with them their own domestic animals. Large populations of feral goats have established themselves in Australia, New Zealand, and the Galápagos Islands, where they have caused serious environmental damage. Despite its many years of service, perhaps we do not feel entirely comfortable with the inquisitive, intelligent, and independent goat, which is why we have found it so easy to demonize.

WILD SIDE
The ancient Greek god Pan was half-man, half-goat, and was known for his uncontrolled sexual appetites.

North American Beaver

Castor canadensis

Native range: North America

Class: Mammal

Size: 35–52 in (89–132 cm) in length

+ *EDIBLE*
+ *MEDICINAL*
+ *COMMERCIAL*
+ *PRACTICAL*

The beaver does not earn its place in these pages because it is one of nature's most superb civil engineers, but because its exploitation between the seventeenth and nineteenth centuries was instrumental in opening up the vast North American wilderness. Hunted for its meat and fur, it was particularly prized for the secretion castoreum, which was used in early medicine.

NATURE'S CIVIL ENGINEER

The world's third largest rodent after the South American capybara and the European beaver, the semi-aquatic North American beaver is one of nature's most accomplished civil engineers. Second only to humans, the beaver reconfigures its environment to suit its own needs. To create its living space, it will fell trees to build dams in order to create a suitable body of water for its den, know as a "lodge." In doing so, it has unknowingly made an important contribution to the conservation of wetlands, much to the benefit of other species. Its role as a conservationist, however, was not well understood until it had nearly been hunted to extinction from much of its native range. From the seventeenth to the nineteenth century, humans harvested beaver populations for their meat, fur, and the bitter secretion called castoreum that was thought to have medical properties. As a result, the original beaver population, which has been estimated at around 60 million animals, has now been reduced to between six and 12 million today.

HYDRO-ENGINEER
Second only to humans, the beaver shapes its environment to suit its own needs.

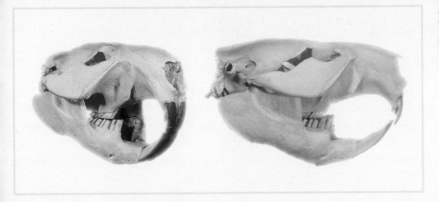

Beavers show a number of adaptations to their unique ecological niche: they have differentiated front and back feet; their webbed hind feet are much larger and are used to propel them through the water; and they have five digits, one of which has two claws that are used for grooming. The shorter front legs resemble small webless hands with sharp pointed claws that they use to carry branches, dig, and tear up vegetation. The beaver's body is insulated by a layer of subcutaneous fat and a thick fur coat. Beaver fur has two different lengths: the surface guard hairs measure 2.5 in (6.5 cm) long and the dense undercoat is about 0.75 in (2 cm) long. Air trapped between the two layers of fur keeps the beaver warm in cold water.

The beaver has small ears that it can close with flaps when swimming. Similarly, it can seal its nose with an internal valve. The beaver's lips meet behind its teeth and are covered in fur; this allows them to carry branches and cut material while swimming, and makes sure they don't swallow water. The beaver has several eyelids, including a thin film that covers the eyes and acts like a pair of swimming goggles. The leathery, flat tail measures 6 to 12 in (15–30 cm) long and 4 to 5 in (10–13 cm) wide. On land they use it to support themselves when tree felling and to balance when walking on hind legs. In the water, beavers can turn their tails in four directions to act as a rudder while swimming. When disturbed, the beaver will slap the water with its tail to warn others of danger.

The beaver's dentition consists of 20 teeth and 16 molars, mainly used for grinding food. The four front incisors have a hard coating on the front, and a soft inner coating. They grow continuously, averaging 2.5 inches

> **The beaver is an animal which has feet like those of a goose for swimming and front teeth like a dog [....] It is called the castor from 'castration,' but not because it castrates itself as Isodore says, but because it is especially sought for castration purposes.**
>
> *Saint Magnus Albertus (c. 1200–80)*

FRONTIER
The exploitation of the beaver for its fur and secretions opened up vast areas of the North American landmass to human settlement.

(6.5 cm) in length. The incisors are ground down and kept sharp by cutting down trees and branches. The beaver's diet consists of fibrous cellulose-rich plant matter, such as bark, wood, sedges, pondweed, and water lilies. However, it is not a ruminant like the cow. Instead of chewing the cud, it eats its food twice. When the food passes through the first time it is compacted into moist green pellets that the beaver excretes. It then eats the pellets a second time to extract the maximum amount of nutrition from its food before excreting them a second time.

Beavers live in small family groups and are fiercely territorial. They build lodges in ponds or lakes from branches and other plant material plastered together with mud. These lodges are designed with an underwater entrance to prevent the entry of predators from the land. If a suitable body of water is not available, beavers will create one by damming watercourses with felled trees and branches, which they cover with mud and stones until they have made a watertight structure. The lodge contains two dens, one for drying off after swimming, and a dry living area for the beaver family.

THE UNKINDEST CUT

TIMBER!
Beavers will cut down mature trees to dam watercourses in order to create a suitable body of water for their lodges.

The Native American people have hunted the beaver for its meat and fur for millennia. It was they who introduced the species to European settlers, exchanging pelts for trade goods. Beaver fur is warm and water-resistant, so it was a popular material for outer garments, such as overcoats, jackets, and hats. European settlers in the U.S. and Canada also ate beaver meat, though this was probably under exceptional circumstances rather than as a regular part of their diet (see box, opposite).

However, the beaver's true appeal to Europeans lay in the medicinal qualities of a secretion known as castoreum, which the beaver uses to mark its territory and to waterproof its fur. The castor glands that secrete castoreum are located near the tail in both male and female beavers.

Beaver testicles were also prized for their medicinal qualities. This gave rise to the odd story, referred to in the quote on page 57, that male beavers would bite off their own testicles to prevent hunters from pursuing them. This is an entirely fanciful piece of ancient invention; as the beaver's testicles are internal it would be impossible for the animal to castrate itself. Native Americans used castoreum to relieve pain, taking it in the same way as we would take aspirin. Castoreum is rich in an analgesic compound that is derived from tree bark, which the beavers eat, and which is also the original source of aspirin. Its medical properties were much in demand in Europe, where it was used to treat headaches, fevers, and hysteria. With the near extinction of the European beaver, hunters turned their attention to its North American cousin, until its survival, too, was threatened.

Today, castoreum still has a number of uses in the perfume and food industries. In the world of high-end scents, known for their fancy names, and bottles, and eye-watering price tags, the fetid secretion of the castor glands are used to give a "leathery" note to a perfume's composition. In other words, men and women using perfume and cologne are unwittingly warning off beavers from their territories. Castoreum is also used as a flavoring agent in the U.S. and Scandinavia—the FDA-approved additive is often labeled as a "natural flavoring."

NATURE'S LOGGER
The beaver plays an important role in managing wetland habitats by felling trees and redirecting rivers.

North Atlantic Herring

Clupea harengus

Native range: North Atlantic and Baltic

Class: Fish

Size: 12–18 in (30–46 cm)

✦ **EDIBLE**
✦ MEDICINAL
✦ **COMMERCIAL**
✦ PRACTICAL

Your raiment, O herring, displays the rainbow colors of the setting sun, the patina on old copper, the golden-brown of Cordoba leather, the autumnal tints of sandalwood and saffron.

Joris-Karl Huysmans (1848–1907)

The north Atlantic herring remains an important commercial fish species to the present day, but during the Middle Ages, the trade in herring was the cornerstone of the wealth and political might of a northern European superpower.

SURVIVAL OF THE MOST NUMEROUS

According to the *Guinness Book of World Records*, the herring is the oceans' most numerous species of fish despite serious overfishing during the 1990s. Living in the waters of the north Atlantic and Baltic Sea, the herring has been an important source of animal protein for coastal communities since prehistory, and it became a major trading commodity during the Middle Ages. The herring was the basis of the economic and political influence of a northern European confederation of city-states known as the Hanseatic League that controlled trade over a large area of what are now the Netherlands, Germany, Scandinavian countires, Russia, and the Baltic states between the thirteenth and sixteenth centuries.

The herring has a three-stage lifecycle consisting of egg, larva, and adult fish. A migratory fish, herring will migrate to its coastal spawning grounds to mate and lay their eggs. Egg fertilization takes place externally—female herring release their eggs and male herring simultaneously release clouds of fish sperm know as "milt." The herring's strategy is to lay a large number of eggs to ensure the survival of a few. Females lay between 20,000 and 50,000 eggs, although large females can lay as many as 200,000 eggs in one spawning. The spawning grounds vary in depth between 60 and 300 ft (20–100 m), and are on level ground. The eggs sink to the bottom and adhere to the ocean floor, forming a dense carpet that can be over an inch thick. One square yard can contain as many as seven million individual eggs.

HERRING POWER
The humble herring provided the basis of the wealth of a medieval superpower.

Although the eggs on the surface have a better chance of survival because of higher oxygen levels, they are also more vulnerable to predators who come to feast on this banquet of free protein.

The eggs hatch into larvae in seven to ten days. The newly hatched herring larvae are transparent and have no scales. They are between 0.2 and 0.3 in (5–7 mm) long when they hatch and carry a yolk sac that provides a mobile food reserve until they are able to start feeding on plankton. Herring larvae are poor swimmers and are carried along by currents, tides, and winds. The larval stage averages six months, after which the larvae metamorphose into juvenile herring, or "brit." Their bodies become deeper and flatter and they grow scales, taking on the silvery color of adults. The brit migrate toward the coastal waters, gathering together in dense shoals. They live in deeper waters during the day, and come to the surface at night to feed. The Atlantic herring matures at between three and four years of age, when they measure approximately 9 in (25 cm) long.

"SILVER OF THE SEA"

It may seem strange that the humble herring, which we usually see floating pickled in glass jars, was a cornerstone of the might of a medieval economic superpower. The Hanseatic League of free city-states, which controlled trade from Germany to Russia, was established in the thirteenth century and endured as a major economic player until the sixteenth. The league controlled the rich fishing grounds around the Falsterbo Peninsula in southern Sweden, which was on the Atlantic herring's migration route from the North Sea into the Baltic Sea. The huge quantity of fish caught between September and October each year were gutted, cleaned, salted, and packed in barrels to be taken to the annual Scania fish market. In a good year, herring exports amounted to 300,000 barrels. The market attracted traders from as far away as Scotland, England, and France, and for 250 years was the major trading gateway for goods from Western Europe destined for Scandinavia and the Baltic region. The decline in Baltic herring stocks was one of the factors that led to the decline of the league in the seventeenth century.

EASY CATCH
In the Middle Ages, the herring were caught in nets during their yearly fall migration from the North Sea to the Baltic.

SALTY SNACK
Baltic herring were gutted, cleaned, and preserved by salting, before being packed into barrels and exported all over Europe.

Pigeon
Columba spp.

Native range: Europe and Asia

Class: Bird

Size: 25–28 in (64–72 cm) wingspan

+ **EDIBLE**
+ MEDICINAL
+ COMMERCIAL
+ **PRACTICAL**

To most of us, the pigeon is a pest whose only function is to bombard passers-by and cars with "guano." But the pigeon is an ancient companion species to humans, whose domestication dates back to prehistory. In more recent times, the pigeon has played a vital role in carrying messages during wartime.

HOMING INSTINCT

The pigeon is a permanent resident of our cities, and it is likely that this was always the case. The pigeon was domesticated between 5,000 and 10,000 years BP in the Near East, just as our ancestors were building their first permanent settlements. Today, an estimated 17 to 28 million pigeons live in Europe alone, making it one of the most abundant feral bird species. The pigeon was first domesticated as a food animal, but after humans discovered that

pigeons had a strong homing ability, they were bred to carry messages. Prior to the development of the telegraph, the pigeon was one of the few rapid means of long-distance communication.

Like all birds, the pigeon is a distant descendant of the giant dinosaurs that ruled Earth during the Jurassic period (199.6–145.5 million years BP). Several species of dinosaurs were feathered and slowly evolved the power of flight over millions of years. In order to be able to fly, birds need a lightweight skeleton and extremely powerful flight muscles. Their musculature requires a constant supply of oxygen-rich air, which necessitates more than the usual mammalian arrangement of two lungs. In addition to their lungs, birds have nine posterior and anterior air sacs. When the pigeon breathes in, half the air passes into the lungs and posterior air sacs, and the other half passes through the lungs and fills the anterior air sacs. The air sacs play no direct role in the exchange

YANKEE DOODLE PIGEON

+

The Dickin Medal is awarded to animals in recognition of gallantry and devotion to duty in wartime. During World War Two, a pigeon named G. I. Joe (1943–61), serving with the U.S. Army Pigeon Service, won the medal for saving over 1,000 lives when he delivered a message to Allied command that the village of Calvi Vecchia, Italy, had been captured by the British, just before it was due to be bombed by Allied planes.

of oxygen and carbon dioxide, which takes place in the lungs, but they maintain a high flow of air, giving the pigeon much more efficient respiration than humans.

Archaeological evidence suggests that it was the Sumerian people of ancient Babylonia (now Iraq) who first domesticated the pigeon, keeping them for their meat, as sacrificial offerings for their gods, and as domestic pets. The pigeon's homing abilities were discovered some time during the first millennium, prompting the ancient Egyptians and Persians to employ networks of carrier pigeons. How pigeons can find their way to and from an unfamiliar location many hundreds of miles away is still a matter of debate. Three theories have been put forward to explain this ability: the first is that the pigeon uses the Earth's magnetic field; the second is that it uses visual clues in the landscape, such as roads and rivers; and the third is that it uses its sense of smell to identify a distinct atmospheric scent trail.

Messenger pigeons were used well into the modern period. During the siege of Paris by the Prussian army in 1871, carrier pigeons relayed messages from the city to as far away as London. Even after the development of radio communications, pigeons still had an important role to play during wartime. Unlike radio signals that could be intercepted by the enemy, messages transported by carrier pigeon were secure unless the bird was shot down. Between 1943 and 1949, 32 pigeons were awarded the Dickin Medal for conspicuous gallantry or devotion to duty while serving in a military conflict (see box, opposite). Today, pigeons are used in the popular pastimes of pigeon fancying and pigeon racing. In 2009 a race was held between a pigeon and a South African Internet service provider to see who could deliver a large amount of formatted data fastest. The pigeon, carrying the data on a storage stick, flew to victory, easily besting its electronic rival.

EVOLVED
In addition to its two lungs, the pigeon has air sacs that improve its respiration.

MOBILE LOFT
During World Wars One and Two pigeons were used widely by both the Allies and the Axis powers for secure communications.

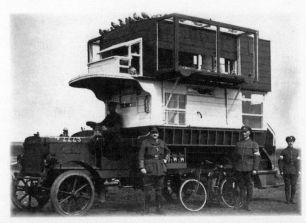

Accept that some days you are the pigeon and some days the statue.

From Dilbert *by Scott Adams (b. 1957)*

Carp

Cyprinus carpio subsp.

Native range: Europe and Asia

Class: Fish

Size: Up to 47 in (120 cm) in length

+ **EDIBLE**
+ MEDICINAL
+ **COMMERCIAL**
+ PRACTICAL

The freshwater carp has been an important source of animal protein since antiquity—both the Romans and the ancient Chinese farmed the carp in artificial ponds. In addition to being a food animal, the carp is bred for sport fishing and also as a decorative species for garden ponds.

RIVER HARVEST

When we think of domesticated animals, we tend to think of mammals, such as cows and sheep, or birds, such as ducks and chicken. Yet the freshwater carp, which is found in rivers and lakes, has been farmed since antiquity in both Europe and Asia. In the nineteenth century, the carp was introduced to North America and Australia as a food animal. However, its introduction into these new habitats resulted in serious environmental degradation, and efforts have been made to eradicate it or control its numbers ever since. Apart from its importance in aquaculture, carp are also bred for sport, and as a pet, particularly in Japan, where they are known as koi (see box).

The common carp's body is covered in large brownish scales. The spiny dorsal fin acts as a deterrent to predators that, together with the anal fins, enables the fish to balance. The tail, pelvic, and pectoral fins, in combination with the body movement, propel the fish through the water. The carp has two feelers on either side of its mouth called barbules that it uses to locate food on the river bottom. Carp have a varied omnivorous diet, feeding both on plants and worms, insects, and crustaceans. They live in small groups of five or more, but are also known to be solitary. They prefer warm water, which heats up their blood and makes them more active. Like the herring, the carp has adopted the strategy of laying a huge number of eggs to ensure the survival of a few.

EASTERN DELIGHT
Carp are particularly popular in East Asia as food animals and garden ornaments.

A female will lay up to 300,000 eggs in one spawning, and up to one million a year. Despite these vast numbers, carp populations remain stable, because the eggs and young carp fall victim to a large number of predators, including wading birds, semi-aquatic mammals, and other fish.

The domestication of the carp took place independently in the East and West during antiquity. The Romans introduced carp throughout their empire; after the collapse of the Western Empire in the fifth century CE, the monasteries disseminated the farming of carp throughout Europe. The breeding of captive carp developed in China around the same period, from where it was exported to Korea and Japan. In areas far from the sea, the carp provided an important source of cheap animal protein. In the present day, the production of farmed carp exceeds the production of any other freshwater fish, with China leading the table of producers. In 2002, carp accounted for 14 percent of world farmed freshwater fish. Carp is eaten in Central and Eastern Europe, and it is a staple ingredient of Jewish cuisine. In Europe, North America, and Australia, the carp is more commonly considered a sport fish. British anglers class the carp among the "coarse fish," and prize it as a challenging catch. *The Compleat Angler* of 1653 described the carp as "the queen of rivers; a stately, a good, and a very subtil fish." In America, by contrast, the carp is classed as a "rough fish," that is, a fish that is not commonly eaten, or is unpopular with the majority of the angling community.

MONSTER CARP
Japanese print featuring the popular hero Kintaro fighting a giant carp.

COLORFUL CARPS

✦

The breeding of ornamental koi carp began in Japan in the 1820s in the town of Ojiya, Niigata Prefecture, northeast of Tokyo. As Japan was closed to the outside world until 1868, koi remained unknown in the West until the early twentieth century, when they were first exhibited at an international exhibition in Tokyo. Koi varieties come in a large range of colors and patterns. The most common colors are white, black, red, yellow, blue, and cream. New hybrid species, including ghost koi and butterfly koi, have been bred since the 1980s.

Cochineal

Dactylopius coccus

Native range: Central and South America

Class: Insect

Size: The female cochineal is 0.2 in (5 mm) long

◆ ***EDIBLE***
◆ MEDICINAL
◆ ***COMMERCIAL***
◆ PRACTICAL

The pre-Columbian peoples of Mexico and Peru used cochineal, extracted from the body of the cochineal insect, to dye their cloth a rich carmine-red color. Until the early nineteenth century, the dye was one of Mexico's most important exports to the rest of the world. Today cochineal remains in use as a colorant in food, beverages, and cosmetics.

REDHEADS

In the modern world, we take rich, vibrant colors for granted, but in pre-industrial times, color was an expensive luxury. Pigments and dyes had to be extracted from natural sources, and the best were rare, expensive products imported from distant lands. Without modern chemical mordants to fix dyes in cloth, colors were often muted or washed out quickly. Certain dyes were prized because they were particularly vibrant and did not fade. Tyrian purple (see pp. 26–27), for example, was the most sought-after dye in antiquity, reserved for centuries for the use of Rome's imperial family and senatorial class. The Aztecs, who ruled what is now modern-day Mexico, used cochineal to color their cotton and maguey fabrics, obtaining the precious dye from conquered cities as tribute. After the Spanish conquest of Mexico, cochineal red, or carmine, was exported to Europe. The new dye was so much better than what was then available that the Spanish quickly expanded Mexican production to meet the growing demand. Until the beginning of the nineteenth century, cochineal production remained a Mexican monopoly, and was one of the country's leading exports.

The cochineal is a soft-bodied, flat, oval-shaped scale insect. The adult male and female are physically very different: the male has wings and is much smaller than the wingless female. The insect has a two-stage lifecycle consisting of juveniles, or nymphs, and adults. The females attach themselves to the pads of the nopal cactus with their sharp mouthparts, and feed on the plant's juices. They are largely immobile and wait for the males to visit and mate with them. After mating, females give birth to tiny nymphs that secrete a waxy white coat to protect themselves from dehydration. The nymphs produce long waxy filaments, with which they will catch the wind and travel to other host cacti. The new colony matures into the adult form to begin its lifecycle

DYESTUFFS
A selection of natural dyes, including dried cochineal insects, are used in Mexico to produce colorful traditional clothing.

once more. The males cannot feed, and die soon after they have mated.

Both the adult and nymph produce red carminic acid as a deterrent to predators, which makes up between 17 and 24 percent of the dry body weight of the insect. Harvesting the insects is a labor-intensive process, as they must be individually knocked, brushed, or picked off the cacti. They are collected when they are three months old and killed by immersion in boiling water, or by exposure to sunlight, steam, or heat. Each of these methods produces a slightly different shade of red or orange. It takes about 70,000 insects to make one pound (454 g) of cochineal dye.

Cochineal quickly displaced all the other red dyes available, gaining a worldwide monopoly. It was particularly suited to dyeing woolen cloth and yarn, which was unknown in Central America until the introduction of sheep by

Can blaze be done in cochineal, Or noon in mazarin?

Emily Dickinson (1830–86)

European settlers in the sixteenth century. The dye was exported as far as the Middle East and India, where it became the red used in the manufacture of Oriental rugs and carpets. Cochineal's dominance in cloth dyeing came to an abrupt end in the mid-nineteenth century with the appearance of cheaper, synthetic chemical dyes.

In the modern world, cochineal is still widely used as a colorant but no longer in the textile industry. The dye is one of the few water-soluble colorants that does not degrade when exposed to heat, light, or air. Unlike many synthetic red pigments, which have been shown to be carcinogenic, cochineal is not harmful to human health. This makes it suitable for use in the food, beverage, and cosmetics industries. Cochineal is found in a wide range of products including alcoholic beverages and sodas, processed meat and poultry products, bakery goods, dairy products, sauces, and candies. A significant proportion of cochineal is used in the cosmetics industry for hair- and skin-care products, lipsticks, face powders, rouges, and blushers.

WHOLESOME RED
Cochineal dye is still used in many foodstuffs, cosmetics, and beverages.

Fruit Fly
Drosophila melanogaster

Native range: Worldwide

Class: Insect

Size: Up to 0.1 in (2.5 mm) long

+ EDIBLE
+ ***MEDICINAL***
+ COMMERCIAL
+ PRACTICAL

The small and quite unimpressive common fruit fly has nevertheless played a crucial role in the development of the sciences of genetics and developmental biology. One of the most frequently used model organisms since the beginning of the twentieth century, the fruit fly carries 75 percent of known human disease genes within its genome, which makes it the ideal model for studying a wide range of human conditions.

MODEL ORGANISM

One of the problems that biologists faced when they attempted to discover the mechanism of heredity in humans is that humans take many years to mature and reproduce. They spend nine months in the womb, reach sexual maturity in their teens, and are unlikely to have offspring until much later. A human-based study of genetic inheritance would take centuries. In order to speed up the process, biologists looked for model organisms that they could substitute for humans. At the turn of the twentieth century, American scientists working at Harvard University hit upon the idea of using the common fruit fly because it was easy to breed in captivity and reproduced quickly. This proved to be an inspired choice, because the fruit fly, though an insect with 300 million years of evolution behind it compared to *Homo*'s measly 2.5 million, carries three-quarters of human disease genes within its genetic makeup.

OLD RED EYE
The fruit fly is an ideal genetic model organism because it is easy to raise in the lab and will go through several generations in a few weeks.

The fruit fly is found in homes, restaurants, and supermarkets—wherever fruit and vegetables are left to rot and ferment. The fly is easily recognizable by it red eyes and tan body with transverse black bars across its abdomen. The female is slightly larger than the male, and the male is darker

FRUIT LOVER
Fruit fly larvae hatch quickly in temperate conditions and feed on fruit sugars and bacteria.

with a black patch on its abdomen. Like other insects, the fruit fly has a four-stage lifecycle, consisting of egg (embryo), larva, pupa, and adult (imago). Once the male has located a female, he will court her by vibrating his wings and dancing. If she accepts him as a mate, she will take his sperm into two receptacles known as spermathecae. At 0.07 in (1.8 mm), fruit fly sperm is the largest in the animal kingdom relative to body size. Copulation takes about 30 minutes, and females will take and store sperm from several males. Research has shown that the last male to inseminate the female has the greatest chance of fertilizing her eggs.

The female produces up to 500 eggs, which she lays near the surface of rotting fruit or other moist, organic materials. At 77°F (25°C), the eggs will hatch within 12 to 15 hours. The larvae feed on bacteria and fruit sugars, and undergo two molts over a period of four days. After the second molt, the larvae enter the immobile pupa stage and will metamorphose into adults four days later. At the optimum temperature of 82°F (28°C), the fruit fly will take one week to complete its developmental cycle from egg to adult, though this can take much longer in cooler temperatures. In warm conditions, the fruit fly will live for an average of 30 days and lay up to 2,000 eggs.

[The fruit fly] has been extremely cooperative in our hands—and has revealed to us some of its innermost secrets and tricks for developing from a single celled egg to a complex living being of great beauty and harmony.

Nobel Prize-winner Christiane Nüsslein-Volhard (b. 1942)

"DAS WAR JA TOLL!"

✦

Work on fruit flies continues to reap rich scientific rewards. In 1995, Christiane Nüsslein-Volhard (b. 1942) won the Nobel Prize in Medicine for identifying the genetic and molecular mechanisms controlling the development of fruit fly embryos. Her findings have advanced our understanding of the evolution of microorganisms and the process of RNA–DNA transcription. She was also the first to identify "Toll" genes and explain their central role in embryo formation. The name "Toll" comes from Nüsslein-Volhard's exclamation "Das war ja toll!" ("That was weird/great!") when she first identified the gene as a result of her fruit fly experiments.

RISE OF THE MUTANTS

Until the early eighteenth century, most laymen and scientists accepted the Christian teaching that animal species had been created fixed and immutable. However, this idea could not explain the huge variation found within species, and the discovery of extinct species such as those of the genus *iguanodon*. The French scientist Jean-Baptiste Lamarck (1744–1829) proposed the theory of the transmutation of species that worked through two mechanisms to explain animal evolution: adaptation to the local environment, and an innate drive for organisms to evolve from simple to complex forms.

In *On the Origin of Species* (1859), Charles Darwin (1809–82) famously put forward the alternative of natural selection as the main driver of evolution. From his observation of the Galápagos finches and other living and fossil species, Darwin proposed that specific traits were selected ahead of others gradually over time. However, what he lacked was a physical mechanism that explained how variation took place within animal populations. Until the early twentieth century, most biologists favored three non-Darwinian theories to explain the evolution process: neo-Lamarckism—the inheritance of acquired characteristics; orthogenesis—an innate drive in organisms to change; or saltationism—evolution through sudden, large mutations.

The scientific community could have saved itself a lot of time and trouble if they had reviewed the work of Gregor Mendel (1822–84), first published seven years after *On the Origin of Species*, but almost immediately dismissed and forgotten. Mendel, a Catholic monk who spent seven years studying pea plants, succeeded in formulating the two basic laws of genetics: the Law of Segregation and the Law of Independent Assortment, but without identifying the role of chromosomes and genes in the process. In 1900, Mendel's ideas on inheritance were rediscovered by the British scientist William Bateson (1861–1926), who coined

UNHERALDED
The importance of Gregor Mendel's work was not appreciated until years after his death.

the term genetics, and the Dutchman Hugo de Vries (1848–1935), who introduced the idea of mutation. De Vries favoured saltationism (evolution through sudden mutation), and it was his theory rather than Darwin's gradual change through natural selection that the American Thomas Hunt Morgan (1866–1945) set out to prove when he began experimenting with fruit flies in 1908.

There are good reasons why Morgan and other early geneticists picked the fruit fly as their model organism. The fruit fly is small and easy to care for, and large populations can be bred in a small laboratory with little outlay in equipment or money. Typically, flies are mated in bottles containing porridge, on which the larvae will feed. Because the fruit fly's developmental cycle takes just one week under optimal conditions, it is possible to produce a large number of generations in a short time. The males and females are easy to distinguish; therefore it is possible to isolate unmated females after pupation to facilitate experiments in genetic crossing. Finally, fruit flies have only four pairs of chromosomes: three autosomes and one sex chromosome.

Morgan used chemicals and radiation to stimulate mutations in fruit flies, and then began crossbreeding experiments to see if he could identify hereditable mutations. After two years of work, Morgan succeeded in creating a series of hereditary mutations, notably a white-eyed male mutant fruit fly. When white-eyed males were bred with red-eyed females, the white-eye mutation skipped a generation. Morgan had identified the first recessive, sex-linked genetic trait. In 1911, he concluded that certain traits were carried on the sex chromosomes, while others were not sex-linked and carried by autosomal genes. Instead of confirming the theory of saltationism, Morgan had finally discovered the physical mechanism that confirmed Mendel's laws, and also Darwin's theory of gradual evolution through natural selection.

INNOVATOR
Thomas Hunt Morgan was not the first to use fruit flies, but he made the breakthrough that unlocked the secrets of genetic inheritance.

Donkey

Equus asinus

Native range: Northeast Africa

Class: Mammal

Size: 36–58 in (91–147 cm) at the withers

+ **EDIBLE**
+ **MEDICINAL**
+ **COMMERCIAL**
+ **PRACTICAL**

Proverbially portrayed as stupid and stubborn, the donkey has in fact been one of humanity's most useful animal helpmates for over five millennia. In addition to providing meat, milk, and hides, the stolid, sure-footed donkey has carried people and goods along the world's trade routes and helped them explore its wildest and most inhospitable regions.

OUT OF AFRICA

If the horse is the sports car of the equid family, the donkey is its pickup truck. For thousands of years the donkey has been doing the heavy lifting for humans in peace and wartime, for trade and exploration. The horse and donkey's earliest ancestor dates back to 54 million years BP. It was a small herbivorous animal about the size of a large dog that was adapted to running. During the Miocene period (23–5.3 million years BP), the equines diversified and took on the appearance of modern species. The modern survivors of the equines, which include horses, donkeys, asses, zebras, kiangs, and onagers, evolved during the Pleistocene period (2.5 million–12,000 years BP) alongside our own human ancestors (see the next entry for a more detailed discussion of the early equids).

The domestic donkey's immediate ancestor is the African wild ass, which, though now listed as an endangered species, is still found in small numbers in Somalia, Eritrea, and Ethiopia. The wild ass's historic range included Sudan, Libya, and Egypt, where archaeologists believe domestication began. The donkey is well adapted to arid and semi-arid environments; as well as being hardier than the horse, it can survive on a much poorer diet. After domestication, the donkey spread quickly across the Near East, Europe, and Asia. In contrast, the donkey came late to the Americas, where equines became extinct around 12,000–8,000 years BP, either because of climate change or overhunting by the waves of humans who migrated across the Alaskan land bridge from Asia. The first domestic donkeys reached American shores with Christopher Columbus (1451–1506) in the late fifteenth century. A few decades later, the Spanish conquistadors took horses and donkeys with them during their exploration and conquest of the Aztec empire. As Central America lacked pack animals, the species quickly became established in the Spanish colonies in the New World.

The donkey, although smaller, is morphologically similar to the horse. Its ears, which are much larger than those of the horse, serve the dual purpose of hearing and cooling the animal in warm weather. Like the cow, the donkey is a grazing animal that feeds on grasses and sedges. It will browse on shoots and bark, like the goat, but only when its preferred food is not available. Although it shares a cellulose-rich diet with ruminants, the donkey does not have a multichambered stomach or chew the cud, but breaks down its fibrous plant diet in its cecum, which is part of its intestinal tract. Unlike feral horses that form herds, wild and feral donkeys are solitary animals, who use their extremely loud bray to keep in contact with others.

The male donkey is called a "jack," and the female a "jenny" or "jennet." Donkeys can interbreed with horses, though the resulting crosses are usually infertile. A mule is the offspring of a jack and a mare, while a hinny is the sire of a stallion and a jenny. Donkeys have also been bred with zebras, producing an animal known under a variety of names including the zebra-mule, zonkey, or zebrass.

PEOPLE-CARRIER
The donkey is the pickup truck of the equine family, used to transport both goods and people.

THE PHARAOH'S DONKEYS
Archaeological evidence from several ancient burial sites suggests that the domestication of the wild ass began about 6,000 years BP in pre-dynastic Egypt. The earliest donkey skeletons found so far were excavated near Cairo and date back to 4600–4000 BCE. Ten skeletons were found interred in a specially constructed brick chamber close to the burial complex of an unidentified Egyptian pharaoh at Abydos (c. 3000 BCE). A comparison of the skeletons with those of modern

ANCIENT ASS
Archaeologists believe the donkey was first domesticated in predynastic Egypt 6,000 years ago.

donkeys and wild asses showed that they were an intermediate form, sharing characteristics of both, but the wear patterns on their spines and joints confirmed that they had been used as beasts of burden. Tomb paintings from dynastic Egypt show both the hunting of wild African asses, and the use of domesticated donkeys as pack animals to transport trade goods and agricultural produce.

Another ancient human artifact that shows the early use of donkeys is the "Battle Standard of Ur," which was not a flag but a wooden box inlaid with a mosaic in shell, limestone, and lapis lazuli. The standard was found in the cemetery of the Sumerian city of Ur (now in southern Iraq), and dates back to 2600–2400 BCE. Divided into three horizontal panels, the upper register depicts the ruler of Ur in front of a four-wheeled chariot drawn by wild asses or donkeys (though some believe the animals could also be horses); the lower register features a battle scene with similar chariots. This is a rare depiction of the donkey used as an offensive animal in warfare. Other ancient cultures preferred the horse, and in later times in the Middle East, the camel was used as a military mount.

The main use of the donkey well into the modern period was as a pack animal. It was particularly suited to the mountainous tracks of ancient Greece and Asia Minor (now Turkey). The Greeks were famously skilled mariners, but unlike the Romans their road-building skills left a lot to be desired. The province of Attica, ruled by the powerful city of Athens, had only three paved roads suitable for ox-drawn carts; hence most transport and trade between Athens and its surrounding villages and towns was assured by donkeys.

CHEERS!
An ancient Greek drinking vessel made in the shape of a donkey's head.

Although donkeys were commonly used in Mexico and Latin America, they were not a popular pack animal in North America. No less a figure than President George Washington (1732–99), dissatisfied with the size and strength of the donkeys then available in the United States, imported larger stock from Europe with which to breed sturdier working mules. The result of his breeding experiments was the American mammoth jack. Washington had another reason to be thankful for donkeys. The first president lost his teeth at an early age and had several dentures made, one of which used fragments of donkey teeth to replace his own.

Even after the introduction of the mammoth jack, the donkey was not widely disseminated in the U.S. until the mid-nineteenth century, when prospectors setting out on America's many gold rushes preferred the sociable, sturdy, sure-footed donkey to the more nervous horse.

By the early twentieth century, donkeys began to be used less as working animals and instead kept as pets in the U.S. and other developed nations. However, they remain an important work animal in poorer regions of the world. The largest populations of working donkeys are found in Latin America, Africa, the Middle East, the Indian subcontinent, and China, which accounts for a quarter of the total world donkey population—estimated to be 44 million animals.

To carry his load without resting, not to be bothered by heat or cold and always be content: these three things we can learn from a donkey.

Traditional Indian proverb

WORKING BEAST
Now kept as pets in the developed world, donkeys are still used as working animals in the developing world.

Horse

Equus ferus caballus

Native range: Central Asia

Class: Mammal

Size: 58–72 in (1.47–1.82 m) to the withers

+ **EDIBLE**
+ MEDICINAL
+ **COMMERCIAL**
+ **PRACTICAL**

HORSEPOWER
The horse's speed, strength, and carrying capacity have made a major contribution to human civilization.

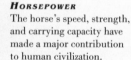

With the horse we come to one of the animals that has had the greatest impact on the development of human civilization. Its importance, however, does not only stem from its production of meat and milk, or its role in transportation, communication, and agriculture, but because it was the preferred mount of warriors from antiquity until the mechanization of warfare in the early twentieth century.

THE FIRST HORSEMEN

Early humans were social animals that predated on herbivores, with little to differentiate them from wolves apart from their tool-making abilities. As hunter-gatherers, they lived permanently on the verge of extinction, dependent for their survival on finding their next meal. With the domestication of the goat, sheep, camel, and cow, humans switched to being nomadic pastoralists and settled farmers who were no longer at the mercy of the whims of nature. They had an insurance policy in the shape of their animals that could see them through the lean times. In the earliest stages of domestication, the horse was another food animal that provided meat, milk, and hides. But when humans discovered how to ride, there occurred another change in the evolution of human civilization. Ironically, horsemen became a new type of predator: they were better, faster hunters, and also fiercer, more deadly warriors, preying on their horseless brethren.

As we saw in the previous entry on the donkey, the equids are an ancient family of mammals that evolved over the past 54 million years. One of the horse's earliest ancestors, the *Hyracotherium*, was a small browsing herbivore, no larger than a medium-sized dog. It had four toes on its front feet, and three on its back feet. Over the next 50 millions years, the equids grew larger and lost the extra toes on their feet, until they were running on one toe like modern equines. By five million years BP, recognizably modern equine species had evolved. They were better adapted for running, with longer legs and single-toed hooves, and their dentition reflected the change in their diets from browsing on soft tropical plant materials to grazing on the dry grasses of the steppes. Like ruminants, modern horses feed on cellulose-rich material,

but unlike cows, they do not have a multichambered stomach or chew the cud. The horse's fibrous diet is first broken down in the stomach, and the nutrients are then extracted in the cecum, which is part of the large intestine.

The early equines were distributed widely across the Old and New Worlds. However, after the arrival of the first humans in the Americas that equines became extinct. There are two theories proposed to explain the extinction: the first is a climatic change that disrupted the equines' food supply; the second is overhunting by humans. Whichever is correct, by around 8,000 years BP, the horse had disappeared from the Americas, only to return there with European explorers in the fifteenth century. There is only one surviving subspecies of wild horse: the Central Asian Przewalski's Horse, also known as the Mongolian wild horse. It is smaller and stockier than the modern domesticated horse, with a thick neck,

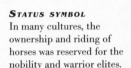

STATUS SYMBOL
In many cultures, the ownership and riding of horses was reserved for the nobility and warrior elites.

stiff mane, and shaggy coat. The only other subspecies of wild horse to have survived into the historic period, the Tarpan, or European wild horse, became extinct in the early twentieth century.

In prehistoric times, humans hunted the horse for its meat, as is evident in the prehistoric cave paintings of France and Spain and the remains of butchered horse bones at Neolithic sites. Exactly how, where, and when the horse made the transition from prey to domesticated herding animal has been the subject of several theories. One of these placed the domestication of the horse in the Near East around 2,500 years BCE, but recent research has pushed this much farther east to Central Asia, and much further back in time to the fourth millennium BCE. Archaeological finds in several sites in the

Central Asian republic of Kazakhstan indicate
that the Botai people, who flourished between
3,700 and 3,100 years BCE, were the first to
domesticate wild horses.

The steppes east of the Ural Mountains in
Northern Kazakhstan were a prime habitat for
large herds of wild horses, which the human population of the area hunted. Three lines of evidence
have led archaeologists to believe that this was
also the earliest, or at least one of the earliest,
sites of the horse's domestication. First, an analysis of horse remains from Botai sites revealed
significant morphological differences from wild
populations, proving that they had begun to breed
horses for specific characteristics. Second, a study
of horse jawbones brought to light wear patterns
consistent with the horses being harnessed or
bridled for riding. And finally, traces of mare's
milk found on pottery suggest that the Botai were
already making the fermented milk drink known
as *kumis* that is still drunk by the people of
present-day Kazakhstan.

Genetic analysis is another method that has been used to study the
domestication of the horse. Genetic material from modern horses is
compared with DNA extracted
from the teeth and bones of horses
found in archaeological sites. The
resulting analysis shows a difference in the genetic variation passed
by the paternal line (Y-chromosome) and that passed by the
maternal line (mitochondrial DNA).
The low levels of Y-chromosome
variability indicates that only a few
wild stallions contributed to the
domestic horse, while many wild
horse mares were part of the early
domesticated herd. Even today, the
horse plays a major role in the life
of the Kazakh people.

IMPERIAL PURSUIT
The Persian game of polo
was exported to India, where
it was adopted by the officers
of the British Raj.

WARHORSE

Without a time machine, we shall probably never know when the nomadic pastoralist horsemen of Central Asia realized that their horses were formidable weapons with which they could attack their settled neighbors. On horseback, they could cover much more ground than an army on foot, and in battle their extra speed gave them an advantage over infantry. The conflict between nomadic pastoralists and settled people would continue for millennia and culminate in the creation in the thirteenth century CE of the huge Mongol Empire, which extended from China to Central Europe.

CHARGED
The horse's greatest impact was on the battlefield, where it increased the speed and maneuverability of troops.

The earliest recorded use of horses in warfare was not for cavalry, however, but as draft animals for war chariots. In the previous entry, we saw that donkeys or wild asses (and, some believe, horses) feature on the 4,500-year-old Standard of Ur, which depicts four-wheeled Sumerian war chariots. Modern reconstructions have shown that these vehicles were slow and difficult to steer. By the second millennium BCE, much lighter and faster chariot designs, incorporating the use of the horse collar, were in use from China to Greece. The ancient world's most renowned charioteers, the Hittites of Anatolia (now central Turkey), used their chariots to carve out an empire in the Near East during the fourteenth century BCE. Hittite war chariots were mobile weapons platforms, carrying up to two bowmen alongside the driver. Horse-drawn chariots were important weapons in Bronze Age ancient Egypt, Minoan Crete, and Mycenaean Greece. Although chariots continued to be used until the first centuries CE, in most regions they had been superseded in battle by cavalry.

Incursions by Central Asian nomads in the Near and Far East stimulated the development of cavalry by settled peoples until it became a permanent feature of all ancient armies. The Greeks and the Macedonians under Alexander the Great (356–323 BCE) used cavalry with devastating effect in their wars against the Persian Empire. Until the first century CE, the Roman legionary fought primarily on foot, although the legions also had light cavalry auxiliaries for scouting and skirmishing. In the imperial and Byzantine periods, however, cavalry grew in importance. The heavy Byzantine cavalry, the cataphracts, anticipated the heavily armored mounted knights of Medieval Europe.

There are not enough Indians in the world to defeat the Seventh Cavalry.
General Custer (1839–76)

The two technical developments that we take for granted in riding, the saddle and the stirrup, were both developed comparatively late. Although ancient horsemen used blankets and felt pads secured by a girth to protect the horse's back and flanks and to provide added comfort for the rider, the framed saddle that distributes weight across the horse's back and gives the rider a more secure seat was not developed until the second century CE. The stirrup, which was first seen in China in the third century CE, did not come into widespread use in Western Europe until the ninth century CE.

The spread of gunpowder weapons in the late Middle Ages and the growing democratization of warfare led to the disappearance of the armored knight on his charger. From the sixteenth century onward, cavalry played a supporting role to the infantry as a highly mobile attack force on the battlefield. With the development of mobile field artillery in the seventeenth century, the horse found a new role moving ordnance quickly from place to place during battles. The horse was still used in offensive charges, but with varying results. A signal disaster was the Charge of the Light Brigade at the Battle of Balaclava (1854) during the Crimean War (1853–56). Immortalized in poetry, the British Light Brigade's charge of highly fortified Russian artillery positions ended with predictable consequences: almost half of the brigade was either killed, wounded, or captured.

Horse, thou art truly a creature without equal, for thou fliest without wings and conquerest without sword.

The Qur'an

With its reintroduction to the Americas at the very end of the fifteenth century, the horse played a major role in the conquest of the Aztec and Inca empires. While the Inca had a pack animal in the shape of the Andean llama, the Aztecs of Mexico had no large domesticated mammals. When they first saw the mounted conquistadors, they believed that they were some kind of terrifying animal–human hybrid. Combined with the firearms and steel armor, the horse gave the Spanish invaders a decisive advantage over their more numerous enemies. Horses soon reached the Native American population of North America, either through trade or the domestication of feral herds. The Great Plains Indians integrated the horse into their lifestyle, using it to hunt the buffalo and to mount a very successful counter-offensive against European settlement during the nineteenth century.

Although tactics and armaments changed considerably over the centuries, cavalry continued to play a decisive role in warfare until the beginning of the twentieth century, when it was rendered obsolete by the advent of trench warfare and the development of the tank and armored car during World War One.

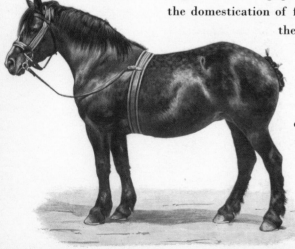

PULLING POWER
Horses, such as this Belgian draft horse, have been bred for their strength.

WORKHORSE

In addition to its military uses, the horse has a long history as a working animal in agriculture, transport, and communication. The horse has been used as a meat- and milk-producing animal in Central Asia, but in Europe, its greatest contribution to farming was as a draft animal for plowing. The introduction of the horse-drawn plow in the seventh century CE greatly increased food production from the heavy clay soils of northern Europe. In North America the horse was an integral part of the open-range ranching system that drove much of the expansion into the Great Plains region during the nineteenth century.

FARMER'S HELP
Prior to mechanization, the horse performed much of the heavy work in agriculture, from plowing to transporting crops.

The horse assured long-distance communication and transport from antiquity until the nineteenth century. Through a network of post horses, messages could be taken over hundreds of miles in a few days. The Persians and the Romans both used this system to maintain centralized control of their vast empires. The last service of this kind was the Pony Express, which briefly operated a mail service between Missouri and California from April 1860 to October 1861 until the completion of the transcontinental railway and telegraph.

Until the advent of the railway, horse-drawn carts, wagons, and stagecoaches provided long-distance transportation of goods and people throughout most of the world. In the burgeoning cities of the nineteenth century, the vast number of horses presented city fathers with an unexpected problem. In the 1880s there were an estimated 150,000 horses in New York City, assuring public and private transportation, and their "emissions" amounted to some 540,000 tons of manure deposited on the city streets. This led prophets of doom to predict that by the 1930s, the world's major cities would be buried under a thick layer of horse dung. The great dung crisis, however, evaporated when the automobile replaced horse-drawn vehicles at the turn of the twentieth century. In the present day, while there are still working horses in the less developed parts of the world, the bulk of the equine population is used for leisure and sporting pursuits.

Falcon

Falco peregrinus

Native range: Worldwide

Class: Bird

Size: Wingspan 31–47 in (80–120 cm)

+ EDIBLE
+ MEDICINAL
+ COMMERCIAL
+ *PRACTICAL*

The falcon was almost lost to the world because of humanity's thoughtless exploitation and abuse of the environment. Its survival bears witness to a new attitude toward the natural world and the need to preserve biodiversity to ensure our own survival.

NATURE'S DIVE BOMBER

The falcon does not earn its place in these pages because of its central role in ancient and medieval falconry, or because it is the fastest bird on the planet, but because, due to human exploitation of the environment, it almost became extinct in many regions of the world. Fortunately, the falcon was brought back from the brink, and its numbers are growing once again. Increasingly the falcon has colonized our urban environments, where our skyscrapers provide it with secure nesting sites and our street canyons are ideal hunting grounds in which it can ambush and kill its avian prey.

The peregrine falcon is an extremely widespread and adaptable species, living on every continent except for Antarctica. Its native range covers all climatic zones from the Arctic to the tropics. Falcons living in warmer regions are usually permanent residents, while those living in the far north will migrate in the winter months. The peregrine has very distinctive slate gray or bluish-black upper plumage, and cream-colored or brown under-plumage, which is distinguished with horizontal black barring and spotting. The claws and beak are black. The female of the species is on average 30 percent larger than the male.

Although the falcon will take small ground-dwelling mammals, it predates mainly other bird species that it will kill on the wing. After locating a prey, it will fold back its tail and wings to achieve maximum streamline, and literally dive bomb its target. A diving falcon will reach speeds as high as 200 mph (320 km/h), and one was recorded at 242 mph (389 km/h). It strikes the prey with its clenched talon, killing or stunning it, and will then turn to catch it in midair. It is this extraordinary skill in hunting that made the falcon one of the principal raptors used in falconry. In the wild, falcons nest on cliff tops and ledges, and in cities, they will choose the tops and ledges of tall buildings. Unlike other birds, falcons do not build a nest from twigs and plant materials. Their nesting sites, or "scrapes," are just a shallow depression in the soil or rock. The female lays between two and five eggs, which she will incubate for 32 days, while the male forages for food. The young are able to fly between 35 and 40 days after hatching.

The hawk, as a lethal agent, is the perfect flower of that still utterly mysterious alchemy—evolution.
From A Sand County Almanac *(1949)*
by Aldo Leopold

Although the falcon is itself predated by larger birds of prey, the greatest threat to its survival has been human activity. It was not because of direct persecution, as with the dodo or the whale, but because of the ill-considered and widespread use of pesticides, especially DDT. An organochlorine compound used to protect crops from pests and also to kill disease-carrying insects, such as the malarial mosquito, DDT accumulates in the food chain, breaking down into more lethal chemicals and increasing in potency as it becomes more concentrated. Falcons are at the top of the food chain and so eat high levels of pesticide residues that then accumulate in their tissues. One of the major breakdown compounds of DDT, DDE, causes the thinning of eggshell and the subsequent death of the fetus during incubation. By the 1970s, the problem was so acute that the falcon had become extinct in large parts of North America and Europe and was on the list of endangered species.

The plight of the falcon and other raptors provided the fledgling environmentalist movement of the 1960s and 70s with one of its early victories when it successfully argued for the control and then banning of DDT in the developed world. Although the pesticide continues to be used in some parts of the developing world, notably in areas of Latin America where North American falcons overwinter, the species has now been reintroduced to much of its native range.

Fallout
One of the unexpected effects of DDT used to kill malaria-bearing mosquitoes and other insect pests was the slow poisoning of birds of prey.

Cat
Felis catus

Native range: Eurasia

Class: Mammal

Size: 18 in (46 cm) in average body length

+ EDIBLE
+ MEDICINAL
+ COMMERCIAL
+ *PRACTICAL*

The cat does not provide any significant produce or work for humans, yet it is one of the most highly valued domesticated species on the planet. What it gives is companionship and affection to its human masters, or should we say, the humans with whom it deigns to share its living space.

BORN FREE

The first evidence for the domestication of the cat dates back 9,500 years, yet it is difficult to understand why this small carnivore has become one of humanity's most favored animal companions. In most cultures, humans do not eat cats, and apart from keeping down the population of vermin within the home, the cat furnishes little or no work. The cat, however, as anyone who has owned one will testify, provides a form of physical companionship that cannot be matched by any other animal. The cat therefore could be the first species that humans kept primarily as a domestic pet for the sheer pleasure of its company. The cat's closeness to humanity means that it features in the myths and religious symbolism of nearly every world culture.

The ancestor of the felids, including the big, wild, and domestic cats, is *Proailurus*, a genus of small carnivores that lived in the forests of Eurasia 25 millions years BP. It shared many features with its feline descendants, including a long tail, sharp teeth, and semi-retractable claws. The direct ancestor of the domestic cat, the wild cat, appeared two million years BP as a carnivore that was superbly adapted to its forest habitat, with a striped or mottled camouflaged coat and excellent night vision. Wild cats survive in many regions of the world but are on the endangered list, not only because of the destruction of their habitats and persecution by humans, but also because of hybridization with domestic cats. At first sight, the wild cat looks identical to a domestic cat, but it shows much less variation in color, shape, and size. Wild species are pale yellow to mid-brown with black stripes or spots. The belly is light gray, and sometimes marked with black spots. Its current range covers isolated regions of Europe, Africa, the Near East, and Central Asia.

What sets wild and domestic cats apart is that the former are extremely wary of humans and will stay away from human habitation. This paradoxically gives us a clue as to how the wild cat may have become domesticated. In the entry on the dog, we came across the concept of self-domestication, whereby animals who were less afraid of humans and more sociable were able to take advantage of the food supply available from the waste heaps of settlements and gradually became integrated within human communities. In a similar way, wild cats could have been attracted to early agricultural settlements, where in addition to food found in waste heaps there were also large populations of rodents feeding on grain stores. Early farmers would have welcomed this undemanding predator, which rid them of damaging pests, and also provided them with companionship.

As cat owners will know, the domesticated cat remains an extremely independent animal, which is quite capable of catching its own food. Unlike other domesticated species, the domestic cat will easily revert to the wild, where it will survive quite happily. The cat retains an anomalous position among domesticated species, most of which are completely dependent on humans for their survival. The cat might be better described as a parasitic species, living with humans as long as the arrangements suits it.

WILD AT HEART
The wild cat shows less variation in size, shape, and color than its domesticated descendants. It is now threatened because of loss of habitat and hybridization.

CAT GODS AND FAMILIARS

Archaeologists believe that our associations with the cat began in the Near East with the development of the earliest settled agrarian communities. The first evidence we have for the keeping of a cat as a pet comes from a burial on the island of Cyprus dating back to 7500 BCE. The tomb contains a high-status male, along with a number of grave goods, and buried nearby were the remains of an eight-month-old kitten. Cats are not native to the island, so the cat would have been brought there from the mainland on purpose. Unless there is a still-unknown ritual reason why the burial included a young cat, one can only conclude that the animal was a beloved pet.

Time spent with cats is never wasted.

Sigmund Freud (1856–1939)

The ancient culture with the closest links to cats is Egypt. The Egyptians worshipped many gods in animal form, including the goddess Bast, or Bastet, who began a career as a fierce lion-headed deity who protected the pharaoh. When another lion goddess displaced her, Bast became associated with the domestic cat. Her cult center was located at Bubastis in the Nile delta, where she had a large temple much patronized by cats (one can only imagine the smell!). When the site was excavated, over 300,000 cat mummies were discovered buried around the temple, indicating the high regard in which the animal was kept. An examination of some of the cat mummies has revealed that many were fakes—bones wrapped in bandages made to look like cats, that the priests of the temple passed off as genuine cat mummies to the unsuspecting pilgrims who flocked to the temple's yearly festival.

The cult of Bast was abolished, along with all other pagan gods, in the fourth century CE. In later periods, the cat got a much more mixed reception. In the Western folk tradition, cats became associated with witchcraft and devil worship. Black cats, in particular, were held to be the familiars of witches, and they often suffered the dreadful fate of their women owners who were suspected of witchcraft. During the fourteenth-century outbreak of the bubonic plague known as the Black Death, thousands of cats were killed as they were thought to bring bad luck and disease. In fact, this led to an explosion in the rat population whose fleas were the major carriers

IDOL
The Egyptians worshipped the cat in the form of the goddess Bast, whose temple was the abode of strays.

of the plague. A last remnant of this fear and suspicion of cats is the superstition that a black cat crossing one's path is unlucky.

The cat has a much better reputation in the Islamic world, where dogs are held to be unclean and are shunned as pets. The tabby cat has a distinct letter M on its forehead, which associates it with the founder of Islam, the prophet Mohammed (570–632 CE). One story has it that the prophet owned a favorite cat called Muezza who had earned his gratitude by saving his life from a snake. One day, when she was asleep curled up on his robe, rather than disturb her when the call to prayer came, the prophet cut off his sleeve.

Although cats are still eaten in parts of East Asia, notably China, and cat fur is still used in various parts of the world to make clothing, accessories, and blankets, the majority of domesticated cats are kept as pets. In 2007, the pet cat population of the U.S. was estimated at 82 million, 10 million more than pet dogs. Cats, like dogs, are now a big business, and they are catered for by a huge range of service companies, caring for cats' needs from the kitty cradle to the grave. However, despite our 10,000-year association with them, and all the care, love, and expense that we lavish on them, cats remain wild hunters at heart. One can imagine that if humanity suddenly disappeared from the planet, the cat would shrug its shoulders, raise its tail, and return to its forest habitat, there to live as its ancestors have done for two million years, forever in search of something small, furry, and squeaky to play with and kill.

INVITING CAT
+

Visitors to Japan will have noticed outside shops, restaurant, hotels, and other retail premises a white ceramic cat with one paw raised. This is the *maneki neko*, the "beckoning" or "welcoming cat," which is believed to attract good fortune, money, and customers. The cat sometimes carries a *koban*, a valuable gold coin used during the Edo period (1603–1867) as a token of its power to attract wealth. There are several legends connected with the origin of the *maneki neko*. One tells of a high-ranking nobleman who, noticing a cat beckoning to him, stopped to pet it. In doing so he escaped an assassination attempt. In contrast to the Western superstitions of bad luck and ill omens, cats in Japan are held to be animals that bring good fortune.

Atlantic Cod

Gadus morhua

Native range: North Atlantic and Arctic oceans; North and Baltic Seas

Class: Fish

Size: Up to 6.5 ft (2 m) in length

+ **EDIBLE**
+ MEDICINAL
+ **COMMERCIAL**
+ PRACTICAL

For five centuries, cod was the mainstay of fishing communities on both sides of the Atlantic, but human greed and a lack of fishing regulation triggered an ecological and social disaster from which the north Atlantic cod population has yet to recover.

"BRITISH GOLD"

While Christopher Columbus (1451–1506) was claiming Central and South America for Spain, John Cabot (c. 1540–c. 1599) sailed to the north of the continent, to what would one day become the Canadian province of Newfoundland and Labrador, where he claimed for the English crown a source of wealth that would long outlive the golden treasures of the Incas and the Aztecs. What he found were the seemingly inexhaustible North Atlantic fishing grounds, where the cod were so numerous that his crew only needed to throw baskets over the side to catch them.

As soon as they had been discovered, the Canadian fisheries attracted mariners from Britain, France, Spain, and Portugal, leading to centuries of conflict that were only resolved at the turn of the twentieth century, when the fishing grounds were placed in the hands of the people of Newfoundland. During the eighteenth century, cod was considered so valuable that one British prime minister referred to it as "British gold," which was to be defended from foreign competition (particularly from the French) at all cost.

The cod is a large carnivorous fish growing up to 6.5 ft (2 m) in length, which feeds on sand eels, crustaceans, shellfish, and smaller fish, including the young of its own species. It is a demersal fish that prefers coastal waters between 20 and 200 ft (6 and 60 m) deep. A sociable species, cod congregate in schools, and they will form large shoals at their spawning grounds during the annual breeding season between January and April. After fertilization and incubation, the plankton-sized eggs hatch into minuscule larvae that are 0.16 in (4 mm) in length. Cod are mature at three to four years of age, by which time they have reached 20 in (50 cm) in length. The adult cod has a sandy- to dark-brown

colored back, with mottled lighter sides and a white belly. A distinctive white lateral line runs from its gills to the base of its tail. In addition to its tail fins, the cod has three dorsal fins, two anal fins, two small, spiny pelvic fins, and two

OVERFISHED
Once the mainstay of the Newfoundland economy, cod was so overfished that its harvesting was banned in 1993.

pectoral fins that assist its locomotion. A long beardlike barbel hanging from its lower jaw is a feeler that helps it locate prey on the sea bottom.

The vikings were the first to harvest cod from the Atlantic ocean and Baltic sea in the early Middle Ages. Much appreciated for its delicate, flaky white flesh, the cod was preserved by salting and drying, making it suitable for long-distance trade between northern and southern Europe. Cod remains a staple of Atlantic—particularly Portuguese and Basque—cookery, and it is also the preferred species for Britain's signature dish of fish and chips. The humble cod also played its part in the struggle for American independence from Britain. In the early eighteenth century, Massachusetts engaged in a lucrative trade with the French, Spanish, and Dutch West Indies, exchanging cod, timber, and other commodities for molasses, which was used to make rum. In 1733, the British government passed the Molasses Act, trying to stifle the trade and to protect its own West Indian sugar interests. The widespread flouting of the act through smuggling and the corruption of royal officials bred in the colonists a spirit of independence that would lead to the American Revolution four decades later.

With incredible quantities, and no lesse varietie of kindes of fish in the sea and fresh waters, as Trouts, Salmons and ... also Cod, which alone draweth many nations thither, and is become the most famous fishing of the world.

Richard Hayes (fl. 16th c.) on the Newfoundland fisheries

In 1951, factory-fishing methods were introduced to Newfoundland waters. The cod catch peaked in 1968 at the unsustainable level of 810,000 tons. Within two decades, north Atlantic cod stocks had been so seriously depleted that the Canadian government imposed a moratorium on fishing, bringing an end to the five-centuries-old way of life of the people of Newfoundland. Despite the 1993 ban, cod stocks in the region have yet to recover. Once an example of nature's bounty, the plight of the cod bears witness to the destructiveness of humanity's abuse of the environment.

Chicken
Gallus gallus domesticus

Native range: Southeast Asia

Class: Bird

Size: 18–24 in (45–60 cm) wingspan

✦ **EDIBLE**
✦ MEDICINAL
✦ **COMMERCIAL**
✦ PRACTICAL

TAME AND WILD
The domestic hen (below) and its wild ancestor, the junglefowl (opposite, top right).

First domesticated in Southeast Asia 10,000 years ago, the chicken is now the most numerous bird species on the planet. Once allowed to roam at will in backyards and barnyards, the chicken is now intensively raised in huge battery farms, sparking concerns about animal welfare, as well as fears of a human pandemic caused by a mutated form of the avian flu virus.

JUNGLEFOWL

Everyone has heard the conundrum: what came first, the chicken or the egg? To which one unnamed wit once replied: "The chicken came first—God would look silly sitting on an egg." However, paleontologists have discovered that it was neither. What came first were the dinosaurs, which are the ancestors of all extant bird species. So next time you dig into a portion of fried chicken, you might like to consider that the animal that selflessly gave its life to satisfy your hunger is a distant cousin of the *Tyrannosaurus rex.* Although at first sight there is little family resemblance, both the dinosaurs and birds laid eggs, and researchers now believe that several species of dinosaur were covered in feathers rather than the scales found on modern-day reptiles.

The bird order began its long evolution during the Late Jurassic period (150–145.5 million years BP) with the appearance of the toothed, birdlike *Archaeopteryx*, and diversified into many different forms during the Cretaceous period (145.5–65.5 million years BP), when they lived side by side with the giant dinosaurs and flying pterosaurs. They survived the extinction event that killed off the dinosaurs and pterosaurs to become the unrivaled masters of the air. The largely ground-dwelling pheasant family, whose modern relatives include quails, pheasants, peafowl, partridges, and the junglefowl, appeared between 25 and 20 million years BP. In comparison, our own lineage *Homo* is a Johnny-come-lately at a mere 2.5 million years BP. Who knows, if evolution had taken a few different turns, an intelligent race of chicken might now be digging into a bargain bucket of Southern-fried human nuggets.

Once thought to have taken place on the Indian subcontinent, the initial domestication of the chicken has been relocated to Southeast Asia, possibly Thailand, around 10,000 BP. Genetic studies have shown that the domestic chicken's ancestors are mainly the Southeast Asian red junglefowl, with a later admixture of DNA from the Indian gray junglefowl. The red junglefowl is a forest-dwelling species, which shows marked physical differences between the cock and hen. The former is not only much larger, but has bright red wattles and comb and brightly colored plumage, which is gold on the neck and back, with long dark blue, purple, and green tail feathers. The hen, in contrast, is a drab brown with no wattles, comb, or long tail feathers, giving her much better camouflage when she incubates her eggs. The cock has the rooster's trademark "cock-a-doodle-doo" call, which he uses to attract mates and warn off any rival males in the area. An aggressive bird, the junglefowl cock uses the long spurs on its feet to fight competitors. Just as with the wild cat, one of the main threats to the survival of the junglefowl is hybridization with domesticated chicken.

No evidence exists to indicate how domestication took place, but it would be easy to imagine that hunter-gatherer people, who hunted junglefowl for meat and raided their nests for eggs, would have realized that a captive bird population would give a more secure supply of both. From Southeast Asia, the chicken was taken northeast to China, where the earliest archaeological evidence of domestication dates back to the sixth millennium BCE, and west to the Indus Valley, where chicken remains dating back to around 2500 BCE have been found in the ancient city of Mohenjo-Daro (now in Pakistan). From the Indian subcontinent, the chicken spread to Africa and Europe, reaching ancient Greece around the seventh century BCE. A great world traveler, the chicken

FINGER-LICKING GOOD

✦

Southern fried chicken has an interesting socioeconomic history. The dish originates in African-American slave cooking. The chicken is seasoned with a mixture of spices not usually found in European cookery and thought to originate in West African cooking. But before fried chicken could become widely disseminated, it required the availability of inexpensive fat for deep-frying, which was provided by new, fatter breeds of domestic pigs, as well as a suitable cast-iron pan, which were both introduced in the nineteenth century. Today, fried chicken has lost its associations with slavery, and is one of the main forms of fast food. As such, it has made its own sizeable contribution to the obesity epidemic that afflicts the developed world.

accompanied human mariners to Polynesia around 3,300 years ago, and evidence suggests that it was taken from there to the Americas, where chicken bones have been found at the Chilean site of El Arenal, dated to 1350 CE—140 years before the arrival of Columbus.

A CHICKEN IN EVERY POT

The domesticated chicken shows the same sexual dimorphism as its junglefowl ancestors. The cock is larger than the hen, with colorful plumage and a red comb and wattles. Hens show much greater color variation than their wild sisters, and in many subspecies females have combs and wattles. The chicken is a social animal that prefers to live in flocks, in which dominant individuals have priority for food and prime nesting sites. Unless specially bred for the "sport" of cockfighting (see below), domesticated chickens are less aggressive than junglefowl. The hen will lay a clutch of up to 12 eggs, which she will incubate for 21 days, maintaining a constant temperature and humidity. The cock plays no part in incubation.

Historically, poultry provided a cheap source of animal protein in the shape of meat and eggs to the poorer members of society, particularly at times when other meats were either scarce or expensive. Compared to the larger meat-producing mammals, such as the cow or sheep, the chicken needs little space and, being an omnivore, can exploit whatever food resources are available in its environment. Chickens are

FIGHT CLUB
The "sport" of cockfighting exploits the cock bird's natural aggressiveness. Fights usually end in the death of one of the birds.

kept on most farms and smallholdings and, well into the twentieth century, many city-dwellers in the developed world kept poultry in their backyards. In sixteenth-century France, the chicken became a symbol of the growing affluence of the peasantry and the artisan class. King Henry IV (1553–1610), nicknamed "good king Henry," promised that he would provide his subjects with a "chicken in every pot" on Sundays.

Today, however, the majority of the 50 billion chickens that are raised every year to produce eggs or meat are intensively farmed, which raises a number of animal welfare and human health issues. Egg-laying birds are housed in cramped battery cages, which allow the animal little movement. Lighting and temperature are artificially maintained at levels that encourage hens to lay all year round. The birds are unable to roam as they would in a barnyard, and their close proximity to other birds makes them prone to cannibalism. To prevent hens pecking one another, part of the beak is sliced off with a heated blade. Broilers, which are raised for meat, live in large climate-controlled sheds. They are routinely fed on antibiotics to prevent disease from the overcrowded and unsanitary conditions as well as growth-promoting chemicals that many campaigners claim are potentially harmful to humans. An intensively farmed broiler will be killed at six weeks of age, while a free-range chicken will live eight weeks, and an organic chicken, 12 weeks.

Whether organic, free range, or intensively farmed, chicken meat and eggs remain two of the most important food staples of world cooking. In the Western tradition, roasting, frying (see box, p. 91), and stewing a whole chicken or chicken portions are the most common ways of cooking, and only the meat is consumed. In Chinese cookery, most of the chicken is used, including the feet, which are considered to be a delicacy. It would be difficult to imagine cooking without eggs, which can be eaten on their own, as well as being the binding ingredient for a huge range of sweet and savory dishes.

EGG FACTORY
In battery farming, chickens are placed in tiny cages within close proximity of one another.

In addition to its role as a food animal, the domestic chicken is also valued as a fighting animal in the so-called "sport" of cockfighting. The practice, which is thought to have originated in the Indian subcontinent in the third millennium BCE, was popular throughout the ancient world, from China to the Greco–Roman world. Today, cockfighting has been outlawed in most of the developed world, but continues in many countries of Asia and Latin America. Bouts usually prove fatal for one of the contenders.

The ancient Romans, apart from eating chickens and watching them fight, also used them to foretell the future. They were used as oracles both in flight and when feeding. A flying chicken appearing from the left was considered auspicious. In the feeding method, the augury in charge of the birds opened the cages in which they were kept, and scattered pulses and a type of cake in front of them. If the chickens stayed inside, squawked, or flew away, the omen was bad, but if they came out and ate the food, the omen was good. In 249 BCE, just before a major naval engagement against the Carthaginians, the Roman commander Publius Clodius Pulcher (d. c. 246 BCE) was enraged when his chicken refused to eat. He ordered that they be thrown overboard, saying, "If they won't eat, perhaps they will drink." He lost the battle, and on his return for Rome was convicted of impiety.

REVENGE OF THE KILLER CHICKEN

The chicken is an unlikely villain for a sci-fi B-movie plot; however, according to the World Health Organization (WHO), domesticated poultry represents one of the greatest threats to human health, far outweighing HIV–AIDS and malaria. The past few years have seen several pandemic fears that have not materialized, notably the great swine flu pandemic of 2009 that never was. However, we only have to look back less than a century for evidence of how devastating a serious flu pandemic can be. Between 1917 and 1920, the Spanish Flu killed between 50 and 100 million people worldwide. The particular tragedy of this pandemic was that it killed healthy young adults, unlike the seasonal flu that tends to affect the very young, the old, and those with underlying health conditions. The cause of the Spanish flu was a highly infectious airborne avian flu virus carried by birds including domestic poultry, which mutated to become transmissible between humans.

PANDEMIC
Between 1917 and 1920, the Spanish flu, a form of avian influenza, killed 50 to 100 million people worldwide.

What the WHO most fears is a similar scenario to Spanish Flu, with a reassortment (recombination) of genetic material from avian, swine, and human flu viruses that would create a new deadly pathogenic strain with the potential to kill millions. The huge number of domestic poultry in the world increases the chances of this happening. The virus causing most concern is H5N1, which has caused the death of millions of birds, and has killed 302 humans at the time of writing. The victims lived and worked in close contact with poultry, and

Avian and pandemic influenza are posing a greater challenge to the world than any previous emerging infectious diseases.
Dr Margaret Chan, Director-General of the World Health Organization

there have been no reported cases of human-to-human transmission. At present, there are no large stocks of vaccine against H5N1, and antiviral drugs, such as Tamiflu, have been shown to have a limited effectiveness against the disease.

The chicken is another animal whose domestication freed humans from the constant need to search for food in order to survive. As such, it played an important role in the development of human civilization. Unlike many other species, the chicken has thrived alongside humans, until it now outnumbers any other bird on the planet. Today, however, the intensive rearing of poultry has transformed the chicken from a boon into a growing threat to human health.

Darwin's Finches

Geospiza spp.

Native range: Galápagos
Islands

Class: Bird

Size: 4–8 in (10–20 cm)

+ EDIBLE
+ MEDICINAL
+ COMMERCIAL
+ **PRACTICAL**

A group of quite unremarkable birds native to the Galápagos Islands were part of the key that Charles Darwin used to unlock the secrets of evolution. Darwin's finches have remained the subject of controversy ever since, cited by both evolutionary scientists and creationists as confirmation of their own views.

THE DIVINE PLAN

We owe the idea that all animal species were created discretely, fully formed, and with no capacity to change to the medieval Christian mindset. According to Genesis, God created the animals on the fifth day of creation, each species "after its own kind," to populate the heavens, waters, and earth. Because God, theologians argued, had created the world with the sole purpose of leading humanity to salvation, everything within it had its appointed form and function according to the divine plan, and there was no reason for anything to change. Coupled with the belief that the world was only 4,000 years old, there was little scope for the long-drawn-out process of evolution.

Creationism has its basis in pre-Christian thought, in particular the works of two ancient Greek philosophers: Plato (c. 428–348 BCE) and Aristotle (384–322 BCE). Plato taught that our world and everything within it are imperfect reflections of a divinely created world of perfect forms. Aristotle established the "Chain of Life" in which all of creation

was arranged hierarchically, with inanimate matter at the bottom, and God at the very top. Although there were dissenting views to be found in the works of other ancient philosophers and in other cultural traditions, there was no intellectual space for these to develop in Europe until the Renaissance, when a combination of scientific inquiry and the rediscovery of ancient learning challenged established church teaching.

By the nineteenth century, despite the fact that a more accurate calculation of Earth's age and the discovery of fossilized remains of extinct animals had undermined the idea of fixed, immutable species, religious orthodoxy remained the accepted wisdom until the publication of *On the Origin of Species* in 1859. Darwin's ideas were not entirely original; he himself built on existing theories and beliefs. His grandfather, the natural philosopher and inventor Erasmus Darwin (1731–1802), had written a poem on the subject of evolution supporting the idea of the mutability of species. In France, the naturalist Jean-Baptiste Lamarck believed that species changed through two mechanisms: an innate drive to complexity, and the inheritance of acquired characteristics from one generation to the other. Lamarckism remained the most popular method of explaining how evolution worked until the discovery of the genetic mechanism of inheritance.

As a young man, Darwin would have seemed an unlikely choice as the father of evolutionary science. Although he was fascinated by geology and natural history as a student, he intended to become a country parson. He believed in what we would call today "intelligent design," whereby the creator had established the laws that controlled the adaptation of species to their environments. In 1831, one of Darwin's professors at Cambridge suggested that the young graduate join Captain Robert FitzRoy (1805–65) on the HMS *Beagle*, which was about to set sail for South America. Darwin would be the expedition's geologist and naturalist and also an intellectual companion for FitzRoy.

Darwin was enthusiastic about the voyage, which he believed would furnish him with evidence about the workings of the creator's grand designs. However, his hopes were almost immediately dashed as his father was dead set against the idea, saying that the voyage would be a waste of time. Had Darwin not gone, it is unlikely that he would have ever written *On the Origin of Species*, and the glory of his discoveries would have gone to another. In the event, Darwin's uncle persuaded his father to let him go, and on December 27, 1831, the *Beagle*, with Charles Darwin on board, set sail from Plymouth for what would turn out to be a five-year circumnavigation of the globe.

ON

THE ORIGIN OF SPECIES

BY MEANS OF NATURAL SELECTION,

OR THE

PRESERVATION OF FAVOURED RACES IN THE STRUGGLE FOR LIFE.

By CHARLES DARWIN, M.A.,

FELLOW OF THE ROYAL, GEOLOGICAL, LINNÆAN, ETC., SOCIETIES;
AUTHOR OF 'JOURNAL OF RESEARCHES DURING H. M. S. BEAGLE'S VOYAGE
ROUND THE WORLD.'

LONDON:
JOHN MURRAY, ALBEMARLE STREET.
1859.

The right of Translation is reserved.

NATURAL SELECTION
Darwin built upon the ideas of others when devising his theory of natural selection.

I have called this principle, by which each slight variation, if useful, is preserved, by the term of Natural Selection.

From On the Origin of Species *(1859)*
by Charles Darwin (1809–82)

A SHOT IN THE DARK

The aim of the voyage was to chart the coasts of South America for the British Admiralty. After crossing the Atlantic, the *Beagle* sailed southward from Salvador de Bahia, Brazil, to Tierra del Fuego at the very tip of the continent, with a stopover at the Falkland Islands. The *Beagle* then rounded Cape Horn and sailed north along the coasts of Chile and Peru, before stopping at its last port of call in the Americas, the Galápagos Islands, 525 nmi (972 km) west of Ecuador. While the ship conducted its survey work, Darwin spent his time ashore collecting geological data, plant and animal specimens, and fossils. In Punta Alta, Argentina, he

made an important find of the fossilized remains of long-extinct South American megafauna, including the giant sloth megatherium, which he noted were related to modern species.

Although Darwin had some experience as a naturalist, his true field of expertise was geology. He collected bird, animal, and plant specimens to take back to England, but sometimes haphazardly, not always bothering to make a note of the exact location of the finds. Fortunately for Darwin, he was not the only amateur naturalist on board the *Beagle*, and FitzRoy and two others also collected specimens of the bird life they encountered. The *Beagle* reached the Galápagos on September 15, 1835. While the ship charted the coastline of the isolated volcanic archipelago, Darwin spent his time on the islands they called at, making geological observations and collecting specimens. The birds that most attracted his interest were the mockingbirds that he encountered on the islands, which he noted were similar to those he had observed on the South American mainland. He also collected specimens of what he described as blackbirds, gros-beaks, finches, and wrens.

SURVEY SHIP
HMS *Beagle* circumnavigated the globe, furnishing Darwin with the evidence that would prompt his theory of evolution.

VARIATION
One of the keys to evolution was the variation in the shapes of beaks between species of finches that Darwin found on the Galápagos Islands.

Seeing this gradation and diversity of structure in one small, intimately related group of birds, one might really fancy that from an original paucity of birds in this archipelago, one species had been taken and modified for different ends.

From The Voyage of the Beagle, *2nd ed., (1845) by Charles Darwin*

The return leg of the voyage included stops in New Zealand, Australia, the Cocos Islands in the Indian Ocean, South Africa, and a final visit to Salvador de Bahia, before the *Beagle* headed north across the Atlantic to reach Plymouth on October 12, 1836. During the five-year voyage, Darwin and his shipmates had collected and preserved thousands of specimens from three continents, including several rather small drab birds that Darwin had found on the Galápagos

GRAND OLD MAN
Darwin after the publication of the groundbreaking book *On the Origin of Species*.

and Cocos Islands. As he did not have the expertise to identify his bird specimens, Darwin entrusted his collection to the leading ornithologist of the day, John Gould (1804–81).

Gould wasted no time in studying the birds, and in January 1837 announced findings that rocked the scientific world and made Darwin something of a popular celebrity. He told Darwin that he had collected 25 new species of mockingbird, and that the birds he had identified as gros-beaks, blackbirds, finches, and wrens, were all species of ground finch, also new to science. Unfortunately, Darwin had failed to label the specimens properly, so he could not immediately identify which islands the birds had come from. However, by looking at the specimens and notes collected by his shipmates, he was able to pinpoint the locations of his own specimens.

The final count was 15 new finch species: 14 from the Galápagos and one from the Cocos Islands. Although ornithologists have since reclassified the birds as members of the tanager family, they are still known as "Darwin's finches." What sets the birds apart are the size and shapes of their beaks, which are adapted to the different food sources available on each island. It was their similarity to South American finches, however, that made Darwin realize that they had not been created independently on the Galápagos but were descended from a common ancestral pair that had come from the continent at some point in the past. The different conditions on the various islands had then led to speciation through the process of natural selection.

THE CREATIONISTS STRIKE BACK

✦

The reader who would like an alternative take on Darwin's finches can consult the relevant article in creationwiki.org, a site that describes itself as having a "unique creationist perspective." Instead of supporting the theory of evolution through natural selection, creation-wiki argues, the finches merely represent genetic variations within a single species caused by environmental change—in other words, a latter-day version of Lamarckism.

Bald Eagle
Haliaeetus leucocephalus

Native range: North America

Class: Bird

Size: Wingspan up to 96 in (2.5 m)

✦ EDIBLE

✦ MEDICINAL

✦ COMMERCIAL

✦ *PRACTICAL*

A part from a role in falconry, the eagle has little practical service to offer humans. In fact, historically, the eagle has been persecuted as a predator of domesticated animals. But it does perform an important role as a symbol of strength, power, and nobility that has made it the emblem of nationhood for many states, including ancient Rome and the United States of America.

THIN ON TOP

The eagle is the first of four animals in this book that have been included not because of their commercial value to humans, but because of their symbolic significance from ancient times to the present day. However, the contrast between our respect for the eagle as an embodiment of strength, power, and courage, and for the animal itself could not be more pronounced. The eagle has been hunted for sport, and egg collectors have raided its nests. Even after it became a protected species, the eagle, like the falcon and other birds of prey, fell victim to pesticides that almost caused its extinction from across much of the continental U.S.

The particular species of eagle that concerns us here is the bald eagle, whose native range covers the U.S., Canada, and northern Mexico. Despite it name, the bald eagle is not thinning on top. The derivation is from the old English word "piebald," which describes an animal with patches of dark and light coloration. With the bald eagle, the head and the fan-shaped tail are white and the body is brown. The plumage of the immature juvenile (up to five years of age) is brown speckled with white. The feet, large hooked beak, and irises of the adult bird are a striking yellow color. As with other species we have encountered so far, the male and female of the species are differentiated by size. In the eagle's case, it is the female that is larger by up to 25 percent.

The bald eagle is classed as a sea eagle. It lives near large bodies of water and rivers, where it can predate for its preferred food, fish, which it

ALL-AMERICAN
The bald eagle is classed as a sea eagle and predates mainly on fish.

snatches from the water with its sharp talons. However, it will also feed on small mammals and other birds. A mated pair chooses a permanent nest site in a large tree, and they will add to the nest every breeding season. Their nests are the largest of any North American bird, averaging 13 ft (4 m) deep, 8 ft (2.5 m) across, and weighing 1 ton; one particularly large nest in Florida was 20 ft (6 m) deep, 9.5 ft (3 m) across, and weighed 2.7 tons. The female will lay clutches of one to three eggs every year, and both male and female take turns incubating the eggs.

Although the bald eagle was first protected in 1918, and the commercial killing of the bird was banned outright in the U.S. in 1940, its population crashed after the introduction of DDT in the 1940s. Like other raptors at the top of the food chain, the bald eagle was particularly vulnerable to chemicals in the environment. Through the process of bio-magnification, large amounts of DDT and its breakdown product DDE accumulated in the birds, making them sterile or causing the shell of their eggs to thin to such an extent that they broke before hatching. By the 1950s, there were only 412 breeding pairs left in the continental U.S. (excluding Alaska). After the introduction of controls on DDT in the early 1970s, eagle populations began to recover, reaching 100,000 by the early 1990s.

He clasps the crag with crooked hands;
Close to the sun in lonely lands,
Ringed with the azure world, he stands.
The wrinkled sea beneath him crawls;
He watches from his mountain walls,
And like a thunderbolt he falls.

"The Eagle" *by Alfred, Lord Tennyson (1809–92)*

LEGEND
The ancient Aztecs were led to the site of their capital by an eagle.

EAGLE OF TENOCHTITLAN

✦

According to legend, when the Aztecs were wandering across the valley of Mexico in the fourteenth century, surrounded by hostile peoples on all sides, they were guided to their new home by an eagle. The bird flew onto an island in the great shallow lake that once occupied the site of modern-day Mexico City and settled on a cactus, indicating that the Aztecs should settle there, protected from their enemies by the waters of the lake. The island grew into the great metropolis of Tenochtitlan, the capital of the Aztec Empire. The eagle remains on the coat of arms of the modern United Mexican States.

HAIL TO THE CHIEF

Had the bald eagle become extinct in the continental U.S. because of human greed and short-sightedness, the irony would not have been lost on the world, because, as my American readers will know, the bird plays such a central role in the iconography of the federal government of the United States. The bald eagle features on both the Great Seal of the United States and the Seal of the President of the United States. The Great Seal, which features on federal documents, coinage, letterheads, military insignia, embassy crests, and on the one-dollar bill, has the American bald eagle in the center with wings outstretched, supporting a red, blue, and white shield. In one talon it holds an olive branch with 13 leaves, and in the other 13 arrows, representing the original thirteen colonies and symbolizing their love of peace but readiness to go to war to defend it. In its beak, the eagle clutches a scroll bearing the motto *E pluribus unum* ("Out of Many, One"), and its head is crowned by a constellation of 13 stars.

The Great Seal of the United States adopted by Congress in 1782 consciously harkened back to ancient Rome, with whose virtues the founding fathers sought to associate the fledgling United States. The Roman eagle, or aquila, was not a symbol of the Roman state, however, but was the emblem carried by the legions. Originally the eagle was one of several animal emblems used by Roman armies, but at the beginning of the second century BCE the other animals were abandoned and only the eagle remained in use. The aquila was made of gold or bronze and was affixed to the top of a long pole, which also carried a piece of

WAR BIRD
The eagle naturally lends itself to use in war propaganda, as these two examples from World War Two show.

cloth emblazoned with the head of the emperor or the letters SPQR (the senate and people of Rome). They were taken into battle, much like a national flag in later periods, and their loss to the enemy was considered the greatest humiliation to be avenged at any cost.

The Roman aquila spawned many symbolic descendants. After the fall of the Western Roman Empire in the fifth century CE, the Eastern Roman, or Byzantine, Empire chose the double-headed eagle as its national emblem, one head representing old Rome, and the other the city of Constantinople, which was also known as New Rome. When the king of the Franks, Charlemagne (c. 742–814), had himself crowned Emperor of the West in the year 800, he chose the Roman imperial eagle as his emblem. From Constantinople, the imperial eagle was exported to the Balkan kingdoms and to imperial Russia, where it remained the heraldic animal of the Romanov dynasty until the Russian Revolution of 1917. In Western Europe, several territories of the former Holy Roman Empire, including the Austro-Hungarian Empire and the kingdoms of Poland and Prussia, adopted the eagle as their national emblem.

There is a strange contradiction in humans that allows them to elevate an animal such as the eagle to represent the full majesty and power of their rulers and governments, yet at the same time let the animal itself be persecuted and almost driven to extinction. Fortunately for the citizens of the United States, the bald eagle has survived and thrives once more. In 2007, the national bird of the U.S. was finally removed from the list of threatened and endangered species.

NATIONAL EMBLEM
Chosen by Congress as the U.S.'s national bird in 1782, the bald eagle features on all federal documents.

AQUILA
The eagle was carried into battle as the standard of the Roman legions.

Leech
Hirudo medicinalis

Native range: Europe and western Asia

Class: Clitellate

Size: Up to 8 in (20 cm) in length

+ EDIBLE
+ ***MEDICINAL***
+ COMMERCIAL
+ PRACTICAL

For thousands of years the bloodsucking leech was a principal tool in the doctor's arsenal against disease. Although bloodletting as a general medical treatment has long been discredited, the leech has found a new role in twenty-first-century microsurgery. The leech has vanished from our daily lives, but it survives as a derogatory term for a human parasite who clings to another for personal gain without giving anything in return.

THE HERMAPHRODITE BLOODSUCKER

This book features several bloodsucking species that prey on humans—the mosquito, the flea, and the louse—but these are unwelcome visitors who steal into our homes and lives uninvited. Medicinal leeches, however, are unique because they were intentionally attached to humans to remove blood. Until the seventeenth century, doctors believed that diseases were caused by imbalances in the body's four "humors," and that bleeding a patient to remove excess blood was one way to restore their balance. Unfortunately for the benighted patients who were already weakened by the original disease, the treatment often proved fatally debilitating. Leeches were such an important part of medical practice that for centuries doctors were known as "leeches" and medicine as "leechcraft."

The leech is part of an ancient phylum of segmented worms called the annelids, which several paleontologists believe to be over 500 million years old, predating even the insects. The leech, like its distant cousin the earthworm, is part of the clitellate class named from the Latin word for "collar," *clitellum*, which is a collarlike segment of the worm's body that is used in reproduction. Leeches are hermaphrodite, meaning that they

MEDICAL FIRST
Among the bloodsucking species, the leech is unique in that it was intentionally attached to humans to remove blood as a form of medical treatment.

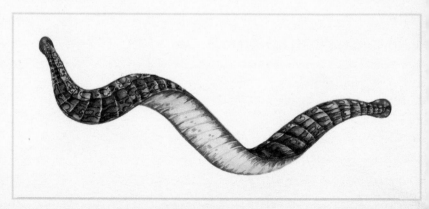

have both male and female sex organs. However, they do not fertilize themselves but reproduce sexually with another leech. Mating leeches will position themselves top to tail, and the "male" leech will inject the "female" leech with his sperm through a type of built-in hypodermic. Once mated, the female leech will lay up to 50 eggs in a humid, shady place near water.

If a leech were made a hundred times bigger, it would be an ideal alien B-movie monster. The greenish-brown leech is equipped with a suckerlike structure at each end of its tubular body. The rear sucker is used for locomotion, while the fearsome front sucker is the business end of the worm. The leech uses 100 sharp jawlike teeth to fasten itself to and pierce the skin of its prey. Once it has hooked onto its victim, the leech releases the anticoagulant hirudin, which will prevent the wound from closing up, and an anaesthetic to ensure that the victim doesn't become so irritated that it tries to remove the leech before it has gorged itself. The leech can take up to ten times its bodyweight in blood. Once it has had its fill, the leech will unfasten its jaws and allow itself to drop off its prey to digest its meal.

RAZOR-SHARP
The leech is equipped with 100 teeth with which it pierces its victims' skin. Shown here, its teeth at high magnification.

The medicinal leech is found in freshwater ponds and ditches across Europe and Western Asia in areas with a temperate climate. Contrary to popular belief, the leech's favorite food is not human blood but the blood of horses and cattle. However, since horses are no longer used in farming, and cattle and horses are furnished with artificial supplies of drinking water, the leech has disappeared from much of its native European range. In the developed countries of Europe, the leech is now considered an endangered species surviving only as a few isolated populations.

As the lean leech, its victim found, is pleased
To fix itself upon a part diseased
Till, its black hide distended with bad blood,
It drops to die of surfeit in the mud.
So the base sycophant with joy descries
His neighbor's weak spot and his mouth applies,
Gorges and prospers like the leech, although,
Unlike that reptile, he will not let go.

Ambrose Bierce (1842–1914)

HUMORING THE PATIENT

In order to understand why leeches were used to bleed patients until the relatively recent past, we have to seek out the roots of Western medical practice in the medicine of ancient Greece and Rome. Like ancient China and India, the Greco–Roman world had its own prescientific medical lore. While Traditional Chinese Medicine (TCM) and Indian Ayurveda have survived into the modern period, traditional Western medicine was replaced by scientific medicine in the mid-nineteenth century.

The Chinese and Indian systems share a belief in a subtle energy (*qi* in TCM and *prana* in Ayurveda) that animates the body. Disturbances in this energy cause mental and physical illness, and the physician restores its balance and flow in the body to return the patient to good health. Just as a Western doctor does today, Chinese and Indian practitioners give lifestyle advice about diet and exercise, as well as prescribe drug therapies. However, the important difference is that Chinese and Indian doctors do not base their diagnosis and treatments on germ theory or an understanding of human physiology. The TCM practitioner believes that *qi* flows through a network of meridians, and in Ayurveda, *prana* is distributed through the body by channels known as *nadi*.

Like their Chinese and Indian counterparts, traditional Western doctors did not know about the role of viruses and bacteria in causing many diseases until the nineteenth century, and because of religious taboos and legal restrictions, they were not allowed to dissect human bodies, so their knowledge of human anatomy was severely limited until the seventeenth century. They did not understand the circulation of the blood that distributes both oxygen and nutrients to the body or the role

STUCK ON YOU
Once attached to the skin, the leech is difficult to remove; it will fall off once it has finished gorging on blood.

of the brain and nervous system in consciousness, thought, and sensation. Instead, they believed that the body was animated by the four substances, or "humors": blood, black bile, yellow bile, and phlegm—each one produced by a different organ, and each with its own nature and functions.

The Greek physicians Hippocrates of Kos (c. 460–c. 370 BCE)—he of the "Hippocratic Oath" that doctors still take today—and Galen (129– c. 216 CE) are credited with systematizing the system by associating the four humors with the classical elements and the seasons to give four basic physiological and mental temperaments that still have some (nonmedical) currency today: "sanguine," dominated by blood made in the liver, associated with air and the spring; "choleric," dominated by yellow bile made in the gall bladder, associated with fire and the summer; "melancholic," dominated by black bile made in spleen, associated with earth and the fall; and "phlegmatic," dominated by phlegm made in the lungs and brain, associated with water and the winter. The ideal was for there to be a balance of the four humors, but external factors such as the time of year and poor diet could cause imbalances to develop, leading to different kinds of disease.

While Hippocrates himself recommended very gentle treatments, such as rest, exercise, and dietary changes, and shunned invasive procedures and strong drugs to restore the balance of the humors in the body, other ancient physicians preferred much more invasive methods including emetics, diuretics, purges, and bloodletting. Galen, who remained one of the most trusted medical authorities until the nineteenth century, believed that there were two separate circulations of the blood: the first of arterial blood that was made in the heart, and the second of the darker venous blood, made in the liver. This led him to believe that blood could stagnate and accumulate in different parts of the body, causing disease, which could be treated by bleeding. The first recorded use of leeches to take excess blood from patients who were too "sanguine" dates back to Greece in the second century BCE.

ANGLO-SAXON LEECHCRAFT

✦

For centuries, doctors were known as leeches, and medicine as leechcraft. One of the earliest English medical texts is known as the *Leechbook of Bald*, which was compiled sometime in the ninth century CE. The book is divided into two parts, the first dealing with external ailments, and the second with internal disorders. The *Leechbook* contains the only reference to plastic surgery mentioned in the Anglo-Saxon period, when it gives a procedure to correct a harelip.

From there the practice was exported to the Roman world, where it was adopted and promoted by Galen and his followers.

After the rise of Islam in the seventh century CE, the main medical heirs of Greece and Rome were Muslim scholars and physicians, who further developed the theory of humorism in two central texts written at the turn of the first millennium: *The Canon of Medicine* by Avicenna (981–1037) and *The Method of Medicine* by Abulcasis (936–1013), both of which contain references to bloodletting and recommend the use of leeches. When these texts were translated into Latin during the Middle Ages, the Greco–Roman–Islamic theory of humorism was reintroduced to Western Europe, where it remained influential for a significant period of time.

DEMON BARBERS

The use of leeches increased throughout the Middle Ages and reached its heyday in the seventeenth century, adding a new terror to being ill. Bleeding with leeches was recommended for a wide range of illnesses, especially those that caused reddening, inflammation, or fever that were taken to be symptoms of the presence of excessive blood in the body. Mental conditions that caused the patient to be too loud or energetic, in other words to be too "sanguine," were also treated by bleeding. Strangely, leeches were also used to treat wounds. Patients who were already weakened by loss of blood were subjected to periodic bleeding, which weakened them further, sometimes fatally. One such case involved a French soldier who had been injured in a duel. His "treatment" over the next month consisted of the removal of 13 pints (6 liters) of blood. Luckily, on this occasion, the patient survived both the injury and the treatment. Bleeding was also used prophylactically to prevent disease, and was routinely used during childbirth and surgery.

Although the British anatomist and physician William Harvey (1578–1657) demonstrated the circulation of the blood by the heart in the 1620s, thereby disproving Galen's erroneous dual-circulation theory, and seriously undermining the whole basis for humoral theory, the practice of bleeding with leeches continued until the late nineteenth century. Such was the demand for leeches in Europe that they became rare in much of their

FIRST-AID JAR
Leeches were kept ready in elaborate containers for use on patients visiting the doctor.

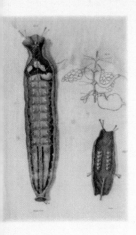

native range—so much so that they had to be imported or bred in captivity.

Doctors were not the only ones to use leeches. In England, barbers were also allowed to practice surgery, providing medical aid to soldiers on the battlefield and to those poorer members of society who could not afford to be treated by "bona-fide" doctors. The barber's pole that is still found outside traditional barbershops is a reminder of the bleeding and surgical services they once provided: The red of the pole represents blood, the white, the tourniquet applied to the arm, and the pole itself, the small wooden stick gripped by the patient to dilate the veins.

The advent of scientific medicine finally brought an end to the routine use of bleeding in the treatment of wounds and infectious diseases. However, in the 1980s, the medicinal leech found a new use in microsurgical procedures such as plastic and reconstructive surgery. In the case of reconstructive surgery, for example, muscle and skin tissues are transplanted from one part of the patient's body to another to replace tissues destroyed in an accident or by disease. It is vital to establish a new blood supply both in and out of the graft, but in some cases, there are problems in reattaching the veins that carry deoxygenated blood away from the area. The veinous blood may pool and clot, causing the arteries bringing oxygenated blood to become blocked, resulting in the death of the grafted tissue. In order to clear the blockages and prevent clots, leeches were applied to the graft. As we saw above, leech saliva contains the powerful anticoagulant hirudin that will maintain blood flow even once the leech has been removed, and the feeding leech will also take any accumulation of excess blood. Now that synthetic hirudin is available, however, the leech has once again been consigned to the museum of medical curiosities.

MISGUIDED
Even after Harvey's discovery of the circulation of the blood, leeches were still employed to remove "stagnant" blood.

ENDANGERED
The demand for medicinal leeches was so high that it became extinct in many areas of Europe.

Iguanodon
Iguanodon bernissartensis

Native range: Europe

Class: Reptile

Size: Up to 33 ft (10 m) in length

+ EDIBLE
+ MEDICINAL
+ COMMERCIAL
+ ***PRACTICAL***

The second dinosaur to be described scientifically, species of the genus *Iguanodon* have undergone several transformations as our understanding of dinosaur anatomy and behavior has evolved. When a partial skeleton was first reconstructed, it was represented as a rhinolike quadruped with a horn on its nose; as more skeletons were discovered, it became a kangaroolike biped, which used its flexible tail to hold itself upright. More recent research has revealed that *Iguanodon* could walk on two or four legs, and held its body and tail horizontal to the ground.

LOST WORLDS REDISCOVERED

Humans have recorded the discovery of fossilized remains of long-extinct animal species since antiquity, but they have interpreted them in different ways, according to their religious and scientific beliefs. The ancient Greeks thought that fossils were an attempt by rocks to reproduce the appearance of life in stone; the Chinese believed that they were the bones of dragons; and medieval Christians that they were the remains of a biblical race of giants. By the seventeenth century, scientists were accumulating evidence that challenged the Church's teachings that the earth was only 4,000 years old, and that the creator had made all species perfect, fixed, and immutable. But it would take until the middle of the nineteenth century before the scientific community finally accepted the true extent of geological time and of the evolution of species.

At the beginning of the eighteenth century, the French naturalist and zoologist Georges Cuvier (1769–1832) was the first to suggest that there had been a time in the history of the earth when reptiles and not mammals had been the dominant species. Cuvier is

MISREPRESENTATION
Iguanodon underwent several transformations before it was correctly reconstructed.

also credited with the idea that animal species could become extinct. He believed that a series of catastrophic events had caused sudden changes in the makeup of the animal populations of the planet. In this he anticipated the theory that the disappearance of the dinosaurs was caused by a massive "killer" asteroid strike in Central America some 65.5 million years BP. Much of the evidence confirming his ideas about a prehistoric "Age of Reptiles" would come in the next two decades, with many of the finds originating in the rich fossil deposits of the south of England.

The first dinosaur fossil fragment to be subjected to scientific scrutiny was the head of the femur (thigh bone) of a megalosaurus, a large meat-eating dinosaur of the middle Jurassic (166 million years BP). Found in a quarry near Oxford in 1676, the fossil was sent to the university, where it was correctly identified as part of a leg bone. However, because the specimen was so much larger than any bone belonging to a living species, it was thought to belong to the race of giants mentioned in the Bible. Further bone and teeth fragments unearthed in the same location in the early 1800s were sent to the English geologist William Buckland (1784–1856), who, with the help of Cuvier, identified them as belonging to a long-extinct giant lizard-like carnivore, which he christened megalosaurus ("great lizard").

While geologists and zoologists were taking the first hesitant steps in identifying ancient reptiles, amateur fossil hunter Mary Anning (1799–1847) was discovering the fossilized remains of marine ichthyosaurs and plesiosaurs in the Blue Lias cliffs near her hometown of Lyme Regis, Dorset, on the English south coast. She prospected for fossils in the cliffs, and sold her finds to collectors and museums from her shop in Lyme. Anning, however, suffered from two serious disabilities that kept her from being fully accepted by the scientific community of

EXTINCTIONS
The French naturalist Georges Cuvier was the first to propose that animal species could become extinct.

PIONEER
While scientists were arguing about evolution and extinction, amateur fossil hunter Mary Anning was unearthing new species from the cliffs of Lyme Regis.

the day: she was a woman, and she was of humble birth (the daughter of a cabinetmaker) at a time when the scientific establishment was dominated by well-to-do gentlemen of leisure. These factors meant that her many contributions to the new science of paleontology were not recognized until long after her death.

IGUANODON MISCONSTRUED

Inspired by Anning's finds to search for the fossils of extinct animals, Gideon Mantell (1790–1852), an obstetrician, and amateur geologist and paleontologist, found several large fossilized teeth in a quarry near the village of Cuckfield, West Sussex, in 1822. There were two things that set apart the Cuckfield finds from Anning's: the teeth belonged to a land-

UPRIGHT
The discovery of 38 specimens in Belgium in 1878 finally proved that iguanodon was partially bipedal.

dwelling animal, unlike the Lyme Regis specimens, which were all marine species; and, unlike the meat-eating *Megalosaurus*, the teeth appeared to be those of a herbivore. Initially, Mantell's report was viewed with skepticism by the scientific establishment. Buckland dismissed the teeth as those of a fish or rhino, and Cuvier, after only a cursory examination, agreed that they probably came from an extinct species of rhinoceros from a much later period.

It was only two years after the find, in 1824, once Buckland had published his description of megalosaurus and seen Mantell's full collection of fossils from Cuckfield, that he conceded that they were reptilian in origin but probably not from a herbivore. Encouraged by this change of heart by one of his main detractors, Mantell sent teeth to Cuvier in Paris, who this time agreed that they were reptilian and quite possibly from a

plant eater. The new creature was as yet unnamed, but in 1824, the assistant-curator of the Royal College of Surgeons drew Mantell's attention to the similarity of the fossilized teeth from Cuckfield with those of the modern iguana, although they were many times larger. Mantell decided to christen his find "iguanodon," meaning "iguana-tooth," and the species was given the binomial *Iguanodon anglicus*, which was later revised to *Iguanodon bernissartensis* when more complete skeletons were discovered in Bernissart, Belgium.

Mantell's 1822 finds were too fragmentary to reconstruct what *Iguanodon* looked like or even how large it was. Initially, he thought it might be 60 ft (18 m) long and shaped like a modern crocodile. However, when a more complete specimen was unearthed in a quarry near Maidstone, Kent, Mantell was able to produce a slightly more accurate description of the skeleton. Nevertheless, he made several mistakes in his observations: although he realized the front legs were shorter than the hind legs, he pictured it on all fours; he thought the long tail was flexible like a lizard's and would be dragged along the ground; and he placed a short horn on its nose.

HOPPING LIZARD
Dollo modeled his *Iguanodon* on kangaroos and wallabies, with a long flexible tail.

Although wrong in many respects, Mantell's vision of *Iguanodon* was closer to reality than the image of the dinosaur that the British public saw in the metal, brick, and concrete dinosaur sculptures that were made for the Crystal Palace Park (see box, p. 114) in the London suburb of Sydenham Hill and unveiled to the general public in 1854. The sculptures were the brainchild of a rival paleontologist, Richard Owen (1804–92), the man who coined the term "dinosaur" (from the Greek for "terrible lizard"). Owen was a creationist, who opposed the idea of evolution. He claimed that the dinosaurs, far from being the ancestors of modern reptiles, were advanced mammallike creatures that had become extinct. He saw *Iguanodon* as similar to modern rhinos and elephants, and the models he had made were of squat quadrupeds, with a short horn on their noses.

Even if we admit [...] that the linear dimensions of the extinct and living animals were not of the same relative proportions, still it must be allowed that the *Iguanodon* was one of the most gigantic reptiles of the ancient world; and a colossus in comparison to the pigmy alligators and crocodiles that now inhabit the globe.

Illustrations of the Geology of Sussex *(1827) by Gideon Mantell (1790–1852)*

INCOMPLETE
The first remains of *Iguanodon* to be identified consisted of a few teeth and bone fragments.

In 1878, Owen's version of *Iguanodon* was finally overthrown when the skeletons of 38 specimens were discovered in a coalmine in Bernissart, Belgium. This remains the largest ever find of *Iguanodon*. The man in charge of their reconstruction was the Belgian paleontologist Louis Dollo (1857–1931). The specimens went on display at the Royal Belgian Institute of Natural Sciences in Brussels in 1882, nine of which Dollo mounted in standing poses rather than on all fours. Dollo modeled his upright *Iguanodon* on wallabies and kangaroos, standing on their hind legs and balancing on their tails. He correctly placed Mantell and Owen's "horn" on the hand where it belonged, as it was in fact a sharp spikelike thumb. However, even he was not entirely correct. He introduced a bend in the tail, whereas later research has shown that the tail was kept straight by bonelike tendons. The only way a living *Iguanodon* could attain a bent-tail posture like a kangaroo would be if its tail had been broken.

Reexaminations of *Iguanodon* skeletons in the twentieth century have shown that it had quite a different stance and mode of locomotion to those imagined by Mantell, Owen, or Dollo. Rather than standing upright on its hind legs and tail like a kangaroo, *Iguanodon* held its body and tail horizontal to the ground. It could walk bipedally on its powerful three-toed hind legs, or, when necessary on all fours with the aid of its shorter arms. The wrist and middle three fingers of its hands are sturdy and relatively immobile and the bones are structured so as to be weight-bearing. It seems likely that young *Iguanodon* were mainly bipedal, but as they grew older and heavier, they spent more and more time on all fours. Paleontologists have estimated that *Iguanodon* could reach a top speed of 15 mph (24 km/h) on two legs, but their anatomy did not allow them to gallop on all fours like horses.

VICTORIAN DINOSAURS

✦

The Great Exhibition of the Works of Industry of all Nations was held in a specially built glass-and-steel structure, the Crystal Palace, in London's Hyde Park in 1851. At the end of the exhibition, the building was dismantled and moved to parkland in the suburb of Sydenham Hill in southeast London. The park that surrounded the Crystal Palace featured the first models of dinosaurs ever made, including two *Iguanodon*, one standing on four squat pillarlike legs, and the other lying on its belly. The models were made on the advice of Richard Owen, and therefore conform to his mistaken conception of the animal as a large quadruped with a small horn on its nose. The sculptures, long neglected and ridiculed once they were discovered to be inaccurate in the late nineteenth century, were restored to their full Victorian splendor in 2002, and can still be enjoyed today as one of the park's main attractions.

The other distinguishing feature of *Iguanodon* that was misunderstood until Dollo's reconstruction was the thumb spike that both Mantell and Owen had interpreted as a horn and placed on the animal's nose. Several theories have been put forward as to its exact function: the first, that it was a weapon for use against predators or other *Iguanodon*; the second, a more peaceful explanation, was that it was used to break open seeds and hard-shelled fruits. In addition to a thumb spike and three fixed fingers, *Iguanodon* had a single prehensile little finger on its hands, which scientists believe it used to manipulate food. As with many dinosaurs, the diet of *Iguanodon* remains a matter of conjecture. It was, as Mantell had correctly interpreted from his original finds, vegetarian, and in addition to its teeth had a horny beak with which it could crop off twigs and shoots.

The tooth in this stage has exchanged the functions of an incisor for that of a molar, and is prepared to give the final compression, or comminution, to the coarsely divided vegetable matters [...] which are found buried with the Iguanodon.

From On the Anatomy of Vertebrates *(1866) by Richard Owen*

As only the second dinosaur to be discovered and described by the fledgling science of paleontology, *Iguanodon* has undergone the greatest transformations of any ancient saurian species. It began life as a mammallike horned quadruped that creationists put forward to argue the case against evolution; it spent some time as the kangaroo of dinosauria; and finally ended up as a far stranger bipedal creature that balanced with the aid of its long, straight tail. Throughout its many incarnations, however, *Iguanodon* has continued to fascinate scientists and laymen alike, sparking and maintaining our enduring love affair with the race of giant reptiles that once ruled our planet.

QUADRUPED
Although completely inaccurate, these reconstructions were installed in the grounds of the Crystal Palace in south London.

Llama

Lama glama

Native range: Andean region of South America

Class: Mammal

Size: 43–50 in (1–1.3 m) at the withers

+ **EDIBLE**
+ **MEDICINAL**
+ **COMMERCIAL**
+ **PRACTICAL**

The llama is South America's only native large domesticated herbivore. Before the introduction of the horse, cow, donkey, goat, and sheep by European settlers, the llama had to fill the roles of beast of burden, meat animal, and dairy and fiber producer. The sole camelid survivor in the Americas, the llama is as well adapted to its high-altitude home as the camel is to the desert environment.

SOLE SURVIVORS

The people of the Old World were spoiled for choice when it came to the domestication of large, productive herbivores. The peoples of Central Asia had the horse; in the Near East and Europe they had the sheep, goat, and cow; and in Arabia, the camel. In the Americas, though there were still equines and camelids at the end of the last glaciation (12,000 years BP), most had become extinct by 8,000 years BP. Researchers disagree as to why these species became extinct, some claiming that they were hunted to extinction by the first human settlers in the Americas, others that their disappearance was due to natural factors, such as climate change.

North American camelids crossed the Isthmus of Panama from North to South America between two and three million years BP, where they not only survived the arrival of humans but thrived in the challenging high-altitude environment of the Andean Altiplano (high plateau) and mountain range. They became the ancestors of the four modern llama species (the domesticated llama and alpaca, and the wild vicuña and guanaco). Llamas were central to the lives of the Native American peoples of the Andes, first as a source of meat and hides, and later as beasts of burden and sources of milk and fiber. After the Spanish conquest in the sixteenth century, llamas were displaced in lowland areas by Old World species such as sheep, cattle, donkeys, and horses, but their adaptation to life and work at high altitudes has ensured that they continue to play an important role in present-day Andean life.

The llama bears a striking physical resemblance to its Old World cousin the camel, but lacks the hump in which the latter stores its body fat. In the cold climate of the Andes, the llama needs an even distribution of body fat to keep itself warm. Like the camel, the llama has two toes embedded in a thick leather sole that protects its feet from rocky ground, and also makes it very sure-footed on uneven or slippery surfaces. Another similarity with the camels is the special environmental adaptations seen in its blood. While the camel is adapted to arid environments to make the best use of limited water resources, the llama, which lives at altitudes of up to 12,800 ft (4,000 m), has adaptations that enable it to make full use of the lower oxygen levels in the air. Llama blood has a higher proportion of red blood cells than the blood of any other mammal, and its hemoglobin absorbs oxygen faster and more efficiently.

Like the goat, the llama has longer, coarse guard hairs on top of a much finer undercoat of downy hair that act together to trap a warm layer of insulating air. Llama coats range in color from white and gray to reddish-brown, brown, dark brown, and black, often in combinations of two colors. The vegetation of the llama's native range is sparse and low in nutrition. Being both grazers and browsers, they will eat a wide variety of plant materials, although they prefer to graze on grass. They are ruminants and chew the cud like cattle, but they have only three stomachs like camels. Llamas are unusual among large mammals in that they do not go in heat but are "induced ovulators," meaning that ovulation takes place 24–36 hours after mating. The llama dam will give birth to one baby llama, or "cria" (derived from the Spanish for "baby"), after a gestation of 11 months. A highly sociable animal, the llama lives in herds led by a dominant female, who controls herd members by spitting a mixture of saliva and regurgitated food.

NOAH'S LLAMAS

◆

According to Inca legend, there was a time when the people became wicked and turned against the gods. One day, two virtuous brothers who lived in the high Andes noticed that their llamas were looking up at the sky. They asked the llamas what they were doing, and the animals told them that the stars had warned them that the gods were sending a great flood to punish humanity. The brothers moved their families and herds to a cave on one of the highest peaks of the Andes. The rain came and did not stop for four months and four days. The Earth and its wicked people were drowned except for the brothers and their families, who repopulated the Earth when the waters finally receded.

SHIPS OF THE ANDES

Opinions are still sharply divided in the scientific community as to when human settlers first arrived in the Americas, and how many migrations took place in prehistoric times. The conventional date is 20,000–17,000 years BP, but several authorities have moved back the first humans crossing from Asia into North America to around 40,000 years BP. What is known is that bands of hunter-gatherers had reached the Andean region by 15,000 years BP (again, other experts give an earlier date). There they encountered the llama, which they would have hunted for its meat and hides. Unlike the extinct equines and camelids of North America, the llama survived the Andean hunter-gathering phase, and around 4,000 years BP, the wild guanaco and vicuña were domesticated, giving rise to the two domesticated camelid species: the llama and the alpaca.

As Andean civilization developed, the role of the llama began to change. At first, the domesticated llama was a source of meat, milk, and fiber, but as small states grew into empires, it became increasingly important as a beast of burden and also as a sacrificial animal offered to the gods and the ancestors. The first great Andean empire was centered around the city of Tiwanaku (Tiahuanaco; c. 300 BCE–c. 1000 CE) near Lake Titicaca (now in Bolivia). Llama remains have been found in Tiwanaku burials, thought to be food offerings for the dead. The llama was also used as a pack animal carrying trading goods and tribute between the upland capital and its coastal provinces. A similar pattern was established by later pre-Columbian Andean states, the largest of which was the Inca Empire.

The Inca began to expand in the early fifteenth century, and their empire reached its greatest extent on the eve of the arrival of the Spanish conquistadors in 1532. It covered a huge area: north from modern-day Ecuador, including parts of Peru, Bolivia, and Chile, and reaching as far south as northern Argentina. The empire's capital was located in the highland city of Cuzco (now in Peru), which was linked to the empire's highland and coastal provinces by an impressive network of paved roads. The Inca encouraged the breeding of both llamas and alpacas, establishing state-owned herds all over the empire.

Although llama meat was still eaten either fresh or as jerky, the animal's main functions during the Inca period were as a source of fiber and as a pack animal. The finer fibers of the vicuña and alpaca were reserved for the nobility, and the coarser llama fiber for the clothing of commoners. The llama's longer guard hairs were made into wall hangings, rope, and *quipu*, a device made of knotted colored cords used to record numerical and other information in a culture that had not developed a writing system. Another important function of the llama in Inca society was as a ritual animal offered to the gods and Inca ancestors. White male llamas were sacrificed to the main Inca deity, the sun god Inti.

The llama is a woolly sort of fleecy hairy goat, with an indolent expression and an undulating throat; like an unsuccessful literary man.

Hilaire Belloc (1870–1953)

After the Spanish conquest, the llama herds went into decline. The conquistadors brought with them diseases that killed many llama, and also rival Old World domesticated species. They also slaughtered many animals for their meat. However, when they began to exploit the mineral wealth of the Andean region, they realized the value of the llama as a hardy pack animal that could carry heavy loads at high altitudes. Llamas remain an important animal in the Andean economy, and have been exported worldwide, as farm animals in their own right, as pets, and as guard animals for sheep.

INCA HERD
The pre-Colombian Inca kept a large national herd and spread the llama throughout the Andes.

Elephant
Loxodonta africana

Native range: Africa

Class: Mammal

Size: 10–13 ft (3–4 m) tall at the shoulder

+ EDIBLE
+ MEDICINAL
+ **COMMERCIAL**
+ **PRACTICAL**

The elephantid family—divided into two, the African and Asian elephants— once had an extensive range across Eurasia. Elephants have served humans for millennia as beasts of burden, war mounts, and circus entertainers, but now sadly feature on the endangered list of species because of the destruction of their habitat and poaching for their meat and ivory.

VANISHING GIANTS

The popular expression "the elephant in the room," meaning something that is obvious to everyone but is not discussed, is an oblique commentary on the fate of the animal itself. As the largest land-dwelling animal on Earth, the elephant is almost impossible to hide and difficult to protect from its human predators, and its ultimate fate, summed up so clearly in the David Attenborough quote on page 125, and still ignored by many governments, may be inexorable decline and extinction. Despite the elephant's more than 2,000 years of service to humanity, its populations have been shrinking since antiquity. Divided into two genuses: the African *Loxodonta* and the Asian (or Indian) *Elephas*, the elephant's original range covered Africa north and south of the Sahara desert, the Near East as far as Syria, the India subcontinent, China, and Southeast Asia. Today the Asian elephant is limited to parts of Western and Southeast Asia, and the African, to sub-Saharan Africa, where their populations are under threat from habitat destruction and ivory poaching.

The elephant is perhaps one of the most instantly identifiable animals on Earth, first because of its great size, and then because of its unique prehensile trunk, a fusion of the upper lip and nose, and its tusks, a modified pair of eye teeth. Asian and African elephants exhibit a number of physical differences: the Asian is smaller, hairier, and with a flatter back than the African, whereas in the African species, both male (bull) and female (cow) have tusks, while only male Asian elephants have tusks. The high level of poaching of African elephants for ivory is selectively breeding elephants without tusks. At present one-third of African elephants are born without tusks, as compared to one percent at the beginning of the twentieth century. As tusks are used in a range of behaviors, including feeding and mating, their disappearance may have a serious and possibly detrimental impact on elephant lifestyles and survival.

Although female and juvenile elephants are highly sociable herding animals, bull elephants tend to lead more solitary lives when fully grown. An elephant herd is composed of between five and 15 related adult females, with their immature offspring of both sexes, led by the eldest female, or matriarch. Cows engage in complex intra- and inter-herd relationships. In contrast, when a bull reaches maturity around 14 years of age, he will leave the maternal herd for good. He may associate with other males in loose "bachelor herds," or spend time living on his own. While female elephants are in heat for a few days each year, bull elephants exhibit a periodic condition of intense sexual arousal known as "musth," when they become extremely aggressive, fight any other male they encounter, and attempt to mate with any receptive female. During musth, even domesticated bull elephants become dangerous and erratic, endangering both humans and other elephants.

HEAVY WORK
The elephant's great strength has made it an ideal draft animal in both war- and peacetime.

As with other widely dispersed species, there is no agreement as to exactly where and when the elephant was first domesticated. According to current archaeological research the three best candidate sites are Shang Dynasty China (1600–1100 BCE); ancient Mesopotamia, where a cylinder seal dating back to 2500 BCE depicts what appears to be a

BATH TIME
Led by a matriarch, the elephant herd displays complex social behaviors and long-lasting relationships.

DEATH PENALTY
Several cultures have
used elephants as a means
of execution. Illustrated here
is a man being crushed to
death in Sri Lanka.

An Execution by an Elephant.

domesticated elephant; and the Indus Valley civilization (3300–1300 BCE), located in modern-day Pakistan. The Indus Valley and the city-states of southern Mesopotamia had important trading links, so it is possible that domestication of the elephant began in India and was taken from there to the Near East and North Africa. The larger, fiercer sub-Saharan elephant was not domesticated in antiquity, but the ancient peoples of Egypt, Numidia, Kush, and Carthage tamed the smaller, now extinct, North African elephant.

THE TANKS OF ANTIQUITY

As in Asia today, elephants in antiquity probably had a role in ceremonies, transportation, agriculture, and industry, but their most important use was in warfare, in which they were used both for logistics and on the battlefield. Due to their great size and strength, elephants were the tanks of ancient armies. The war elephant was a weapons platform that could carry several soldiers in a protective turret, known as a *howdah* in India; and a mass elephant charge, though not as fast as a horse charge, could have a devastating impact on infantry and cavalry, especially if the enemy troops had never encountered elephants before. During the Roman invasion of Britain in 43 CE, the appearance of a single armored battle elephant carrying archers and slingers is said to have routed a terrified native army.

Against more experienced armies, however, the elephant was not always such a formidable weapon. Elephants could be easily panicked with the use of fire or if their driver, or *mahout*, was killed. A panicked or wounded elephant could run amok, killing as many of its own troops as the enemy. Although proverbially thick-skinned, elephants could also be disabled and killed by spears and arrows aimed at their unprotected flanks and bellies. They were also vulnerable to heavy projectile weapons such as catapults and ballistas. At the Battle of Thapsus (now in Tunisia) in 46 BCE, Julius Caesar (100–44 BCE) ordered his men to disable the enemy's charging war elephants by hacking at their legs with axes.

The first recorded confrontation between Western troops and elephants occurred at the Battle of Gaugamela (331 BCE), in which the forces of Alexander the Great (356–323 BCE), king of Macedon, faced the Persian army under Darius III (c. 380–330 BCE), whose forces included a division of 15 Indian war elephants.

Despite the initial panic caused by the unfamiliar beasts, Alexander won a decisive victory that brought the whole of Persia under his rule. After Gaugamela he incorporated the captured elephants into his own army.

When Alexander reached the Indian subcontinent, he faced armies that could field a much larger number of elephants than the Persians. At the Battle of the Hydaspes River (326 BCE), he overcame a force of up to 100 war elephants pitted against his own infantry and cavalry. Despite this victory, Alexander turned back rather than face more powerful Indian rulers who had thousands of war elephants under their command. Although the presence of the elephants was only one factor in Alexander's decision to retreat, it would be interesting to speculate what their absence might have meant to world history, had the whole of northern India fallen under Hellenistic rule.

During Rome's republican period (509–27 BCE), the fledgling imperial power faced two foes that made use of war elephants to devastating effect: the Greek kingdom of Epirus, and North African Carthage (now in Tunisia). In the third century BCE, the southern part of Italy and Sicily were not under Roman rule. The area, known as Magna Grecia (Greater Greece), was a loose assemblage of independent Greek city-states, and Sicily was divided between the Greeks and Carthaginians. In 280 BCE, when a dispute erupted between the Greek city of Tarentum and Rome, the Tarentines appealed to Pyrrhus of Epirus (c. 319–272 BCE) for help.

ROYAL MOUNT
In India and Southeast Asia, the elephant is the ceremonial mount of kings and princes.

To prove himself as a major player in Mediterranean politics, Pyrrhus led a large army into southern Italy. This included 20 war elephants loaned to him by the Greek ruler of Egypt, Ptolemy II (309–246 BCE). For five years Pyrrhus battled with the Romans in Italy and the Carthaginians in Sicily. Although he was generally successful, his victories were secured at such a high price, and his army was so exhausted and depleted, that in 275 BCE he quit Italy for good. Pyrrhus' failed Italian campaign is remembered to this day in the expression "Pyrrhic victory," meaning a costly success that ultimately leads to failure.

With the Greeks in Italy subdued, Rome had one more enemy to overcome before it could claim mastery of the western Mediterranean: the powerful trading empire of Carthage that ruled territory stretching from Spain in the West to the borders of Ptolemaic Egypt in the East, and included the Balearic Islands, parts of Sicily, and Sardinia. The conflict between the two cities led to three wars fought between 264 and 146 BCE. During the second Punic War (218–201 BCE), however, it was Rome's survival that was on the line when Carthage's leading general, Hannibal (248–c. 183 BCE), led his army, including several dozen war elephants, from Iberia (Spain), through southern Gaul (France), and across the Alps into northern Italy. Although he took the Romans by surprise, and scored several notable victories, Hannibal was no more successful in Italy than Pyrrhus had been six decades earlier. He was forced to withdraw and was defeated at the Battle of Zama (202 BCE) near Carthage, despite having deployed 80 war elephants against the Roman army.

While elephants disappeared from warfare in the Western world in the first century CE, they continued to be used in parts of Asia until the nineteenth century. In India, they were used by native rulers in their wars against the British in the eighteenth century, and in

SUPERSIZED

♦

Elephants are intelligent and learn quickly, a fact that has made them popular as circus performers since Roman times. During the nineteenth century, hundreds of elephants were imported to be attractions in European and American circuses.

The most famous of these was Jumbo (1861–85), a large African elephant from the French Sudan (now Mali). He was brought to Paris Zoo as a baby and was transferred to London Zoo in 1865, where he was christened Jumbo. In 1882, Jumbo was sold to the American showman P. T. Barnum (1810–91), despite a campaign in the British press that he should be kept in the UK. His fate in the U.S., however, was not a happy one. Although he was a great hit when exhibited at Madison Square Garden, New York, in 1885, he was killed by a locomotive while crossing the tracks at St Thomas, Ontario, Canada. The giant Jumbo is still remembered today in our use of his name to mean anything "supersized," from planes to people.

Southeast Asia, the twelfth-century Khmer, builders of the great temple city of Angkor Wat (now in Cambodia), and their successor states, Burma (now Myanmar) and Siam (now Thailand), made extensive use of war elephants. The last recorded use of war elephants in the region was in Indo-China (now Laos, Cambodia, and Vietnam) in the late nineteenth century, when the Vietnamese used them during their war of resistance against the French. As with the horse and camel, the military elephant was superseded by motorized vehicles in the twentieth century.

The question is, are we happy to suppose that our grandchildren may never be able to see an elephant except in a picture book?
British naturalist and documentary maker David Attenborough (b. 1926)

Nature's plastic

Apart from its roles as a war mount and circus performer, the elephant has had a far more unfortunate function—at least from the point of view of the elephant—in human history, as one of the main suppliers of ivory. Soft and translucent, ivory has been an ideal medium for artists, who have crafted it into exquisite statues, bas-reliefs, jewelry, and small objects such as boxes, pipes, seals, and *netsuke*—a traditional Japanese accessory. In addition, prior to the invention of plastics, elephant ivory was used to make a wide range of things, including billiard balls and piano keys. Although plastic and synthetic ivory substitutes are now widely available, the illegal trade in poached ivory continues to meet demand in East Asia, endangering the survival of both Asian and African elephants.

With the collapse of elephant populations in the 1980s, the U.N. imposed the first moratorium on ivory sales in 1989. However, the ban has been flouted by criminal gangs, and was partially lifted in 2002 to allow several countries in Southern Africa to sell their stockpiles of confiscated ivory. Conservationists argue that this was a retrograde step, as any lifting of the ban merely encourages criminals to attempt to "launder" their illegal supplies through legal channels. In addition to poaching, the elephant is threatened by the disappearance of its habitat, particularly in Asia, where the growth of the human population has led to forest clearance for agriculture and logging. It is a sad fact of twenty-first-century life that our overcrowded planet may have no room for these gentle giants—the world may not be big enough for the both of us.

THREATENED
The greatest threat to the survival of the elephant in the modern world is ivory poaching.

Earthworm

Lumbricus terrestris

Native range: Europe

Class: Clitellate

Size: 3.5–12 in (9–30 cm) long

◆ EDIBLE

◆ MEDICINAL

◆ COMMERCIAL

◆ ***PRACTICAL***

The humble earthworm is a vital part of the biosphere, which, by making our fields and pastures more productive, has improved the lot of humanity since the development of agriculture.

"INTESTINES OF THE EARTH"

Many readers may be surprised to find the common earthworm in these pages alongside much more obviously useful species such as the pig, sheep, cow, or horse. However, as Charles Darwin (1809–82), who made a special study of them at the end of his life, realized, earthworms play a central role in the proper functioning of the terrestrial ecosystem. He called them the "intestines of the earth," and wrote: "When we behold a wide, turf-covered expanse, we should remember that its smoothness, on which so much of its beauty depends, is mainly due to all the inequalities having been slowly levelled by worms. The plow is one of the most ancient and valuable of man's inventions but, long before it existed, the land was in fact regularly plowed, and still continues to be ploughed by earthworms. It may be doubted whether there are many other animals that have played so important a part in the history of the world as have these lowly organised creatures."

Like the leech, the earthworm is a tubular annelid worm consisting of 100 segments. It has five pairs of heartlike structures that pump blood along its body, and a primitive brain, all of which are clustered around the "head," which is fatter and darker than the "tail." The earthworm has no eyes or ears, but it is sensitive to light and vibrations. Like other clitellates, earthworms have a collarlike clitellum two-thirds along their bodies toward the tail, which they use to mate. Although they are hermaphrodites, having both male and female sexual organs, earthworms reproduce sexually. When mating, two worms line up and remain locked together at the clitellum until they have exchanged and stored each other's sperm, a process can take two to three hours. Once they have separated, each worm secretes a cocoon into which it places its eggs and the sperm of the other worm. The newly hatched worms

SNACK DOWN UNDER

◆

There is probably not a single animal on Earth, no matter how unappealing to our eyes, which isn't regarded as a tasty snack somewhere. The same is true of the earthworm, which is appreciated as a gastronomic delicacy by the Maori people of New Zealand, where it is known as *noke*.

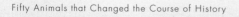

emerge as miniature adults minus the sex organs, which develop within two to three months. They live around three years in the wild, but have been known to live up to ten years in captivity.

Earthworms—there are up to six million per acre—live underground in burrows, which can be up to 6 ft (1.8 m) deep. They emerge at night to feed on organic material. Their beneficial impact on the soil is threefold: physical, biological, and chemical. As they burrow through the ground, earthworms create channels that keep the soil structure open, allowing the penetration of both air and water, and thus preventing soil compaction. As they feed, they take organic material, such as dead plant matter and animal excrement, underground, increasing the amount of humus in the soil and making it more fertile. In addition to enriching the soil with organic humus, earthworms swallow soil particles, which are digested in their intestines and excreted as worm casts. An analysis of casts reveals that they are richer in several minerals, including nitrogen, potash, and phosphates, than the surrounding soil. The earthworm, being at the bottom of the food chain, is itself an important source of food for a range of other animals, including birds, mammals, insects, and other invertebrates.

Small, invisible, and ignored by the vast majority of the human population, the earthworm is a key player that maintains both the health and proper functioning of the terrestrial biosphere on which life on Earth depends. Without the earthworm's ceaseless biological and mineral recycling, our fields and pastures, and the herbivores who depend on them, would be far less productive, making it much more difficult for humanity to meet its ever-growing food requirements.

EARTHMOVER
Burrowing underground, the earthworm increases the aeration and fertility of the soil by burying organic material.

SNACK TIME
The earthworm is itself an important source of food for many other animal species found in our fields and gardens.

Spanish Fly

Lytta vesicatoria

Native range: Southern Europe and Central Asia

Class: Insect

Size: 0.6–0.9 in (15–22 mm) long

✦ Edible

✦ **MEDICINAL**

✦ Commercial

✦ Practical

IRIDESCENT
Like other brightly colored insects, the Spanish fly's gaudiness is a warning of its toxicity.

This entry on the Spanish fly gives us an insight into the lighter and darker sides of human life, as the crushed body of this small beetle has been used as an aphrodisiac and a poison.

LADYKILLER

Throughout history, various plants and animal parts, ranging from oysters and celery to a rhino's horn and a tiger's penis, have been thought to stimulate the human sexual appetite and improve sexual performance. Several of these substances come from animal species considered to be particularly virile, such as the rhino and tiger, while others merely have a shape reminiscent of the sexual organs, such as oysters and celery. Scientific evaluations of traditional aphrodisiacs, however, have shown that their only true sexual potency exists within the mind of the taker—in other words, they are a placebo. In a few cases, however, the reputed aphrodisiac can produce a real physical reaction in the body, though not necessarily the one intended by those taking it. The dried and crushed body of the insect known as the Spanish fly was once believed to have aphrodisiac properties, but unfortunately it is also an extremely powerful poison that can prove deadly if ingested in high doses.

The Spanish fly is not a fly at all but an attractive iridescent greenish-blue beetle that is found on various shrubs and trees, including the ash, elder, and privet, in central and southern Europe and central Asia. The larval form of the insect is parasitic to several species of wild bee: the larvae climb onto flowers and attach themselves to bees collecting pollen and nectar. Once in the bee's nest, they devour their host's larvae and food stores.

The Spanish fly belongs to a large group of beetles known as "blister beetles" that secrete the chemical cantharidin, which causes blisterlike lesions on direct contact with skin. While the chemical is used by the beetle to protect itself and its eggs from predators, its irritant properties have also given it the reputation of being an aphrodisiac. The problem being for many would-be seducers that the dose considered sufficient to light the fires of another's passion might also prove to be fatal, as cantharidin is also highly toxic to humans.

One of the most notorious cases concerning the use of Spanish fly as an aphrodisiac concerns the French sexual dissident, known to us as the Marquis de Sade (1740–1814), whose name was given to the sexual fetish, sadism. In reality, de Sade was more of a fantasist and pornographer than a sexual abuser, but at a time when sexuality was rigidly controlled by the Church and state, his unconventional sexual tastes led to accusations of immorality, blasphemy, and sodomy. In 1772, when de Sade was visiting the southern French port of Marseilles, he engaged several prostitutes for an orgy, and they later accused him of giving them aniseed-flavored pastilles containing powdered Spanish fly. The Marquis promptly fled the country, and was convicted to death in his absence for attempted poisoning and sodomy. He was later pardoned and returned to France, but he was never far from trouble and incarceration. He finished his days in an insane asylum.

> **The U.S. Food and Drug Administration says there are no such things as aphrodisiacs; that it is all in the mind.**
>
> *Burke Owens (b. 1947)*

The toxic properties of the Spanish fly were also noted by those who took a direct approach to removing, as the author Terry Pratchett so colorfully put it, "the inconvenient razorblades in the candyfloss of life." In seventeenth-century Italy, when the only way to obtain a divorce was to petition the pope, unhappy wives had recourse to Aqua Tofana (Tofana water), a colorless and odorless mixture that might have contained a combination of arsenic, lead, belladonna, and Spanish fly, to poison their husbands. The potion was made by Giulia Tofana (d. 1659), and is thought to have sent as many as 600 men to an early grave.

Turkey

Meleagris gallopavo subsp.

Native range: North and Central America

Class: Bird

Size: 5–6 ft (1.5–1.8 m) wingspan

✦ **EDIBLE**

✦ MEDICINAL

✦ **COMMERCIAL**

✦ PRACTICAL

MISNOMER
Although it shares its name with a Near-Eastern country, the turkey has no relationship with the Old World.

Turkey was on the American menu a long time before the arrival of the Pilgrim Fathers. The bird was first domesticated by the Maya of Central America, and was a favorite at the Aztec dining table. A major commercial fowl today, the turkey is traditionally eaten at Christmas and Thanksgiving.

TALKING TURKEY

When the bald eagle was selected as the national bird of the United States of America in 1782, after a six-year-long discussion by Congress, there was one dissenting voice raised in opposition. Benjamin Franklin (1706–90) wrote to his daughter that the eagle was a poor choice because he deemed it to be of "bad moral character," as it stole food from other raptors, while the turkey was a "Bird of Courage, and would not hesitate to attack a Grenadier of the British Guards who should presume to invade his Farm Yard with a red Coat on." We shall never know whether he was entirely serious, but the thought of the U.S. president's aircraft emblazoned with a turkey, snood and wattles flying in the wind, is an image that is worth relishing for a few moments.

The turkey is second only to the chicken as the most numerous domesticated bird species on the planet and, according to current archaeological knowledge, has been farmed for over two millennia. While turkey is eaten at most times of year, it is particularly associated with two Western festivals: Thanksgiving and Christmas.

The turkey evolved in North and Central America, with an ancestral line dating back to around 23 million years BP. A distant relation of the Asian junglefowl and domesticated chicken, the turkey exhibits a similar sexual dimorphism in terms of size and plumage. The male, or cock, is larger than the female, or hen, and has brighter plumage, with patches of iridescent red, purple, green, copper, brown, and gold on its black plumage, while the female is duller and restricted to shades of brown and gray. As with the junglefowl, this increases the hen's camouflage when she is incubating her eggs. Males have fleshy growths on the head, throat, neck, and beak that become engorged with blood when they become excited. A long, fleshy, tubelike structure called a snood hangs from the cock's beak. The male has a fourth toe, or spur, which it uses to fight other males. While the heavier domesticated turkey is a very poor flier, its wild cousin is able to fly into trees to escape a predator.

The name "turkey" is a complete misnomer, as the bird has no relationship whatsoever with the country of that name. When the turkey was first imported from Mexico to Europe by the Spanish, the English thought it was similar to a species of Old World guineafowl called "turkey fowl" or "turkey cocks" that were named thus because they were imported into Europe through Ottoman Turkey. The name stuck, and when English settlers traveled to North America, they brought with them domesticated European turkeys, unaware that they were bringing the bird back to its native land.

The earliest evidence of the domestication of the turkey comes from Mayan sites in the early centuries of the Common Era. The turkey was an important source of food for the Aztecs of Mexico, who lacked any large herbivores for meat. In North America, the turkey played both symbolic and practical roles in Native American culture: it was used as a totem, an animal representing various tribal groups or clans; it was harvested for its meat and eggs; and its feathers were used for ceremonial headdresses and cloaks.

A TURKEY ISN'T JUST FOR CHRISTMAS

Although many (including this writer) would argue with Ambrose Bierce (see quote, p. 132) when he says that turkey makes for "pretty good eating," it has become the bird of choice for the high feast days and holidays of the Anglo-Saxon world, notably Christmas and Thanksgiving. December 25th, though it was intended to celebrate the date of Christ's birth, was probably chosen because it coincided with the day the pagan Romans celebrated the winter solstice.

Thanksgiving Greetings

TURKEY, n. A large bird whose flesh when eaten on certain religious anniversaries has the peculiar property of attesting piety and gratitude. Incidentally, it is pretty good eating.

Ambrose Bierce (1842–1914)

The centerpiece of the traditional Christmas day family lunch is roast turkey cooked with chestnut or sausage meat stuffing and gravy, and served with roast potatoes and boiled winter vegetables, typically Brussels sprouts and carrots.

The turkey seems to have scored an early hit with the British, as it appeared on Christmas menus as early as the sixteenth century—a part of the Christmas-day feasts served to King Henry VIII (1491–1547). For the next 400 years, it jockeyed for position with the Christmas goose, becoming firmly established as the nation's favorite in the late Victorian period. The tradition of the Christmas turkey was exported from England to the rest of the Anglo-Saxon world, and you'll find the bird on tables from the snowy banks of the St Lawrence and the Potomac to the sun-drenched Christmas beach barbecues of Sydney and Auckland.

The second feast day during which turkey takes the lead role is Thanksgiving, celebrated in the U.S. on the fourth Thursday in November. As readers in the U.S. will most probably be aware, the first Thanksgiving celebration can either be traced back to Virginia in 1619 or, more often, to Plymouth, Massachusetts, in 1621.

After many adventures and several false landings, the Mayflower Pilgrims landed at Plymouth Rock on December 21, 1620, but with insufficient stores to get them through their first New England winter. The colonists would have faced certain starvation had they not secured the help of two Native Americans: Squanto (c. 1580–1622) and Massasoit (Ousamequin) (c. 1581–1661), leaders of the Wampanoag confederacy. Squanto was a member of the Patuxet tribe, a tributary of the Wampanoag, who had been kidnapped and forcefully taken to Europe by British sailors in 1614. They intended to sell him into slavery in Spain, but he was rescued and made his way to London where he learned to speak English. He returned to his native land in 1619, only to find that most of his own tribe and many of the Wampanoag had been wiped out by epidemics of European diseases against which they had no immunity. He taught the colonists where to fish for eels and find shellfish, and how to grow the native staple, corn (maize). Just as importantly, he acted as their interpreter in their negotiations with the Wampanoag. Massasoit signed a peace treaty with the Pilgrims and provided them with food stores during their first winter. His efforts proved successful, as the Pilgrims survived.

In the late summer or fall of 1621, the Pilgrims celebrated their first successful harvest with three days of feasting to which they invited 90 Native American guests. Although now seen as the First Thanksgiving, at the time the celebration was more akin to a traditional English harvest festival. The menu of the modern Thanksgiving meal reflects the food served in Plymouth in 1621. The festival is also known as "Turkey Day," as the bird is the main course, served with stuffing, mashed potatoes with gravy, sweet potatoes, cranberry sauce, sweetcorn, and squash, with pumpkin pie to follow. The meal represents a fusion of local ingredients cooked and served in the European manner. Thanksgiving and the turkey remain focal points of traditional American family life and values today. In a way, Ben Franklin was right to suggest the turkey as the U.S.'s national emblem, not because of its unimpeachable morals and courage, but because it symbolized the creation of a new national identity with its roots in Europe but its future firmly fixed in the New World.

JAMIE'S CRUSADE

✦

In 2005, British TV chef Jamie Oliver (b. 1975) launched his campaign for a healthier diet for Britain's school children with his hit show *Jamie's School Dinners*. In his sights were mass-produced processed foods that contained high levels of sugar, salt, artificial colorings and flavorings, and trans-fats. The product that became emblematic of the whole school-dinner debate was the "Turkey Twizzler," a reconstituted turkey-meat product manufactured by the Bernard Matthew's food company. After the program was aired, schools and catering companies banned the Turkey Twizzler from their menus, and falling sales and adverse publicity forced the company to discontinue the product later that year.

Cobra

Naja naja

Native range: Indian subcontinent

Class: Reptile

Size: 6–8 ft (1.8–2.4 m) long

+ EDIBLE
+ MEDICINAL
+ COMMERCIAL
+ **PRACTICAL**

SELF-DEFENSE
The cobra's distinctive hood acts as a visual deterrent to predators.

In Judeo-Christian and Islamic mythology the snake is a symbol of evil and is associated with the devil, but in other religious traditions it is not always demonized. In Hinduism, the cobra is worshipped as a deity in its own right and cobralike beings called *nagas* play an important role in many of its myths and legends.

SHORT-SIGHTED SNAKE

The Indian cobra is not used for food and, with the exception of snake charming, has given no commercial service to humans. In fact, over the millennia, this venomous reptile has claimed many millions of human lives in its native India. However, like the lion and the eagle, it is an animal of enormous symbolic significance in the two major native religions of the subcontinent, Hinduism and Buddhism.

The Indian cobra is also known as the "spectacled cobra" thanks to a distinctive set of markings on the back of its flared hood, which resemble an old-fashioned pair of eyeglasses known as a pince-nez. The Indian cobra is a smooth-scaled snake that varies in color from black or dark brown to yellowish-white. The body is generally covered with a speckled white or yellow pattern, sometimes forming irregular bands, and the belly is white or yellow with a wide, dark band at the neck. The cobra has a distinctive hood that opens to make the animal look larger to predators. The cobra is also unusual among snakes in that is can "stand"—raising its body vertically—which is another way it intimidates would-be predators.

Cobras feed on small mammals, amphibians, birds, and other reptiles. Their fondness for rats and mice brings them into contact with human settlements, which explains the high number of human fatalities from cobra bites in India. Cobra venom is a powerful neurotoxin that, if untreated, will lead to muscle paralysis and death from respiratory or cardiac failure in less than one hour. In spring and summer, the female Indian cobra will lay a clutch of between ten and 30 eggs in rat holes or termite mounds. The eggs hatch after 50–70 days. Newborn cobras measure between 8 and 12 in (20–30 cm) and are exact replicas of the parents, with fully functional venom glands.

CHARMED LIFE

In the Christian, Jewish, and Islamic traditions, the serpent is an evil creature associated with the devil, but in India and Southeast Asia, humans have a far more complex relationship with cobras, which are identified with a mythical race of beings known as the *naga*. In India's Hindu tradition, nagas are nature spirits who live in springs, wells, and rivers. They bring rain, and thus fertility, but can also cause floods and drought. In southern India, where

LEGENDARY
The myths of India are full of references to cobras, either as forces for good or of evil.

cobras are a daily hazard in rural areas, they are nevertheless revered and honored in domestic rituals and annual festivals. In some areas, where the people believe they are descended from nagas, a cobra will never be killed, and a dead snake is cremated like a human being.

The nagas appear in several episodes of the great Hindu epic, the *Mahabharata*, in which they are sometimes portrayed as the evil "persecutors of all creatures," and at others as a force for good. One of the chapters explains the nagas' bitter enmity with Garuda, a Hindu divinity who was part-man, part-eagle. The nagas and Garuda were step-siblings, sharing the same father, the sage Kasyapa. He had two wives: Kadru, who wished to have many offspring, and Vinata, who wished to have only a few very powerful children. Kadru laid 1,000 eggs, which hatched into the nagas; Vinata gave birth to two sons, the charioteer of the Sun, Surya, and the winged Garuda.

In a plot device that is typical of Hindu epics, Vinata makes a bet with Kadru, which she loses, and becomes Kadru's slave. As a result, Garuda is duty bound to obey Kadru's

> **I've always liked reptiles. I used to see the universe as a mammoth snake, and I used to see all the people and objects, landscapes, as little pictures in the facets of their scales.**
>
> *Jim Morrison (1943–71)*

naga children. In order to be released from servitude, he promises to steal *amrita*, the elixir of immortality, from the gods. He defeats the gods in battle and takes the elixir, but on his way back to the nagas he is intercepted first by the gods Vishnu and Indra, who persuade him to join their side against the nagas by promising him immortality. Garuda delivers amrita to the snakes and is released from slavery, but he tricks them into waiting before they drink it. Indra then swoops down and takes back the elixir, denying the snakes immortality. From that time onward, Garuda and the nagas become bitter enemies, and Garuda, like a real eagle, feeds on the nagas. In other Hindu myths, the nagas are the allies and not the

PROTECTOR
In this image of the god Vishnu and his consort Lakshmi, the giant cobra is a benign protector.

enemies of the gods. The god Vishnu is often portrayed as reclining on or being sheltered by a giant naga. Similarly, the elephant-headed Ganesh and the god Siva are often pictured wearing necklaces or belts of snakes, or sometimes seated on them.

Nagas also appear in Buddhist myths and legends as beings with magical powers. They are said to guard Mount Meru, the holy mountain at the center of the universe, and also to live in the human realm. In some legends, nagas are capable of assuming human form. One story tells of a naga in human form who came to the Buddha to ask him for instruction in the eightfold path to enlightenment. The Buddha told the naga that the path was only open to human beings and that he could not be ordained a monk. He promised, however, that the naga would be reborn as a human in its next life.

SNAKE OIL SALESMEN

Probably one of the most enduring images—or should we say visual clichés—of the Indian cobra is as the snake used by Indian snake charmers. A favorite of Hollywood movies, snake charmers are under threat from modern entertainment media such as TV and cinema, but there are still said to be around a million snake charmers in India. Typically the snake charmer keeps his snake in a basket, which he sets down in a public space before the performance. He removes the lid and begins

CHARMED LIFE
Snake charmers do not "charm" cobras with music but use a number of tricks to control their snakes.

to play a flutelike instrument called a *pungi*. The cobra emerges from the basket, and extends its hood, appearing to the audience as if it is ready to strike the charmer. Instead, the snake sways from side to side, seemingly in time with the music. Apparently hypnotized, the snake never strikes its master, and will allow him to kiss its head and handle it.

The reality of snake charming, however, is very different, and pretty grim for the snake itself. Cobras are naturally shy, and will only attack if surprised or threatened. When the charmer opens the basket, the cobra is startled by the light and will stand and extend its hood. The snake charmer may even use his pungi surreptitiously to prompt the snake to emerge from the basket. However, the snake's auditory system does not allow it to hear the music played. Its swaying is actually a response to vibrations from the sound and the charmer's foot tapping, and the movement of the pungi. When the charmer ceases playing and tapping, the cobra will fold its hood and gradually fall back into the basket.

Snake charming is a hereditary occupation in India, so charmers are used to handling snakes from childhood. They often work as pest-controllers, removing snakes from homes. In the past, they were also healers, specializing in charms against snakebites and also in treating them. Snake charmers are rarely if ever bitten, but they have several tricks to ensure their own safety. The simplest method they employ is to sit just out of striking distance of the snake. However, charmers also employ more dishonest and cruel means, such as defanging the snake, or partially sewing up its mouth so that only its forked tongue is visible. This treatment leads to the early death of the snake from infections or starvation.

Like the other symbolic animals featured in this book, the cobra has an ambiguous position in human culture. As a symbol of strength, speed, and power, it is revered and even worshipped as a divinity in its own right; but as a living animal, it is rightly feared for its deadly venom and is often cruelly persecuted and exploited.

GUARDIAN OF LOWER EGYPT

✦

Those lucky enough to have visited the archaeological museum in Cairo will have seen the astounding gold and lapis lazuli funerary mask of Tutankhamun (1341–1323 BCE) up close. The Boy King's headdress features a *uraeus*, a pairing of two animals: the head of a vulture and a standing cobra. The snake represents the goddess Wadjet, who was the protector of Lower Egypt and patroness of the Nile. The uraeus was worn only by the gods and the pharaoh, and became a symbol of Egyptian kingship, much like the crown and scepter of Western monarchs.

Common Rabbit
Oryctolagus cuniculus

Native range: Iberian peninsula

Class: Mammal

Size: 8–20 in (20–50 cm) long

+ ***EDIBLE***
+ *MEDICINAL*
+ ***COMMERCIAL***
+ *PRACTICAL*

The domestication of the European rabbit has had a mixed impact on the world. Although it has been valuable source of protein, especially during periods of hardship, such as wartime and economic depression, its introduction to certain countries, notably Australia, has been disastrous for the environment and native wildlife.

CONEY LAND

According to one controversial linguistic theory, Spain owes its name to an ancient misidentification of the wild European rabbit. The Phoenicians, who came from the coasts of the Levant (now Lebanon), were the great merchant-explorers of the first two millennia BCE. They settled the Western Mediterranean, establishing their most famous colony in Carthage (now Tunisia). When they first explored southern Spain, they came across wild rabbits, which they mistook for hyraxes—animals native to their home in the Near East. The resemblance between the two species is only passing as the hyrax does not have the rabbit's long ears or

powerful back legs. Nevertheless, they called the country *i-shaphanim* ("the land of the hyraxes"), which the Greeks converted into *Spania* and the Romans into *Hispania*, and which in due course morphed into the Spanish *España*.

Unlike the majority of the food animals covered in this book, the rabbit is raised commercially for its meat and fur and also hunted for food and sport. Rabbits have also found a role as household pets alongside cats and dogs. Proverbially an extremely fertile species, the rabbit reproduces at such a rate that its populations have to be controlled by predation or hunting. However, in countries where the species was introduced in the nineteenth century, and where it has no natural predators, the harmless-looking bunny has proven to be a dangerous pest, damaging the environment and endangering the survival of local wildlife. In response, humans unleashed the terrible plague of myxomatosis that temporarily decimated both feral and domestic rabbit populations.

The European rabbit is the ancestor of all modern domesticated rabbit breeds. It is smaller than the domesticated rabbit, averaging 13–18 in (34–45 cm) in length. In the wild, rabbits live in colonies known as warrens. The females (called "does") excavate burrows as nests in which to bear

CUNICULTURE
The first reliable evidence of rabbit breeding dates back to the Roman period.

their young, which they then link with interconnecting tunnels. Rabbits emerge at dawn and dusk to feed, principally grazing on grass, but they will also browse on other plant matter, including crop plants, shrubs, and saplings. Rabbits have a complex hierarchical social system, with dominant males and dominant females. Unlike the child's picturebook image of the lovable, cuddly bunny, wild rabbits can be extremely aggressive and fights for dominance between males (bucks) often lead to serious injury or death. Despite their vulnerability to predation and hunting, rabbits maintain and increase their numbers by upping their reproductive rate and literally "breeding like rabbits." Females are ready to mate at three to four months of age, and thereafter can produce up to seven litters of two to 12 offspring per year.

BUNNY BOILERS

There is no definitive archaeological evidence about where and when rabbits were first domesticated. However, like other herbivores that later became domesticated farm animals, they were the prey of our hunter-gatherer forebears, who consumed their meat and used their fur for clothing. Rabbit bones are associated with early human campsites and settlements, but these could be the result of hunting rather than the breeding of rabbits, or cuniculture. The first reliable evidence of rabbit farming dates back to the Roman period, when rabbits were kept in large walled enclosures. Selective breeding is thought to have begun in the Middle Ages in Europe, leading to the great diversity of modern breeds that are raised for their meat and fiber, and kept as domestic pets and show animals.

Although it will never rival the commercial exploitation of cattle, sheep, and pigs for meat, the rabbit has been a useful source of protein in periods of adversity and economic hardship because it can be raised in the home with little outlay in space and resources. Rabbits were bred for their meat during the Great Depression in the U.S. (1929–39) and during the two world wars in Europe. Rabbits are also hunted in rural areas, both for their meat and as a form of pest control. Rabbit meat is leaner than either pork or beef, though the author's own childhood memories of rabbit stew are of a plethora of tiny bones that had to be picked out to get at the meat.

What is a country without rabbits and partridges? They are among the most simple and indigenous animal products; ancient and venerable families known to antiquity as to modern times; of the very hue and substance of Nature, nearest allied to leaves and to the ground.

Henry Thoreau (1817–62)

Rabbits are also raised for their hides and fiber, though again, the quantity produced is insignificant when compared to leather from cattle and wool from sheep. Historically, rabbit skins were made into clothing and accessories, but today, several breeds of Angora rabbit are bred for their fiber, which is spun and made into clothing, often with admixtures of other yarns. The Angora rabbit's wool is said to be five times warmer than sheep's wool. A final commercial use of the rabbit is as a test subject for medical research and the testing of new drugs.

POPULATION EXPLOSION
With no natural predators, a warm climate, and plentiful food, the Australian rabbit population reached 600 million by the turn of the twentieth century.

PETS AND PESTS

Because of its size, sociability, and temperament, the rabbit has been kept as a domestic pet since the nineteenth century, as an alternative to the dog and cat that has proven to be particularly popular with younger children. Like cats and dogs, rabbits are shown in competition all over the world, with prizes awarded for the best in breed. A more recent competitive pastime involving rabbits that emerged in the 1970s is rabbit showjumping, which is modeled after horse show jumping. Led by their owners on a leash, rabbits are made to jump different kinds of fences along a set course, with top points awarded to a rabbit that clears all the obstacles.

The seemingly harmless rabbit, however, is not a universally welcomed visitor, especially in areas where the local ecosystem does not have a mechanism to control its numbers. In the nineteenth century, a dozen wild and domesticated rabbits were imported from the UK to the state of Victoria in eastern Australia and released into the wild. With no natural predators among the native marsupials, plentiful grazing and agricultural crops, and a warm climate that allowed them to breed year-round, the rabbits did what came naturally, reaching an astounding 600 million by the turn of the century. Various control methods, such as hunting, poisoning, and the construction of a fence to halt the rabbit's expansion across the continent failed miserably.

The solution was found half a century later, with the release of the *Myxomatosis cuniiculi* virus into the feral Australian rabbit population. The effects were immediate and devastating: within a few years the rabbit population had plummeted from 600 to 100 million animals. The virus was accidentally released in Europe in the early 1950s, killing 90–95 percent of the rabbit populations in France and the UK. However, the near elimination of the rabbit across much of its European range has consequently affected its natural predators, who are now also on the endangered list. In recent years rabbit populations in Australia and Europe are again on the rise, as the surviving rabbits have a genetic immunity to the disease.

LITERARY RABBIT
Beatrix Potter's Peter Rabbit stories have charmed children since they were first published in 1902.

"WHAT'S UP, DOC?"

✦

The nonchalant, carrot-munching Bugs Bunny walking up to Elmer Fudd who is pointing his gun at the rabbit hole waiting for the "wabbit" to appear, and saying, "Eh... what's up, doc?" is probably many urban children's first sight of a rabbit. Tex Avery's (1908–80) Bugs Bunny is one in a long line of rabbit characters that have entertained generations of children. One of the most enduring is Beatrix Potter's (1866–1943) Peter Rabbit, who first appeared in 1902. One of the most successful rabbit stories, and probably the one closest to the real life of the animal, is Richard Adams' (b. 1920) *Watership Down* (1972).

Sheep

Ovis aries

Native range: Western Asia

Class: Mammal

Size: 24–35 in (60–90 cm) tall at the shoulder

+ **EDIBLE**

+ MEDICINAL

+ **COMMERCIAL**

+ **PRACTICAL**

Baa, baa, black sheep,
Have you any wool?
Yes sir, yes sir,
Three bags full.

*Traditional English
nursery rhyme*

The sheep was the second animal species to be domesticated by humans after the dog. Apart from being bred for its milk and meat, the sheep is the main source of wool, still one of the most common natural fibers used in the textile industry. Historically, sheep have been the mainstay of the economies of many cultures, from ancient Greece to present-day Australia. In addition to its commercial importance, the sheep features in the myths, rituals, and iconography of many of the world's religious traditions.

MOUFLON DRESSED AS LAMB

For many people, lamb probably comes third in the meat stakes (no pun intended) after beef and pork (and maybe even after chicken for the more health-conscious). But historically, as the first large herbivore to be domesticated, the sheep played a crucial role in teaching our ancestors how to domesticate and selectively breed herding animals instead of hunting them. The successful domestication of the sheep led to the domestication of other herbivores. In addition to providing humans with a source of protein and fat in the form of meat, sheep also produce milk that is ideally formulated to be manufactured into cheese. Meat and milk, however, account for only part of the sheep's significance to the development of human civilization.

Until the late Middle Ages, when silk and cotton cloth became more widely available in Western Europe, the only materials worn by the majority of the population were leather, linen, and wool. As we have seen in earlier entries, fiber can be obtained from a variety of animals, including goats, rabbits, and camels, but with selective breeding, the sheep has become the animal that produces the largest quantities of white wool. The sheep's importance as an edible and commercial species has made it an important symbolic animal in many cultures. Sheep have been associated with divinity since antiquity, when the ram was one of the forms of the Egyptian god Amon-Ra. In the Jewish tradition the sheep was the preeminent sacrificial animal offered to Jehovah in the Temple of Jerusalem, which developed into the Christian concept of Jesus as the sacrificial "Lamb of God."

All modern breeds of domesticated sheep are descended from wild sheep, or mouflon, whose original range stretched westward from the Balkans to the Caucasus. The mouflon is quite unlike a modern sheep in appearance and coloration: it has a short reddish-brown coat with a distinctive black stripe and a light-colored belly and lower legs. The males and some females carry an impressive pair of curled horns. The domestication of the mouflon is thought to have begun around 8500 BCE in Iraq or Iran. Archaeological finds from the region show that selective breeding began around 7000 BCE. By 6000 BCE, domesticated sheep were found in the Balkans, and within a few hundred years, they had reached the western Mediterranean. By the Bronze Age (3300–1200 BCE), the sheep had spread all over Europe, and had become the mainstay of the agricultural economy of many cultures.

BLACK AND WHITE
While the mouflon is brown, sheep were bred to be white or sometimes black.

In historical times, the sheep family, or ovines, had no native representatives in the Americas. After the arrival of humans on the continent, the only surviving large herding herbivores were the buffalo of North America and the llamas of South America. The Spanish introduced the merino sheep to Central and South America in the sixteenth century, while the British, French, and Dutch brought their own breeds of sheep when they settled North America. The sheep played a role in the settlement of the American West during the nineteenth century, when it was introduced to the Great Plains, leading to conflicts between cattle and sheep ranchers over land and grazing rights.

Like its cousin the goat, the sheep is a ruminant herbivore, but unlike goats that prefer to browse, sheep are primarily grazers. Sheep use a combination of repeated chewing of its partly digested food (chewing the cud) and the action of microorganisms in their four-chambered stomachs to extract the maximum amount of nutrition from grass. The sheep is a social animal with a strong herding instinct, which together with its small size made it an ideal choice for domestication. After humans had made the transition from a hunter-gatherer lifestyle to settled agriculture and nomadic pastoralism, the sheep provided a vital source of protein in the form of meat and milk. Although lamb and mutton remain popular in certain parts of the world today, notably in the Arab countries, Australia, New Zealand, the West Indies, and India, their consumption has declined when compared to pork, chicken, and beef in Europe and the U.S. Sheep's milk, which is higher in fat and solids than cow's milk, is not usually drunk fresh but is widely used to make cheese and yoghurt. The best-known sheep cheeses include feta (Balkans), Roquefort (France), Manchego (Spain), and ricotta and Pecorino (Italy).

YARN
The sheep produces the largest quantity of animal fiber.

WOOLLY JUMPERS

The sheep's ancestor, the mouflon, is short-haired with a reddish-brown coat, while domesticated sheep have long crimped fleeces that are generally white—although species can vary in color from white to brown and black. This means that humans began to breed sheep selectively for longer, lighter coats several thousand years BCE. The exact date when this took place is unknown because, unless preserved by special conditions, such as in the dry tombs of Egypt or the peat bogs of Europe, cloth does not survive, so the archaeological record has few ancient textiles. The earliest example of European woolen cloth was found in a bog in Denmark and dates back to the late Bronze Age (c. 1500 BCE). However, it is likely that wool was first spun into thread and woven at a much earlier date.

In classical times, the Greeks wore woolen garments in both summer and winter. In warm weather, men and women would wear the short tunic, or chiton, which was supplemented by a cloak, or himation, for cold weather. Weaving was an occupation reserved for women and was carried out in the home—a pattern that would persist all over Europe until the mechanization of textile production in the eighteenth century. One of the most important festivals of ancient Athens, the Panathenaia, featured the weaving of an ornate *peplos*, a floor-length woolen gown, for the statue of the patroness of the city, the goddess Athena.

The traditional Roman garment, the toga, consisted of 20 ft (6 m) of woolen cloth that was worn by men over a Greek-style linen chiton. Originally a capelike garment worn by soldiers, artisans, and farmers, the toga became longer, more cumbersome, and looser, until it was only worn at court or on special occasions—the equivalent of our own Sunday best. During the republican and imperial periods, there were several types of toga varying in color from plain white to purple with gold embroidery, which were used to indicate differences of age and status. During the Byzantine period (4th–15th c.), the elite preferred expensive silks and linen to woolen garments. In contrast, in Europe during the early Middle Ages (c. 5th–9th c. CE), wool remained the material worn by the vast majority of the population, though clothing styles varied between the more Latinized regions and those settled by Germanic peoples. The former adhered to the long Roman tunic, while the latter favored short tunics and leggings.

From the twelfth century onward, raw wool and woolen cloth were the main commodities driving the European economy. The principal centers of wool production were Spain and

SPINNER
Clothing can be made of sheep's hide or from its spun wool.

HARD-HEADED
The wild sheep is equipped with an impressive pair of horns.

England, and the main manufacturing centers were the Low Countries (now the Netherlands and Belgium) and the city-states of northern Italy. The trading and financial networks established by the wool trade during the later Middle Ages (12th–15th c.) can be seen as the embryonic signs of an emerging capitalist market economy. Hence, the vast global commercial, industrial, and financial edifice that has emerged since the Industrial Revolution was built on the back of the humble sheep.

In the eighteenth century, cotton replaced wool in the manufacture of many garments, especially those worn against the skin; however, wool remained in demand for external clothing, such as men's suits and coats, as well as household items such as blankets, carpets, and upholstery fabrics. The real challenge to wool came in the postwar period with the introduction of synthetic yarns. With the fall in demand, prices collapsed, and production quickly followed. As a result, many sheep farmers in the major producing countries switched from wool to meat production. In recent decades, technical innovations, such as the development of washable wools and a change in fashion favoring natural materials, have led to renewed demand for woolen garments.

LAMB OF GOLD

As an animal of such enormous economic importance, the sheep features as a potent symbol in the myths, rituals, and iconography of many religious traditions. In ancient Egypt, one of the forms of the creator god Amon-Ra was the ram. Alleys leading to several temples in Egypt were lined with ram-headed sphinxes . The people of Babylonia (now Iraq), who developed one of the world's first urban civilizations and were gifted astronomers, drew the constellations in the heavens, and established Aries, the ram, as the first sign of the astrological zodiac. In the unrelated Chinese zodiac, which associates a different animal for every year within a twelve-year cycle, the ram features as the eighth animal.

The most famous ancient Greek myth featuring a ram is the story of Jason and the Golden Fleece. Jason, leader of the Argonauts—a group of heroes that includes Herakles (Hercules)—sets out on a quest to acquire the magic fleece from the Kingdom of Colchis (now the Republic of Georgia on the Black Sea coast). After many adventures during his

HELLO, DOLLY!

✦

It is somehow fitting that the first herbivore to be domesticated and selectively bred by humans should also be the first mammal to be cloned successfully. Dolly the sheep (1996–2003) was produced from an adult cell taken from a sheep's mammary gland. She was born in Scotland in 1996 and lived for seven years until she was put down because of serious health problems. Dolly's cloning proved that animals could be cloned from any body cell, and not just an embryonic stem cell. Explaining their choice of name, one of her creators explained: "Dolly is derived from a mammary gland cell and we couldn't think of a more impressive pair of glands than Dolly Parton's."

outward journey, Jason arrives in Colchis only to find its ruler deeply (and rightly) suspicious of his intentions. However, with the help of the king's daughter, Medea, he defeats the dragon that guards the fleece, escapes from the king's men, and takes the fleece and Medea back to Greece. One explanation suggested for the origins of the legend is the practice of using lambs' fleeces to sift gold from the waters of streams and rivers of Colchis. Hence the story is not about a noble quest for a divine artifact but a mythological retelling of an ancient Greek piratical raid for treasure.

Sheep were among the animals sacrificed to the pagan gods of Greece and Rome, and were the principal victims offered to Jehovah at the Temple in Jerusalem. The sheep features in several episodes in the Old Testament. God tests Abraham by ordering him to sacrifice his son Isaac, but the boy is saved at the last minute by the appearance of a ram caught in a thicket, which Abraham sacrifices in his place. This event is celebrated in Islam in the Eid ul-Adha festival, when a goat or sheep is sacrificed and its meat is distributed to the poor. During the Israelites' captivity in Egypt, they are saved from the Angel of Death, who carries away the first born of every Egyptian family, by daubing their doors with lamb's blood. The practice, and accompanying imagery, of the sacrificial lamb was converted in Christian theology into the representation of Christ as the *Agnus Dei*, the Lamb of God. Jesus Christ, part-human and part-divine, is sent to die on Earth to atone for the sins of humanity.

Human civilization would exist without the sheep, as it emerged perfectly well without it in the Americas. However, many aspects of our culture and daily lives would be radically different. Though proverbially stupid, easily led, and vulnerable, the domestication of the sheep enabled humans to develop a more secure, settled way of life, and eventually became one of the economic bases for the development of Western capitalism.

GOLD DIGGER
The legend of the Golden Fleece refers to the use of fleeces to sieve gold in ancient Georgia.

INNOCENT
In medieval Christian iconography, the lamb is a symbol for Christ the Redeemer.

Chimpanzee
Pan troglodytes

Native range: West and Central Africa

Class: Mammal

Size: Up to 4.3–5.6 ft (1.3–1.7 m) tall

+ EDIBLE
+ *MEDICINAL*
+ COMMERCIAL
+ *PRACTICAL*

The chimpanzee is our closest living relative; while we are not directly descended from chimps (or any other great ape), they share many traits with us, including a range of social and emotional behaviors, as well as tool-making abilities. Our similarities with our primate cousins have made us realize that we are not so unique and deserving of the unquestioned lordship of creation.

MOCKMAN

Until Darwin's *On the Origin of Species* (1859) and *The Descent of Man* (1871), most laypeople were secure in the knowledge that "Man" was quite distinct from the animals. Humans were unlike the "lower" animals in so many different ways that the idea of Darwin's proposed "common descent" was absurd. First, there were the technological accomplishments of human civilization, from the stone-age ax to the steam engine; then came language, abstract thought, artistic creativity, and complex emotions, such as love and altruism. The belief in human uniqueness was buttressed by two millennia of Christian teachings that God had created Adam and Eve in his own image and the animals as their servants.

When the animals that humans compared themselves to were the slow, dim-witted sheep and cattle, the savage, bloodthirsty wolf and lion, or the bizarre, exotic giraffe and rhinoceros, it is easy to understand how they could set themselves apart from the "animal kingdom." However, when Europeans began to explore their world, they made discoveries that did not quite fit with this comfortable worldview. For one, they came across humans that did not look or behave like them, and they also found animals—the great apes of Africa and Asia—that were remarkably human in appearance and behavior. They solved both these problems by classifying humans who seemed too different

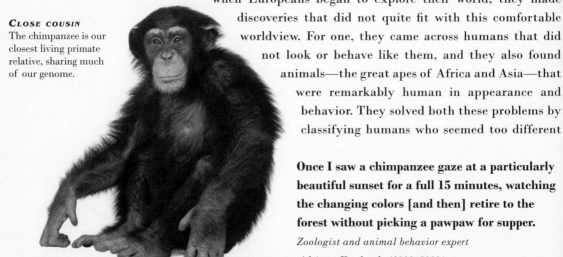

CLOSE COUSIN
The chimpanzee is our closest living primate relative, sharing much of our genome.

Once I saw a chimpanzee gaze at a particularly beautiful sunset for a full 15 minutes, watching the changing colors [and then] retire to the forest without picking a pawpaw for supper.

Zoologist and animal behavior expert
Adriaan Kortlandt (1918–2009)

from "civilized" man and the great apes as "lesser" human species, giving birth to the racist pseudo-science eugenics.

Although the chimpanzee and human lineages diverged some six million years BP, the chimp is our closest living relative. Evidence of our close familial relationship comes from the 95 percent overlap of the human and chimp genomes. Long before the advent of genetic science, however, the chimpanzee's similarity to humans had been noted by the Luba people of the Democratic Republic of the Congo, whose name for the ape can be translated as "mockman." The first mention of chimpanzees in Western records dates back to the sixteenth-century writings of a Portuguese navigator, and when the first chimps were brought to Europe in the seventeenth century, they were thought to be a race of exotic pygmy humans. During the next few centuries, chimpanzees were brought to Europe and exhibited as curiosities in zoos and circuses, but they were not studied scientifically. When Darwin published *The Descent of Man* in 1871, which proposed that animals and humans were descended from a common ancestor, he was caricatured in one newspaper as having the head of a man on the body of a chimpanzee (shown above)— a jibe that was based on the popular misconception that the book claimed humans were descended from the great apes, rather than being their taxonomic cousins.

Our image of the chimpanzee has been distorted by its many representations in TV and film as the cute sidekick of African explorers and loincloth-wearing lords of the jungle. In a popular British advertising campaign for tea, chimpanzees are made to playact dressed in human clothing and, until the event was abolished for reasons of animal welfare and good taste, London Zoo held a regular "chimps' tea party" as an entertainment for its human visitors. A fully grown

DESCENT OF MAN
Some readers of Darwin's *On the Origin of Species* mistakenly thought he claimed that we were descended from the great apes.

GOING APE

✦

Michael Jackson (1958–2009), adored by his legion of loyal fans but known as "Wacko Jacko" to his detractors, was famous for his "friendship" with a chimpanzee called Bubbles (b. 1983), which he purchased from an animal-testing facility in Texas when the chimp was eight months old. The chimp was his constant companion during the 1980s, accompanying the singer on his foreign tours and mixing with the stars at Hollywood parties. In an interview in 2003, Jackson revealed that he had been forced to part with Bubbles because the now fully grown chimp had become too aggressive, and he feared for the safety of his son, Prince Michael II. Bubbles has survived his celebrity owner, and now lives a much more sedate life in the Center for Great Apes in Wauchula, Florida.

male adult chimpanzee is a deceptively
large and fierce creature. Up to 5.6 ft
(1.7 m) in height, it is as tall as many
adult humans; it appears much
smaller, however, because it spends
most of its time on all fours, walking
on its knuckles and only standing to
its full height when confronting a
rival male or a predator. With five times
the upper body strength of an average man and a
much longer reach, the chimp is a fearsome opponent, and there have
been several cases of pet chimps seriously injuring adult humans, and of
wild chimps snatching and eating human infants. Like humans, chimps
are omnivorous and in addition to fruits and vegetable matter they will
eat insects, grubs, and small mammals and other monkeys.

PRIMATE PRIMER

Although chimpanzees were studied in captivity in the early twentieth
century, it was not until the middle of the century, when they were
observed in the wild, that the full range of their abilities and behaviors
were properly understood. Starting in 1960, the pioneering British
anthropologist and primatologist Jane Goodall (b. 1934) lived with a
community of forest chimpanzees in Tanzania. What she witnessed
rocked the zoological establishment and the wider world. Her most
startling discoveries were that chimps made and used rudimentary
tools and that they cooperatively hunted small monkeys as food.
However, perhaps even more startling was Goodall's claim that the
chimps exhibited extremely complex, humanlike emotions, such as
curiosity, grief, altruism, and love. Goodall's chimps also had a dark

side. Like humans, they were capable of
extreme violence against one another,
and Goodall witnessed acts that we
would call murder and infanticide if
they had taken place in the human
world. Chimps have since been observed
using sharpened sticks as weapons to
fend off leopards, which are their main
predators.

Language is often cited as one of the
faculties that differentiate us from other
animals. Although all animals communi-

cate to some degree, this is usually as a response to a direct stimulus in their environment. For example, the arrival of a predator will generate an alarm call. However, to use the same scenario, humans can discuss the existence of predators in abstract terms, and decide on a strategy to escape any danger they may face. In the wild, chimpanzees employ a wide range of nonverbal means of communication such as body language, hand gestures, vocalizations, and facial expressions, but whether these demonstrated a capacity for abstract thought that matches our own was not clear. It was a problem that researchers Allen and Beatrice Gardner set out to investigate in the 1960s.

Chimps lack the finely tuned voice box that gives humans their capacity for modulated speech. They could never learn to speak as they do in *The Planet of the Apes* movies. But like humans, they have agile prehensile hands with which they could be taught to communicate in the same manner as people with hearing or speech disabilities. The Gardners taught a young chimpanzee female called Washoe (1965–2007) American

SOCIABLE
Chimps exhibit complex social behaviors and are credited with emotions such as love and grief.

Sign Language (ASL) and claimed that she successfully mastered 350 ASL signs, which she in turn taught to her offspring. They concluded that chimps were capable of abstract thought and that they exhibited another quality that was once considered to be uniquely human—self-awareness. However, later attempts at repeating the experiment with other chimpanzees have proved less conclusive, and researchers now think that rather than using language spontaneously to express their thoughts and feelings, the signing chimps might merely be imitating their human handlers. Although chimpanzees might not be as close to humans as some researchers initially thought or hoped, they exhibit a range of abilities and behaviors that has demonstrated once and for all that humans are not as unique as they'd like to think they are.

Lion
Panthera leo

Native range: Europe, Africa, and Western Asia

Class: Mammal

Size: 4.5–8 ft (1.4–2.5 m) long

Like the eagle, the lion's importance to human civilization is largely symbolic. The lion represents strength, courage, and nobility, and has been used as a symbol of royalty since antiquity. Real-life lions, however, have been hunted for sport, incarcerated in menageries and zoos, and turned into circus performers. Once one of the most common mammals after humans, the lion is now an endangered species.

KING OF THE ANIMALS

The lion is a species that plays a hugely symbolic role in the spheres of religion, politics, and art, but whose range has been in decline since the end of the last ice age because of pressure from humans, and whose survival in the wild looks increasingly uncertain. Lions have been deified and worshipped in their own right, but their most common association is with the role of king and the institution of monarchy—thus the "king of the animals" also stands for the lion's human counterpart. However, the contrast between the respect given to the lion as a symbol and the treatment accorded to the species could not be greater.

LION KING
The lion has a symbolic significance that far outweighs its actual role in human life.

The lion has been hunted for sport or as a ritual test of manhood since ancient times. But they have also been persecuted by humans who saw them as a threat to their herds of cattle and sheep. Thousands of lions have been taken from the wild to be kept in unsanitary, unsuitable conditions, first in the menageries of the rich and powerful, who saw the ownership of lions as a visible expression of their power, and then as the leading attractions in zoological gardens that brought the exoticism of Africa and Asia to the shores of Europe and North America.

SPORT OF KINGS
Ritual lion hunts symbolized the king's power and his duty to protect his subjects.

Lions evolved in Africa between one million and 800,000 years BP, and spread widely across the planet, colonizing most of Europe, Asia, and the Americas. At one time, they were the most common mammalian species after humans. The inexorable rise and spread of the human population, however, has been mirrored by a decline in the lion's range and numbers. In prehistoric times, the two species were natural rivals as hunters of large herbivores, and later lions would be considered a threat to the herds of nomads and settled farmers. The lion disappeared from the Americas around 10,000 years BP, though it is not known whether this was caused solely because of human activity or because ecological changes made their prey less available.

The lion is the only big cat to exhibit clear sexual differences between the male and female. The male is larger, stronger, and more heavily built than the female, and also has a distinctive mane of hair around his head. The mane, while it makes the lion look larger and protects the vulnerable area around the head and neck from injury, also makes him a less able hunter as it is cumbersome and also makes him overheat during a chase. However, true to his reputation as the "king" of the animals,

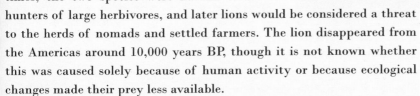

This desert is the lion's home, the monarch's royal lair;
From hence, when stars are out, he gallops to the plain,
Beneath the herdsman's very beard the cattle spoil to gain.
Isaac McLellan (1806–99)

the male lion spends most of his time in indolence, letting his harem of "queens" do the actual work. Although lions have a reputation as fierce hunters, bringing down large prey such as zebra and wildebeest, they obtain up to 40 percent of their food requirements from scavenging or stealing prey from other predators.

Lions live in family groups known as "prides," consisting of two to four adult males and between four and 20 adult females and their immature offspring of both sexes. When lion cubs reach maturity, they either

MAIN ATTRACTION
The first lion-taming acts
date back to the late
nineteenth century.

have to challenge their fathers and uncles for dominance of the pride or are expelled, while the females remain with their mothers. In order to mate, excluded males will have to take over an existing pride by challenging and defeating its dominant males. If the newcomers are successful, they will normally kill the immature cubs sired by their predecessors. In this they are not unlike our own historical kings, who, after winning the crown from a rival, did not hesitate to liquidate his or her inconvenient heirs.

GUARDIAN LIONS

The lion is a fierce, aggressive hunter, so it would seem natural that it became associated in ancient times with humanity's most aggressive pastime: warfare. The ancient Egyptians and their neighbors worshipped several lion gods, including the goddess of war Sekhmet, whose most common representation was as a woman with the head of a lioness. She protected the pharaoh in battle and attacked his enemies with fiery arrows. Sekhmet was honored in rituals at the end of a battle to ensure the conclusion of hostilities and, at her annual festival, her priestesses and devotees drank excessive quantities of beer in order to pacify the goddess' wrath, which might otherwise lead to the destruction of humanity. A more peaceful image of the lion as a protector deity is found in Hindu mythology. Narasimha, an avatar, or incarnation, of the god Vishnu, is represented as a being that is half-man and half-lion. A popular deity in the south of India, Narasimha is worshipped as "the Great Protector" who comes to his devotees' aid in times of need.

WAR GODDESS
The ancient Egyptians represented war as the lion-headed goddess Sekhmet.

The lion as a protector spirit is a common motif that is found all over the world. In the ancient Near East, lions or human–lion hybrids known as "sphinxes" guarded the gates of cities, temples, and royal palaces in Egypt and Assyria (now northern Iraq). The world's most famous sphinx stands guard by the pyramids of Giza, near the modern Egyptian capital of Cairo, although the exact function of the enormous sculpture remains a mystery. Much eroded by time, the sphinx has the body of a lion and the head of a pharaoh, possibly that of the builder of the Great Pyramid, Khafra (d. 2532 BCE). Sphinxes line the alleys leading to many Egyptian temples, notably the temple complexes at Luxor and Karnak.

Visitors to the British Museum in London can see a pair of Assyrian lamassu, impressive winged lions with human heads that once guarded the gates of the palace of Ashurnasirpal II (d. 859 BCE) in Nimrud (now northern Iraq). The huge sculptures were made specifically to awe the visitor, and make them fully aware of the power of the Assyrian monarchy. In a neighboring room, a series of bas-relief panels in the museum, excavated in the palace of the Assyrian king Ashurbanipal (685–c. 627 BCE) in Nineveh, depicts a royal lion hunt. In both ancient Assyria and Egypt the lion hunt was a ritual event that symbolized the king's power and his duty to guard and fight for his people. The scenes show captive Near Eastern lions, now long extinct, being released, chased by the king in his chariot, and finally killed with a bow and arrow. Similar motifs of guardian lions are found in the palaces of the Persian Achaemenid Empire (6th–4th c. BCE; now Iran).

As shown by the lions that guard the city gates of the Bronze Age city of Mycenae in Greece, the lion was a potent symbol in Greek mythology and iconography. Greece was the westernmost part of the lion's European range, and the animal was still present during the fifth century BCE. The slaying of the Nemean Lion was the first of Hercules' 12 labors. In the most common version of the story, the hero tries to kill the lion by shooting it with his bow, only to discover that the beast's hide is impervious to human weapons. He follows the beast to its lair, where he first stuns it with his club, and then strangles it to death. Wishing to have the animal's weapon-proof hide for himself, Hercules unsuccessfully attempts to skin it with his knife. The goddess Athena appears to him and tells him to use the lion's own claw to skin it.

Another Greek myth tells of the Sphinx, a creature that had the body of a lioness, the wings of an eagle, and the

WIDESPREAD
The lion was once one of the most common large mammal species on Earth.

head of a woman. She guarded the approaches of the city of Thebes and asked any traveler unfortunate enough to meet her the famous riddle: "What creature walks on four legs in the morning, on two at midday, and on three in the evening?" The monster devoured those who could not answer the riddle. The Sphinx is finally bested by the hero Oedipus, who answers: "Man, who crawls on all fours as a baby, walks on two legs as an adult, and then walks with a walking stick in old age." Defeated, the Sphinx kills herself by throwing herself off a cliff.

Although the lion's range never extended eastward as far as East and Southeast Asia, guardian lions are found at the entrance of many Asian temples and palaces. The idea of a lion as a protective deity was introduced to Asia with the various schools of Indian Buddhism. However, because Asian artists had never seen real lions, their representations are far from naturalistic. The Chinese lion dance is a tradition performed during the celebrations for the lunar New Year. Dancers, wearing a highly ornate and colorful costume that only bears a very passing resemblance to a lion, dance through the streets, stopping at houses and businesses where they are faced with a choice between two auspicious objects: a green vegetable known as *cai*, which is a homophone for the Chinese word for good fortune, and an orange to which has been tied a red envelope—the color red being considered particularly lucky in China. The lion will

HUNTRESS
Contrary to popular opinion,
it is the lioness that is the
better hunter.

"eat" the cai and then "spit" it out, arranging the leaves so they form an auspicious Chinese character. The lion is then rewarded with the red envelope that contains money. The lion's visit is believed to bring good fortune to the house or business.

In medieval Europe, the lion became closely associated with royalty, particularly in England, whose royal standards have featured one or more lions since the reign of William the Conqueror (1028–87). The Three Lions' crest favored by the crusading English king, Richard I (1157–99), nicknamed "the Lionheart" for his courage and military prowess, was later adopted as the English coat of arms. The Three Lions remains the emblem of the England soccer and cricket teams.

INTO THE LION'S MOUTH

Unlike other mammals featured in this book that were hunted for food before they were domesticated, the lion was hunted to control its numbers and protect livestock, for sport, and for ritual or ceremonial reasons, as in the royal lion hunts of Assyria described above. The only lion hunt of this kind to survive into the modern period is a rite of passage performed by young warriors of the Maasai people of East Africa. Historically, a lone warrior would set out to kill a male lion to prove his manhood, but concerns over falling lion numbers mean that only group hunts are allowed today. The Maasai do not eat lion meat but keep the mane and tail. The mane is made into a headdress that is worn on ceremonial occasions, and the tail is kept as a symbol of a man's warrior status.

A far less edifying spectacle was the use of lions in the Roman arena—repeatedly mythologized by largely apocryphal stories of Christians being thrown to the lions—but probably more correctly of the lions themselves being the victims of dogs and armed men who baited and slaughtered them for the enjoyment of the crowd. Lion-baiting with dogs continued in Europe until it was banned in the early nineteenth century. Although no longer killed for a bloodthirsty public, lions were henceforth "tamed" as part of circus shows. Two men pioneered lion taming in the nineteenth century: the Frenchman Henri Martin and the American Isaac Van Amburgh, who performed for the young Queen Victoria (1819–1901) in 1838.

Louse
Pediculus humanus

Native range: Worldwide

Class: Insect

Size: 0.04–0.1 in
(1–3 mm) long

+ EDIBLE
+ *MEDICINAL*
+ COMMERCIAL
+ PRACTICAL

The louse is one of many parasitic insect species that has found its ecological niche—and its meal ticket—on humans. In the present day, lice are at best an annoyance and at worst an acute embarrassment, but in the past they have made their mark on human civilization in more sinister ways, as the vectors of deadly epidemic diseases.

NIT PICKING

The two closely related species of lice dealt with in this article are the body and head louse. The much more embarrassing pubic louse belongs to a more distantly related species, so we shall, so to speak, draw a veil over the offending insect. Historically, both head and body lice infestations were common among the general population. Head lice prompted the wearing of wigs among the European elites from the sixteenth century onward, establishing a visible distinction between the elite and the common people that would have far-reaching political consequences in the late eighteenth century. Lice infestations remain a common problem in the modern period, especially among young children of school-going age, who seem to be veritable head lice magnets. With modern hygiene, body lice are now much rarer, but in the past, they were responsible for spreading several epidemic diseases.

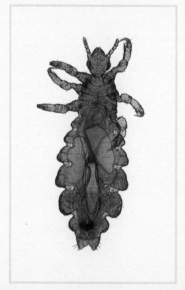

MINI-KILLER
Sometimes it is the smallest creatures that are the most dangerous to humans.

Head lice, as anyone searching for them in the hair of their children will know, are small wingless insects that are a drab gray color, though with a marked reddish tinge once they have gorged on their host's blood. After mating, the female will attach her eggs to the base of a hair with a tough gluelike secretion that will enclose both the hair and egg, leaving a small hatch for the nymph to breathe and emerge. Their favorite egg-laying areas are the nape of the neck and just behind the ears. The nymphs emerge after six to nine days, leaving the now empty egg case attached to the hair. Nymphs are miniature adults that

feed on their host's blood and undergo three molts before they become fully mature.

An adult female louse lives for about four weeks, during which time she can lay between 50 and 150 eggs. Body lice have an identical lifecycle to head lice but have evolved to live and lay their eggs on the fibers of human clothing. Lice cannot fly or hop, meaning infestations are transmitted through direct contact, of hair in the case of head lice, and of clothing or other textiles in close contact with the infected person's skin in the case of body lice. Treatment of body lice consists of washing clothes and bedding at high temperatures to kill the eggs and nits, regular bathing, and the application of insecticide. Treatment of head lice include antilice shampoos, shaving the head, and every mother's least favorite, the louse comb.

DISCOMFORT
Chronic lice infections made our ancestors shave their hair and replace it with wigs.

MISERIES OF WAR

As if war wasn't miserable enough, it is usually accompanied by that other human curse, epidemic disease. The unsanitary conditions of military camps, armies on the march, and sieges are the ideal breeding ground for lice. The two main diseases transmitted by body lice (as opposed to head lice, which is not a disease vector) are typhus and trench fever. Trench fever, as its name indicates, is particularly associated with World War One (1914–18). During the war, up to one-third of British troops and up to one-fifth of the German and Austrian troops are thought to have suffered from the disease. Trench fever is not fatal in most cases but it is extremely debilitating, causing fever, headaches, and pain in the legs and back. The condition is bacterial in origin and therefore has disappeared as a major health issue since the introduction of antibiotics.

REVOLUTIONARY ITCH

✦

Although some readers might find it farfetched, the louse played a bit part in the French Revolution of 1789. Head lice were an increasing problem in the cities of early-modern Europe. One solution favored by the rich was to shave off their own hair and replace it with a wig, which was easier to de-louse.

In the dying days of the French monarchy, wig fashions became ever more extravagant, with powdered wigs piled high on the heads of both men and women. The wig became a symbol of the hated aristocrats, who lost both their wigs and in many cases their heads in the ensuing revolution.

The head louse glues its eggs
to the hair, and the empty
egg cases remain even after
the larvae have hatched.

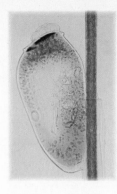

The second disease spread by body lice, epidemic typhus, is far more serious, and before the development of vaccination and antibiotics, killed millions of people worldwide. The symptoms of epidemic typhus include headache, a sustained high fever, muscle pain, delirium, and a distinctive red rash that begins on the chest and spreads to the rest of the body. The exact cause of ancient epidemics is difficult to identify with any certainty because of the rudimentary medical knowledge of the time. During the protracted Peloponnesian War (431 to 404 BCE), fought between the two ancient Greek city-states of Athens and Sparta, Athens was visited on three occasions by a plague, thought by many scholars to be epidemic typhus. The plague carried away many of its citizens, including its leading general and de-facto ruler, Pericles (495–429 BCE), today remembered as builder of the Parthenon. The death of Pericles signaled a change in Athens' fortunes, and ultimately sealed its defeat at the hands of Sparta.

Typhus epidemics have been a feature of wars until the mid-twentieth century. The first reliable description of the disease dates to the late-fifteenth-century siege of Granada during the Reconquista (reconquest) of Spain from the Moors. Soldiers in the besieging army suffered from fever, delirium, and a telltale rash over their bodies. The Spanish army lost 3,000 men in action but 17,000 to the epidemic. During the Thirty Years' War (1618–48), up to eight million German soldiers died of a combined epidemic of typhus and bubonic plague. During Napoleon's (1769–1821) retreat from Russia in 1812, far more French troops died from typhus than from enemy action. Probably the costliest typhus epidemics in history occurred during and immediately after World War One. Millions died on both the Eastern and Western fronts, and after the war an estimated 20–30 million cases of the disease led to three million deaths among the already weakened civilian population of Europe. The largest death toll from typhus during World War Two (1939–45) occurred in the Nazi death camps, where inmates were kept in overcrowded, unsanitary conditions, and were denied access to treatments.

TRENCH CUT
Soldiers in World War One shaved their hair in an effort to control lice infections.

Le Barbier dans la branchée

MISERIES OF PEACE

Although lice infections were particularly prevalent in wartime, lice-born typhus was also a serious problem in the overcrowded cities of Europe and North America right until the end of the nineteenth century. In England, typhus was known as "jail fever" because it affected prisoners kept in dirty communal cells. A prison outbreak in Oxford in 1577 led to a citywide epidemic that killed 300 citizens of the town, including the judges who had tried the infected prisoners. In eighteenth-century England, when a man could be hanged for stealing a loaf of bread (and another 240 capital offenses), more prisoners died from jail fever than the hangman's noose. Typhus epidemics were also prevalent during times of famine. During the nineteenth century, Ireland was afflicted with several devastating famines accompanied by typhus epidemics. The greatest death toll occurred during the Great Irish Potato Famine (1845–52), when an outbreak of typhus killed up to a third of the population of several Irish provinces.

> **An ape, a priest, and a louse, are three devils in one house.**
>
> *Traditional proverb*

As can be seen from the entries on the mosquito and the flea, some of the world's smallest creatures can be the deadliest to humans in terms of mortality count. Although insect-borne epidemics are now a thing of the past in the developed world, they continue to have a devastating impact on the development of human civilizations in the poorer areas of the world, where they remain an endemic threat.

Seal

Phoca spp.

Native range: Arctic regions of the northern hemisphere

Class: Mammal

Size: 4.5–5 ft (1.4–1.5 m) in length

✦ **EDIBLE**
✦ MEDICINAL
✦ **COMMERCIAL**
✦ **PRACTICAL**

WORLDBEATER
The seal can swim at 12 mph (19 km/h), a speed that would leave an Olympic swimmer standing in the water.

As a species found all over the northernmost latitudes, seals were a vital resource for humans as they migrated from Asia into the Americas. Commercial seal hunting, which began in the eighteenth century, made a significant contribution to the economic development of eastern Canada, but in the twentieth century it became one of the most controversial wild-animal harvests.

"TAKE FOUR TRIMMED SEAL FLIPPERS"

While I was at college, my Canadian roommate received a cookbook from his folks who thought that he might be missing the culinary traditions of his homeland. As we thumbed through the pages ever more disbelievingly, we paused at "Newfoundland Seal Flipper Pie," which read: "Take four trimmed seal flippers; brown in a skillet; add onions and gravy; cover and bake for 2–3 hours; make pastry and cover flippers and bake for a further 30 minutes; serves 6–8." Unfortunately we couldn't find seal flippers at the local all-night mart, or even the specialty butcher or fishmonger, so we settled for our usual takeout pizza.

Our reaction to seal flipper pie is probably pretty typical for a couple of city kids whose only experience of meat comes prepackaged in cellophane, or more likely on a bun with relish and pickles, and with fries on the side. But what was so disturbing about eating a seal flipper? Was it that baby-seal toy I was given as a kid, or was it because they look disturbingly like human beings in a wet suit? Seal meat and blubber, however, have been on the menu for thousands of years, and without them, it is unlikely that the peoples of the Arctic and many of the larger predator species, such as the polar bear and killer whale, would have survived.

Exactly how and when the Americas were settled is still hotly debated. One of the main theories is that people from Asia migrated in small boats following the coasts until they reached Beringia, an area now submerged but that was dry land during the last glaciation (110,000–10,000 BP), and finally the North American coast

in what is present-day Alaska. During their long journey east, these sea-borne hunter-gatherers would have survived by hunting the local wildlife, including the several species of seal native to the Arctic. In historical times, the seal has been an important commercial species for meat, oil, and fur, and latterly the subject of an intense controversy pitting animal rights activists against sealers and the Canadian government.

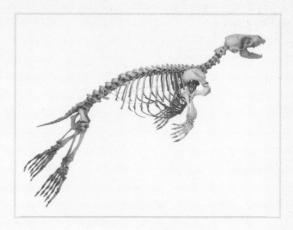

The common, or harbor, seal ranges in color from light or yellowish gray with dark spots, to black, gray, or brown with light rings or spots. Like the beaver, it has coat of coarse guard hairs over a finer downy coat that traps a layer of air to keep the seal warm in cold water. Its distinctive v-shaped nose can close when it is underwater. Superbly adapted for underwater life, the seal can dive to 300 ft (90 m), and stay under for 30 minutes. Descended from land-dwelling mammals that returned to the sea, the seal is a quadruped with webbed front and rear flippers, each with five toes. It uses its hind flippers to propel itself through the waters and can reach a top speed of 12 mph (19 km/h) that would make the likes of Michael Phelps at race pace look as if they were treading water. The seal's sense of sight and hearing are actually better underwater than they are on land, and it uses its long whiskers, or vibrissae, as a sense organ to detect movement of its prey.

QUADRUPED
The seal's terrestrial ancestry can be seen in the four limbs of its skeleton.

HOME AND DRY
Traditional Inuit summer tents were made of seal or caribou skin.

GO EAST, YOUNG MAN

The European settlers of the Americas came from the east and traveled westward to the New World, but the first Americans came the other way, eastward from Asia. During the last glacial period, when much of the northern hemisphere was covered in ice sheets, sea levels were much lower than today, and eastern Siberia and Alaska were linked by a land bridge known as Beringia (now the Bering Strait). There are two main theories about how humans first reached North America: on foot across Beringia, or in small boats following its coastline. It is possible that newcomers to the continent could have taken both routes at different periods.

COOL FASHION
Sealskin was much in demand for clothing in the cool, damp climates of Europe and North America.

Either way, the earliest Americans were nomadic hunter-gatherers dependent for their survival on the animal species they encountered. Our presumed coastal migrants would have lived off the plentiful resources of the sea, including the large population of seals, which would have provided meat and blubber for food and hides for clothing. Thus their lifestyles would have been similar to the Arctic peoples traditionally known as Eskimos, but more properly called the Inuit and the Yupik (for brevity, I shall henceforth refer to them as the Inuit). In historical terms, the Inuit are relative newcomers to the Arctic regions. They originated in western Alaska, and from around 1000 CE spread eastward across the Arctic, displacing the earlier inhabitants of the region. They reached eastern Greenland by the fourteenth century CE.

Although the lifestyles of the Inuit have undergone considerable change in the past 50 years, and are likely to change even more with the warming of Earth's climate, historically, they followed a hunter-gatherer lifestyle, preying on land and sea mammals, in particular the Arctic seal species, such as harbor, ringed, and harp seals. In addition to providing meat and blubber for the Inuit diet, the seal also provided its hide for the manufacture of footwear, clothing, and of the outer skin of the kayak, and oil for lamps. Prior to the introduction of modern housing, certain Inuit populations lived in sealskin tents during the short summer months. The traditional Inuit outer garment is the anorak, which is a hooded jacket made of seal or caribou skin, waterproofed with fish oil. The *amauti* is a modified anorak that accommodates mother and baby,

IMMIGRANTS
One settlement theory of the New World holds that seagoing nomads followed the coasts from Asia to Alaska.

ensuring that the child is kept warm and sheltered from the wind. The Inuit are excluded from the various national and international regulations controlling seal hunting, recognizing the animal's unique place in their culture.

HUNTING CONTROVERSY

Prior to the introduction of firearms, the Inuit hunted seals from their kayaks, netting them or spearing them with a harpoon while they were in the water, or by waiting on the ice for a seal to surface at a breathing hole. They only took what they needed for subsistence, and made use of every part of the animal. In the sixteenth century, European fishermen who came to exploit the rich fishing grounds off Newfoundland began to hunt seals for food and to earn extra income from the sale of pelts and oil during the winter off-season. By the middle of the eighteenth century, the growing demand for seal fur for clothing and seal blubber to be made into lamp and machine oil led to the development of a full-scale commercial seal fishery in Newfoundland. At first, sealing was conducted in small boats, but by the 1790s, fleets of large wooden sailing ships were sailing from St John's Newfoundland on the annual seal hunt.

WARM AND SNUG
The Inuit *amauti* is designed to allow the mother to carry her child and shelter him or her from the elements.

The heyday of the industry was roughly between 1810 and 1860, with many annual catches exceeding 500,000 harp seals. The record years were 1831 (680,000), 1832 (740,000), and 1844 (686,000). The largest hunt by number of vessels was in 1857, with 370 ships crewed by 13,600 men. During this period, the seal hunt was second only to cod fishing in economic importance to the region. In 1863, sail made way for steam, and by the turn of the twentieth century, wood made way for steel-hulled vessels. These heavier, steam-powered vessels could travel faster than sailing ships and force their passage through the ice to reach the seal herds. However, the human cost of the industry was high: between 1800 and 1865, 400 vessels and 1,000 men were lost while hunting seals.

Despite the introduction of motorized vessels, skin and blubber processing machinery, and the introduction in 1921 of spotter planes to locate seal herds, the industry had entered a phase of inexorable decline. Although there were a few catches in excess of half a million animals in 1871 and 1876, stocks had been seriously depleted by years of over-exploitation and catches began to fall. More importantly, the development of kerosene for lighting, and then the switch from oil lamps to electricity, meant a collapse in demand for seal oil. The industry continued to decline through the Great Depression, when world trade stagnated, and the two world wars, when sealing ships were requisitioned for war service. The seal fisheries began to recover after World War Two, thanks to a growing demand for seal fur and leather. An average of 310,000 seals were taken annually between 1949 and 1969, leading to a halving of the harp seal population by 1970.

Harp seals, once known as *Phoca groenlandica* (the Greenland seal), are now classed scientifically as *Pagophilus groenlandicus* (the "Greenlandic ice-lover"). The seal's common name comes from the harp-shaped markings on the adult male's back. Each spring between February and March females congregate on ice floes to give birth. The pups are born with a fluffy white fur coat that gives their name of "whitecoats." After two to three weeks this develops into a "lanugo" coat consisting of long guard hairs over a soft undercoat of curly, woolly fur. For the first month of its life, a harp-seal pup is extremely vulnerable, as it cannot swim and is entirely dependent on its mother for food. Literally stranded on the ice, seal pups are also at the mercy of their greatest predator—man.

The industry grew, bringing foreign investment and employing not only sealers but shipbuilders, carpenters, sailmasters and refiners who extracted the prized oil from seal blubber.

The Canadian Encyclopedia, *"Sealing"*

Firearms have long since replaced the traditional harpoon in seal hunting. However, when a seal is harvested for its pelt, a misplaced shot might ruin the animal's economic value so the seal is often killed by the more "traditional" method of crushing its skull with a heavy club known as a *hakapik*. The hakapik is fitted with a metal hammerhead and a hook at one end. The hammer is used to crush the skull without damaging the valuable pelt, and the hook is used to drag the carcass away for skinning. The annual seal hunt attracted worldwide attention when it was featured in a French-language TV documentary, *Les Phoques de la Banquise* (*Seals of the Icefloes*), which showed scenes of whitecoats being bludgeoned to death on the ice. In response, the Canadian government was

ICE DWELLER
The Greenland seal is one of several species found in the Arctic.

forced to establish regulations governing the use of the hakapik: "Every person who strikes a seal with a club or hakapik shall strike the seal on the forehead until its skull has been crushed [....] No person shall commence to skin or bleed a seal until the seal is dead, [when it] has a glassy-eyed, staring appearance and exhibits no blinking reflex when its eye is touched while it is in a relaxed condition."

Despite this clear humanitarian concern on the part of the authorities, worldwide opposition to the seal hunt continued to grow, leading to antihunt campaigns during the 1970s, celebrity involvement, direct action by animal rights groups, such as Greenpeace, and finally a ban by the European Commission on all products derived from whitecoats in 1983, followed by a Canadian ban on hunting whitecoats in 1987. Although the economic returns of the seal hunt have been seriously diminished because of a fall in demand for pelts, it has gained in importance for the region since the 1992 moratorium on cod fishing. The Canadian government is caught between the rock of international condemnation and the hard place of needing to sustain the economy of Newfoundland—a situation that means the annual seal hunt will continue for the foreseeable future.

HIT BY THE BLONDE BOMBSHELL

✦

Starting in the 1950s, campaigners recruited the help of celebrities to oppose the annual seal hunt. One of the most passionate is the former French movie actress and sex symbol, the "Blonde Bombshell" Brigitte Bardot (b. 1934), who became an animal rights campaigner after retiring from the world of stage and screen in 1973. In 2006 Bardot traveled to Ottawa to lobby the Canadian government to end the hunt. Other notable opponents include former Beatle, Sir Paul McCartney (b. 1942) and his former wife, Heather Mills (b. 1968).

Oyster

Pinctada radiata

Native range: Indian and Pacific oceans

Class: Mollusk

Size: 2–2.6 in (50–65 mm) long

+ **EDIBLE**
+ MEDICINAL
+ **COMMERCIAL**
+ PRACTICAL

I n popular usage, the word "oyster" confuses the several different edible species found on dining tables worldwide with the pearl-producing species. Although both types of oysters are covered in this entry, the headline species is the principal pearl oyster, *Pinctada radiata*.

NEOLITHIC SURF-AND-TURF

The author of *Gulliver's Travels*, Dean Jonathan Swift (1667–1745), probably expressed the opinion of many when he said, "He was a bold man that first ate an oyster." We shall never know who that bold man, or more likely woman (as it was the women who collected much of the food in hunter-gatherer societies) was, but waste heaps from prehistoric coastal sites all over the world contain the remains of the Neolithic equivalent of surf-and-turf, mixing the bones of land animals with oyster shells. The oyster, as well as being a good source of protein, vitamins, and minerals, was plentiful and not too difficult to harvest, and unlike a mammoth or an aurochs, did not run away or stampede toward you. Of course, what Swift was referring to was not the oyster's appearance, which is repulsive to many, but the unfortunate ability of a bad oyster to kill you stone dead, especially in the days before refrigeration.

SEA GEMS
Pinctada radiata is native to the Indian and Pacific oceans but was introduced accidentally into the Mediterranean through the Suez Canal.

Its succulent, translucent flesh, however, is not the only bounty provided by the species of oyster; the other is, of course, the pearl. Natural pearls are extremely rare, and have been highly prized since antiquity. Their exorbitant cost meant that they were worn only by the richest and most powerful men and women. Since the late nineteenth century, however, the discovery of how to cultivate pearls has made the gem quite commonplace—tarnishing the luster of the ever rarer and vastly more expensive natural article.

Although confuted into one animal by the common appellation "oyster," edible and pearl oysters are actually unrelated species. The most common edible oyster is the Pacific, or Japanese, oyster (*Crassostrea*

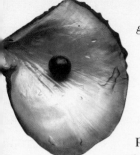

gigas), while the most sought-after seawater pearl oysters belong to the genus *Pinctada*.

Anyone who has eaten an oyster in Europe or the U.S. will be familiar with the light grayish-brown, ridged shell of the Pacific oyster. The inner shell is white without a trace of mother of pearl, or nacre. And no matter how many edible oysters you shuck and eat, you will never find an iridescent pearl. The pearl oyster has a much thinner, more compressed, squared-off, spiny shell, which varies in color from brown to red with a bright, pearly interior. Originally found in the Indian and Pacific oceans, from the Red Sea to Japan and Australia, the species was introduced accidentally into the eastern Mediterranean, probably by boats traveling through the Suez Canal. It is found attached to rocks, crevices, and algae at depths of 15–80 ft (5–25 m). Both edible and pearl oysters are now widely cultivated to make up for the decline in wild stocks because of overfishing and pollution.

BIG APPLE OYSTERS

Our early ancestors were nomadic hunter-gatherers who left little material evidence of their time on Earth, as they did not build towns or alter the landscape through forest clearance or cultivation. What they did leave for future generations to find were their waste heaps, known to archaeologists as "middens." The Whaleback Shell Midden created over 1,000 years by the Native American peoples near the Damariscotta River, Maine, was originally 30 ft (10 m) deep, more than 1,650 ft (500 m) long, and 1,320–1,650 ft (400–500 m) wide and consisted mainly of oyster shells. Similar shell middens exist all over the world from the UK to Australia, testifying to the oyster's natural abundance and its importance to the early human diet. Although oysters are not particularly rich in calories, they contain essential minerals and vitamins. Compared to other more mobile or aggressive prey species, the edible oyster represents an easy catch. Hence, when other food sources failed, oysters were always available to tide humans over.

BEYOND PRICE
Natural pearls are so rare that they were valued as highly as mineral gemstones.

During the nineteenth century, current residents of the Big Apple will be surprised to learn, New York Harbor was one of the largest producers of oysters in the Western world. Millions of oysters were fished annually by New York's oystermen and consumed by the working population of the city, who snacked on the tasty mollusk much as they do now on McDonald's, KFC, and Burger King. The increasing demand finally exhausted the oyster beds, and a combination of disease from introduced species, increasing levels of water pollution, and sedimentation had destroyed the city's oyster beds by the early twentieth century.

ONE IN A MILLION
Only a tiny percentage of pearl oysters will contain pearls. The main source of natural pearls today is the Persian Gulf.

Wild oysters are still harvested today. In shallow water, they are collected by hand or with simple instruments such as rakes. In deeper water, oystermen use long-handled rakes or tongs to reach the beds. For deeper waters still, fishermen use a scallop dredge towed by a boat. However, the increasing scarcity of wild oysters has turned them from a cheap source of protein for the working masses to a delicacy served by the half-dozen on silver platters in restaurants.

To make up for the fall in supply of wild oysters and to meet the ever-increasing demand, humans turned to aquaculture. Oyster cultivation was first attempted in antiquity. The man credited with its invention in the Western world is the Roman engineer and entrepreneur Sergius Orata (fl. c. late 1st c. BCE), who built a system of canals and locks to control the tides and established the oyster beds in the Lucrine Lake south of Rome. Oyster cultivation, along with many other things in Roman times, was lost to the world for centuries, to be rediscovered or reinvented much later. Modern oyster aquaculture dates back to the late nineteenth century. The two most commonly used methods are release and bagging. In the former, oysters are bred onshore and released once they are able to attach themselves to a natural or manmade bed where they are left to mature. They are then harvested like wild oysters. In the bagging method, the oysterman places the young oysters in bags or on racks suspended in the water, which simplifies the task of harvesting, as they can be raised to the surface when the oysters are fully grown.

After the depletion of native oyster stocks in the U.S., foreign oyster species were introduced in the late nineteenth century. Unfortunately, this did not always have the desired effect. The introduction of East Asian species to the once oyster-rich waters of Chesapeake Bay between Maryland and Virginia also brought diseases that led to the near extinction of the native *Crassostrea virginica*, whose numbers were already severely depleted by overfishing. The Pacific oyster was introduced to the West Coast in 1929, where it has become established in coastal waters from Canada to California. The species is now the mainstay of the North American oyster industry. At present, the Pacific oyster accounts for three-quarters of all cultivated oysters consumed in the world, with the largest producer being China.

WITH A SLICE
For many, the only way to eat an oyster is raw with a squeeze of lemon juice.

I will not eat oysters. I want my food dead. Not sick. Not wounded. Dead.
Woody Allen (b. 1935)

Oysters can be eaten raw, smoked, boiled, baked, fried, roasted, canned, pickled, steamed, or broiled, as well as used to make a variety of soups, chowders, and beverages. Every culture has its preferred ways of preparing oysters, but the simplest and, according to many, the only way to eat an oyster is to open the shell and swallow the live contents with a squeeze of lemon. The assumption that oysters are only safe to eat when there is a letter "r" in the month (September–April) is unfounded in biology but does ring true in so much as oysters were more likely to spoil in the warmer summer months of the northern hemisphere prior to the introduction of preservatives and refrigeration. To be 100 percent safe, an oyster must be eaten alive, which means that its shell must be tightly shut or close when tapped. Oysters are filter feeders and naturally concentrate any bacteria present in the water in which they live. Oysters from the U.S. Gulf Coast, for example, may contain the pathogen *Vibrio vulnificus*, which is more deadly in terms of

HEADLINER
Although most commonly worn on necklaces or as earrings, pearls have also been made into elaborate pieces of jewelry such as this ornate imperial Chinese headdress.

number of fatalities per case than either *Salmonella* or *E. coli*. With modern medical treatments, fatalities from bad oysters are now thankfully extremely rare occurrences, though food poisoning is still common in countries where oysters are eaten raw.

PEARLFISHERS

Pearls are made by a variety of sea- and freshwater mollusks, but the most sought-after are produced by the several varieties of oysters of the genus *Pinctada*, which produce

HANDPICKED
The collection of natural pearls is extremely labor-intensive, as oysters have to be opened and checked individually.

both white and black pearls of various sizes and shapes. The most valuable pearls are perfectly spherical, but they can also be pear- or teardrop-shaped, or irregularly shaped (called "baroque" pearls). The most common misconception is that pearls are created around pieces of grit or sand that have gotten lodged in the shell. The usual trigger for pearl formation is organic material, such as a parasite that has attached itself to the mantle when the oyster was open for feeding or breathing, or a piece of the oyster's own tissue that has become detached after an unsuccessful attack by a predator.

In both cases, the oyster creates a pearl sack to isolate the irritant, over which it deposits layer after layer of calcium carbonate, in the form of the mineral aragonite mixed with an organic compound called conchiolin. The combination of aragonite and conchiolin is called "nacre," or mother-of-pearl. The oyster secretes many layers of nacre,

MOTHER OF PEARL
Calcium carbonate, mother of pearl, also known as nacre, is a chemical naturally secreted by many species of shellfish.

leading to the formation of a pearl over a period of years. Due to the haphazardness of the process, natural pearls come in a variety of shapes and sizes, and perfectly round ones are extremely rare and therefore particularly expensive.

For thousands of years, the most highly prized seawater pearls were harvested by divers in the Indian Ocean, Persian Gulf, Red Sea, and the South China Sea. After the conquest of Latin America, the Spanish discovered a rich source of pearls around the islands of Cubagua and Margarita, off the coast of Venezuela. Pearl fishing is extremely labor- and time-consuming work, as the oysters have to be individually opened and checked, and only a tiny percentage yield a usable pearl. Natural pearls are the organic equivalent of natural gemstones, such as diamonds, sapphires, and rubies, that are coveted by the wealthy and powerful and are traded over vast distances, from East Asia to Europe.

In the late nineteenth century, the production of pearls was revolutionized by the work of an obscure British marine biologist called William Saville-Kent (1845–1908). After an unexciting career working at the British Museum and various English aquariums, Saville-Kent moved to Australia, where he worked as Commissioner of Fisheries for Queensland and later for Western Australia. Clearly not a party animal, he spent his leisure hours experimenting with different methods to stimulate the production of pearls in oysters. He himself did not profit from his discovery. It was the Japanese who patented his work and went on to dominate the cultured pearl industry for much of the twentieth century.

To create a cultured pearl, a piece of mantle from a donor is introduced into the oyster, around which it will create a pearl sack. The tissue graft can be accompanied by the introduction of a spherical bead, to produce a round pearl, or beadless, if a different shape is required. Natural and cultured pearls can only be differentiated with the help of X-rays that reveal the presence of a bead, but a beadless pearl may be mistaken for a natural one, and may need closer examination in order to determine its exact origin. Such is the power of human ingenuity that we have taken a marvel of the natural world and made it commonplace. And although it is undoubt-edly a good thing, and properly democratic that pearls should no longer be the preserve of the super-rich and within the reach of the common man and woman, I can't help feeling that by doing so, we have lost a little more of the magic and reverence that we used to feel for the wonders of nature.

IN THE ROUND
The most sought-after natural pearls are spherical. These come in many different hues, including white, black, yellow, and pink.

Bat

Pipistrellus pipistrellus

Native range: Europe, North Africa, and Asia

Class: Mammal

Size: 7.5–10 in (19–25 cm) wingspan

+ EDIBLE
+ MEDICINAL
+ COMMERCIAL
+ **PRACTICAL**

ATYPICAL
The bat is unique among mammals in that, during periods of inactivity, it will roost while hanging upside down by its feet.

As the only mammal capable of true flight and equipped with its own in-built sonar, the bat is a fascinating animal in its own right. However, it has a whole other existence in the realms of the human imagination as a creature of unmitigated evil, associated with the ultimate creature of the night, the vampire.

SEEING WITH YOUR EARS

There are two distinct bats: the animal bat that, for the most part, lives a blameless nocturnal existence, subsisting on a diet of insects or fruit (and, OK, maybe a little bit of blood from time to time); and the bat of the human imagination that lives in the outer darkness. If the former has some truly remarkable natural adaptations to its ecological niche, the latter has been gifted with just as extraordinary an array of supernatural associations. According to horror-film lore, the vampire, the

unholy dead who stalks the living to feed on their blood, can change him- or herself into a bat. But the bat does not have a universally bad press. In Chinese iconography the bat is a symbol of long life, and in the world of comic books, the man in the bat suit, although he has undergone several sinister transformations lately, still fights for truth, justice, and mom's apple pie.

Although several mammals have learned how to glide, the bat is the only mammal that has mastered true flight. Unlike birds, which flap their entire forelimbs, or wings, to create the necessary lift to enable them to fly, bats flap their extended digits. If we were to picture this in human terms, you'd have to imagine that you had fingers several feet long covered by a thin membrane made of skin. The finger bones of bats are much flatter and lighter and more flexible than our own, otherwise they would snap under the strain of flight, and the skin of the membrane is more elastic. Lacking the bird wing's covering of feathers, the bat's wing is lighter, giving the bat better maneuverability, but also making the wing more delicate and prone to tearing. Luckily the membrane can regrow and heal itself quickly. Finally, the bat's wing, like our own fingers, is covered with touch-sensitive organs that give it constant feedback about airflow that enable it to fly more efficiently and instantly locate prey that fly into its wings.

The dry whisper of unseen wings, Bats not angels, in the high roof.
"In a Country Church" by R. S. Thomas (1913–2000)

Although we say "blind as a bat," bats are not actually blind, and they will use their vision to orient themselves. But vision alone would serve them poorly at night and in the darkness of the caves they retire to during the day. The perceptual system that allows them to navigate and locate prey in darkness is known as echolocation, or "biosonar." In order to create a "sound map" of its surroundings, the bat emits an ultrasonic pulse from its mouth that it compares to the returning echoes it picks up with its highly sensitive ears. Bats use two distinct echolocation methods: in the first they emit a short burst of ultrasound and wait for the echo to return before emitting another burst; in the second they emit a continuous ultrasound pulse and analyze the changes in frequency caused by their own movement. Equipped with this extraordinary sensory apparatus, the bat literally "sees" the world with its ears. As with other species in this book, there are hundreds of species of bat, differentiated by size, diet, and perceptual system. The headline species chosen for this entry is one of the most common bat species in the Old World: the small insectivorous common pipistrelle.

HAND GLIDER
Unlike birds that flap their whole limbs, the bat uses its outstretched fingers to support its wings.

MONSTER
The cinematic vampire has evolved from the grotesque Nosferatu to the well-healed aristocratic Vampire Lestat.

GOING BATS

Because of its nocturnal habits and rather sinister appearance, the bat has always been associated with the dark side, but there was no direct link between the many vampire legends of Eastern and Central Europe and the bat until the discovery of blood-sucking species in the sixteenth century. There are three species of vampire bat, all native to Latin America. In addition to the nocturnal adaptations common to all bat species, the vampire bat has specialized heat receptors in its nose that allow it to locate the areas where the blood flows closest to the skin. In addition to sensitive hearing that will pick up its victim's breathing, the vampire may also be able to see in the infrared spectrum.

Vampires will prey on humans, but they tend to prefer animal blood. When feeding, the vampire will use its canine teeth to shave any hair from the skin, and then use its two sharp upper incisors to make a small incision. The bat's saliva contains an anticoagulant that will prevent the wound from closing and a vasodilator that will increase blood flow to the area. An adult bat will take about 1 fl. oz (20 g) of blood in a single meal. Being bitten by a vampire bat will not, of course, turn you into a vampire or a bat, and the tiny amount taken is unlikely to kill you through loss of blood. However, as a small number of bats carry rabies, if their bite is left untreated, it carries the risk of serious illness and death.

The association between the bat and the vampire was not immediate. The human vampire makes his first appearance in a work of English fiction, *The Vampyre* (1819), written by John Polidori (1795–1821). The story of the composition of the novella is in itself quite unusual and merits retelling. Polidori, a doctor by training, was engaged by the Romantic poet Lord Byron (1788–1824) as his personal physician and accompanied him on a tour of Europe. In the unseasonably cold and wet summer of 1816, Byron and Polidori were staying at a villa on Lake Geneva, Switzerland, along with

ROMANTIC
John Polidori created the image of the well-heeled aristocratic *vampyre*.

several other English literary luminaries, including the poet Percy Bysshe Shelley (1792–1822) and his fiancée Mary Wollstonecraft Godwin (1797–1851). One evening after the group had listened to a reading of horror stories, Byron suggested that they each write their own ghoulish tale. In response, Mary Shelley wrote *Frankenstein* (1818), and Polidori began *The Vampyre*, whose antihero, the urbane British aristocrat Lord Ruthven, was to become the model for the many later well-heeled fictional vampires.

Although vampires, both male and female, were popular characters in the Gothic literature of the nineteenth century, the one portrayal that defined the genre and the character was the novel *Dracula*, written in 1897 by Bram Stoker (1847–1912). Stoker worked as the business manager for the leading actor of the Victorian period, Henry Irving (1838–1905). Although he toured the world with Irving, Stoker never visited Count Dracula's supposed Transylvanian lair. An avid reader of horror fiction, Stoker researched the vampire legends of Central Europe before writing his own novel as a series of diary entries and letters by the major protagonists, along with fictional ship's logs and newspaper articles.

In Stoker's novel, a young English solicitor called Jonathan Harker travels to Romania to arrange the sale of several London properties to a mysterious nobleman, Count Dracula. The hapless Harker soon discovers that he is the prisoner rather than the guest of his unusual host. Dracula, as we all know now, turns out to be a vampire, who can change at will into a wolf or bat. The novel went on to inspire hundreds of films, beginning with the 1931 *Dracula*, starring the Hungarian actor Bela Lugosi (1882–1956) as the bloodsucking count. In the movie, Dracula morphs into a bat on several occasions to prey on his victims, firmly establishing a convention that endures in today's many cinematic and literary portrayals of vampires.

SPILLS AND CHILLS
The vampire has been a popular character in pulp fiction since its creation in the nineteenth century.

BIRTH OF THE DARK KNIGHT

✦

While the bat's association with vampirism places it firmly on the side of evil, it has been rehabilitated by its selection as the secret identity of the crime-fighting hero "Batman." The Caped Crusader made his first appearance in "The Case of the Chemical Syndicate," in issue 27 of Detective Comics, published in May 1939. At the age of eight, the future Batman, Bruce Wayne, sees his parents gunned down by a small-time criminal. He swears to avenge their deaths and rid his hometown Gotham City (aka New York) of evil, and trains to become a vigilante. However, he realizes that his skills alone will not be enough. When a bat suddenly flies through the window, Wayne gets the inspiration for the persona that will strike fear in the superstitious and cowardly criminal heart.

Reindeer

Rangifer tarandus

Native range: Arctic regions of America, Europe, and Asia

Class: Mammal

Size: 33–59 in (85–150 cm) tall at the shoulder

+ *EDIBLE*
+ MEDICINAL
+ *COMMERCIAL*
+ *PRACTICAL*

For thousands of years, the reindeer has been equivalent to the cow and horse of the people of the Arctic. Only partially domesticated, the reindeer provides a model of how our ancestors learned to exploit the large herbivores that are now our principal farm animals.

CATTLE OF THE ARCTIC

For many people, the mention of reindeer will conjure up images of Yuletide mall displays, Chris Cringle B-movies, and cutesy cartoon Rudolphs with flashing neon noses. The flesh-and-blood animal, however, is the species that has enabled humans to survive in the Arctic by providing food, clothing, and transportation. Unlike the cow or horse, the reindeer has never been fully domesticated. Historically, it was not bred in captivity, and its appearance and behavior has altered little despite its thousands of years of contact with humans. As such it may exemplify the proto-domestication phase that our ancestors went through with wild cattle, sheep, goats, and horses after hunting and before they embarked on full-scale domestication and selective breeding.

Like many animals that live in the northern latitudes, the reindeer shows a number of adaptations to the cold. Its coat has two distinct layers: a longer surcoat of long guard hairs, and a denser woolly undercoat. The reindeer's large nostrils allow incoming air to be warmed before it is taken into the lungs, helping to maintain the animal's internal temperature. Its hooves change with the seasons: in the summer, when the ground is wet and spongy, the footpads soften to give the animal more traction; in winter, the footpads tighten and shrink, giving it better purchase on the ice and making it easier to dig for food in the snow with the exposed rims of its hooves. Reindeer are ruminants, with a four-chambered stomach, but they only have access to grasses in the summer months; in the winter, they survive mainly on lichens and moss they find buried under the snow. A migratory species, the reindeer will assemble in huge herds of up to half a million animals and travel thousands of miles in search of fresh pastures.

ARCTIC NOMADS
The Sami people of the
European Arctic developed a
unique relationship with the
reindeer.

PEOPLE OF THE REINDEER

The European people most closely associated with the reindeer are the Sami, who live in the northern regions of Sweden, Norway, Finland, and in the Russian Kola Peninsula. The Sami have lived in the region for at least 5,000 years, and maybe for as long as 10,000. In addition to herding reindeer, the Sami are also fishermen. Although the reindeer was never fully domesticated, they were tamed for milking, as well as for use as mounts, draft animals for carts and sleighs, and beasts of burden. The Sami herders continue to travel with the reindeer herds during their annual migration, tending them and protecting them from predators. There are striking similarities between the Sami's relationship with the reindeer and that between the Plains Native Americans and the buffalo: the reindeer provided antlers for tools, weapons, and ceremonial purposes; hides for clothing, footwear, and tents; and meat, which remains a popular alternative to beef and pork in the Scandinavian countries and Alaska. In the North American context, the native reindeer species, the caribou, played a vital role in the lives of the Inuit people.

Why does Scrooge love Rudolph the Red-Nosed Reindeer? Because every buck is dear to him.

American joke

When an animal is economically important to a culture, it will feature in its myths and religious rituals. Before their conversion to Christianity, the Sami were polytheists who worshipped a large pantheon of gods and goddesses. Each clan and family had its own protective deity, known as a *seita*. The seita was represented by a stone, a pile of stones, a tree-stump, or a post displayed in a prominent place in the community. The seita protected the clan and its reindeer, and they also gave instructions on how to catch wild reindeer; in exchange, parts of the reindeer, or reindeer calves were given as offerings. The principal deity of the Sami was Beivve, the goddess of the sun and mother of mankind. At the winter solstice on December 21, a white reindeer would be sacrificed to her to ensure that the winter would end.

One of the foundational myths of the Sami, which explains how evil came into the world, is the story of two brothers, Attjis and Njavvis. Attjis married the daughter of the evil Moon god Mano. The marriage signaled the end of a golden age for the first humans, and the sun goddess Beivve withdrew and hid in the mountains. Attjis' new wife immediately began to sour the relationship between the two brothers. Attjis deprived his brother of his land and herds and even usurped his place in the family tent, so that Njavvis and his wife were reduced to being Attjis' servants. However, the mild-mannered Njavvis never complained when Attjis took the best of their communal hunts for himself. When his wife complained to him about Attjis' behavior, Njavvis would reply, "A brother cannot hate his brother."

ROCK ART
Humanity's ancient relationship with the reindeer is evidenced by these prehistoric rock carvings from Norway.

One day when Njavvis went hunting reindeer alone, he caught a single animal. Because he was hungry and his wife was pregnant, he started to skin and butcher the reindeer alone, instead of waiting for his brother. At that moment, Attjis found him and complained bitterly that Njavvis planned to cheat him of his share of the prize. Njavvis countered that Attjis could have the whole animal if he let him take one cut of meat for his hungry wife. It was now Njavvis' turn to reproach his brother for his behavior. "First you took my lands, then my home, though our father taught us that a brother should not hate his brother," he said, "why have these things come to pass?"

Instead of being ashamed by Njavvis' reproach, Attjis was filled with bitterness and anger. Driven mad by the gods of the moon and of the underworld, he picked up the dead reindeer's antler and struck Njavvis, killing him instantly. As Njavvis' blood soaked into the earth, evil was released into the world. In despair, Beivve hid her face, and her pale reflection, the Moon, took her place. However, at that moment, the heart of the reindeer that was buried in the earth at the beginning of time was so moved by the murder that its trembling shook the entire world. Attjis was blown off the earth and landed on the moon. When the moon shines brightly, if you look closely, you will see Attjis still holding the reindeer antler.

After centuries during which the Sami were forcibly assimilated by the different nation-states that their lands and the migration routes of their herds straddle, only a few thousand still follow the ancient nomadic ways of their forebears.

Dodo
Raphus cucullatus

Native range: Mauritius

Class: Bird

Size: 3 ft (1 m) tall

◆ *EDIBLE*

◆ MEDICINAL

◆ COMMERCIAL

◆ PRACTICAL

EXTINCT
The dodo exemplifies the destructive impact humans can have on a closed ecosystem.

There are few species more iconically representative of their sad fate than the dodo. We still say, "dead as a dodo," even though the species was wiped out over three centuries ago. The dodo was not the first species to have been driven to extinction by humans, but its disappearance in less than 100 years after its first sighting by Europeans dramatizes the negative impact humanity has had on the environment.

ISLAND GIANTS

Extinction is part of the natural order of things. Creatures evolve to fit a specific ecological niche, but if that niche disappears because of climate change or the animal is squeezed out because of pressure from a competitor species, then it becomes extinct. There have been untold millions of extinctions since life began on earth, and they continue to happen in the present day, but we tend to register only the headliners, such as the extinction of the dinosaurs, the woolly mammoth, and, of course, the subject of this entry, the dodo.

"Dodo"—even the name seems to mark it out for its tragic fate. The exact derivation of the name, however, is uncertain. The Portuguese visited the island of Mauritius in 1507, but they made no mention of the bird. Nevertheless, some historians suggest that dodo is derived from the Portuguese word *doido*, meaning "fool" or "madman." The next Europeans to reach the island were the Dutch in the early seventeenth century, and a visiting ship's captain's journal described a bird called the *dodaerse*. The name has been interpreted in two ways: the first associates it with the Dutch word *dodoor*, meaning "sluggard" or "dolt," and the second, with *dodaars*, meaning "knot-arse," referring to the distinctive tuft of feathers on the bird's rear end.

The Dodo never had a chance. He seems to have been invented for the sole purpose of becoming extinct and that was all he was good for.

American humorist Will Cuppy (1884–1949)

An alternative Dutch name for the dodo was the *walghvogel*, the loathsome bird, which is believed to be a reference to the unpalatable taste of its flesh.

DEAD END
The ancestors of the dodo flew to Mauritius, but with no natural predators, the bird grew larger and lost the power of flight.

The dodo was a flightless member of the pigeon family that evolved on the island of Mauritius in the middle of the Indian Ocean. Although there are no complete specimens of the dodo, in several artists' representations they have grayish-brown plumage, a large hooked bill, stubby wings, thick yellow legs, and a distinctive tuft of tail feathers. The dodo was a fruit eater, and nested on the ground. Although it was incapable of flight, its ancestors must have arrived on the island by flying. When the proto-dodos first flew to Mauritius, they found an environment where food was plentiful and the predators that had driven their ancestors to the safety of the skies and trees were absent. Evolution then worked in reverse, transforming birds into a ground-dwelling species that became so large that they were incapable of flight.

Mauritius, although known to Indian, Arab, and East African sailors since the tenth century, was not settled until the seventeenth, when the Dutch established the first permanent settlements on the island. Humans were responsible for the extinction of the dodo less than a century after their arrival, but not because they hunted them for food. Several period sources describe the meat of the dodo as tough and unpalatable. However, where humans go, so do any number of their companion species, such as pigs, dogs, cats, and monkeys, as well as that most accomplished animal freeloader, the rat. Unaware of the serious impact that the introduced species might have on the island's fragile ecosystem, the Dutch made no effort to control the new immigrants, who found a ready supply of food in the vulnerable ground nests of the dodo. At the same time, forest clearances for agriculture reduced the dodo's habitat. As soon as the first human landed on its island home, the trusting dodo was doomed, and within 80 years, it was extinct.

DO-DO-DODGSON

✦

Two centuries after the extinction of the dodo, the bird made an appearance in Lewis Carroll's (1832–98) *Alice's Adventures in Wonderland* (1865), as one of the many strange creatures that Alice meets on her journey through the fantastical realm of Wonderland. It has been suggested that the author caricatured himself as the dodo in the book, because a lifelong stammer left him unable to pronounce his own name.

Rat

Rattus spp.

Native range: Asia

Class: Mammal

Size: Up to 10 in (25 cm) in length

+ **EDIBLE**
+ **MEDICINAL**
+ COMMERCIAL
+ **PRACTICAL**

If we had to decide which among the 50 animals listed in this book is most closely associated with humans in the modern world, it would probably have to be the rat. The association, in most cases, is involuntary, because the rat has long been an unwelcome guest living off humanity's agricultural production and waste, giving only disease in return. In certain cultures, however, the rat is an important food item, and in the twentieth century it has a role in scientific research as a model organism in psychological, medical, and genetic research.

"YOU DIRTY RAT!"

Even if Hollywood actor James Cagney (1899–1986) never delivered the immortal line "You dirty rat!" it does sum up most of humanity's estimation of the species as a loathsome pest. Rats have made themselves at home in our homes and cities, where they have found shelter from the elements and predators, and a plentiful supply of food in our kitchens, trash cans, and dumpsters. The rat is the most successful mammalian species after humans, and it has been calculated that in our great metropolises, you are never more than 9 ft (3 m) away from a rat. Estimates of the UK rat population put it at around 80 million, outnumbering humans by about 1.3 to 1. And the rat population of New York might be as high as 100 million. But the rat also has its defenders and allies. In many parts of Asia, the rat is an important additional source of protein; and it is widely used in scientific research as a model organism standing in for humans.

When we talk about rats, we are actually referring to two separate but related species of rodents, the black rat (*Rattus rattus*) and the brown

Rats!
They fought the dogs and killed the cats,
And bit the babies in the cradles,
And ate the cheeses out of the vats,
And licked the soup from the cooks' own ladles,
Split open the kegs of salted sprats,
Made nests inside men's Sunday hats,
And even spoiled the women's chats,
By drowning their speaking
With shrieking and squeaking.

"The Pied Piper" by Robert Browning (1812–89)

rat (*Rattus norvegicus*). Both species originated in Asia, but the black rat reached Europe first, becoming widespread in northern Europe at the time of the Roman Empire (1st c. CE onward). The brown rat arrived much later, in the early modern period. Despite its Latin name, *norvegicus* (Norwegian), it has no early relationship with Scandinavia. Once it had reached England—possibly as early as the sixteenth century in ships returning from the Near East—it quickly displaced the black rat population. The brown rat was established in continental Europe by the eighteenth century and made the transatlantic crossing to the New World around the 1750s.

The brown rat is the larger, more powerfully built, and more aggressive of the two species. It has a brown or dark gray coat of coarse fur, with a lighter belly. The tail is roughly the same length as the body, with both averaging around 10 in (25 cm). The smaller black rat varies in color from black to light brown, with a lighter belly, and a longer tail in relation to its body. While both species are social animals, they display several behavioral differences. The black rat is a climbing species that is at home in trees and roof spaces, while the brown rat lives in underground burrows and is happiest in a semiaquatic environment such as a river bank or

HELL ON EARTH
The rat was one of the animal vectors that spread the bubonic plague in Europe during the Middle Ages.

sewer system. Brown rats display a complex social hierarchy that has made them a species adopted by certain schools of comparative psychology as models for human behavior.

Although rats do spread infectious diseases in human populations, as we shall see in the article on the flea, its role in the medieval Black Death has been greatly exaggerated. The black rat was only one of the carriers of the flea that is the primary vector for bubonic plague. The rat, it seems, is a much-maligned creature. Intelligent and sociable, it has been chosen by some as a pet, though it will never rival the cat and dog in popularity.

YO! RAT

In Terry Pratchett's *Discworld* series of fantasy comic novels, the rat is the favorite dish of the dwarf population of the city of Ankh-Morpork. In one book, an enterprising businessman launches a chain of fast-food restaurants called "Yo! Rat"—an ironic reference to the British "Yo! Sushi" restaurant chain. Although Westerners would only eat rat in the direst of circumstances—say, when they'd run out of cats and dogs—it remains a prized food item in several cultures. Although not necessarily the same species that are found in Europe, the rat is part of the culinary traditions of India, China, Southeast Asia, Australia, and Polynesia. Until it was replaced by rabbit, rat was also an ingredient of the signature Spanish rice dish, Paella Valenciana.

The rat was the first animal domesticated specifically for scientific purposes in the early nineteenth century. The now familiar white lab rat was not originally bred for science but for the "sport" of rat baiting, in which the spectators bet on how long it would take a terrier to kill a number of wild rats held captive in a pit. During the twentieth century, the rat was a favorite subject of behavioral scientists in experiments to try to discover whether intelligence, memory, and other traits were learned or inherited. In a famous series of experiments conducted in the early 1940s, Robert Tryon (1901–67) tried to prove that intelligence was inherited rather than acquired. The experiment consisted of a maze into which he introduced laboratory rats. Depending on how quickly

NEAR NEIGHBOR
In any major city of the world, we are never more than a few feet away from rats, which have made their homes in our buildings, parks, and sewers.

the rats ran the maze, they were labeled as "bright" or "dull" rats. Tryon then selectively bred bright males with bright females and dull males with dull females over several generations, before swapping the offspring of the bright parents with those of the dull parents to see if this would affect their ability to negotiate the maze.

He reported that the bright rats performed better than their dull brethren; however, as many sociologists and psychologists have since pointed out, this did not actually prove that intelligence and learning ability were inherited. What Tryon might have actually selectively bred was better peripheral vision, for example, which would have accounted for the bright rats' better performance in the maze without making them any more intelligent than the dull rats. In any case, the great weakness of animal experiments is that though they may demonstrate psychological abilities or traits in test animals, there is no compelling reason to believe that the findings are applicable to other animal species or humans.

In the twenty-first century, rats continue to play an important role in medicine, in the fields of drug testing and genetic research. Rats and humans share about 99 percent of their genome, so the rat is an excellent model organism to study human gene functions. Several strains of lab rat have been created to study specific human diseases. The Zucker rat serves as a genetic model for obesity and high blood pressure. Zucker rats are either very lean or very obese, reaching twice the weight of normal animals. The Biobreeding Diabetes Prone rat is bred to develop Type-1 diabetes, and is used to understand the development of the disease and test possible treatments. The latest lab rat to be created is the "knockout rat" because it is genetically engineered so that a single gene can be turned off, thus mimicking human genetic diseases.

CHARISMATIC RAT

✦

The rat is the first animal sign of the twelve-year Chinese zodiac. People born in the year of the rat are said to be forthright, tenacious, intense, meticulous, charismatic, sensitive, intellectual, industrious, charming, eloquent, sociable, artistic, and shrewd. The dark side of the rat character is expressed in people who are manipulative, vindictive, self-destructive, envious, mendacious, venal, obstinate, critical, over-ambitious, ruthless, intolerant, and scheming.

Scarab Beetle

Scarabaeus sacer

Native range: Mediterranean basin

Class: Insect

Size: 0.9–1.2 in (2.5–3 cm)

✦ Edible

✦ Medicinal

✦ Commercial

✦ *Practical*

Many animals have been used as symbols of deities, often because they are associated with great power, strength, or beauty. The ancient Egyptians' reverence of the scarab beetle, however, was based on its apparent ability to be born from dead matter, and the resemblance of the ball of dung that it rolls to the movement of the Sun across the sky.

NATURE'S "NIGHT SOIL" DISPOSAL OPERATIVE

The Egyptians worshipped what is to our eyes one of the ancient world's strangest pantheons of gods and goddesses, many of which had hybrid human–animal forms. Their choices were not random, however, as they sought in the shapes, behavior, and lifecycles of the animals around them symbolic representations of the divine world. Thus they associated their greatest divinity, the sun god Ra, with a rather humble insect, the scarab, or dung beetle. In addition to its mythological and ritual importance to the ancient Egyptians, the scarab beetle is valued today because it provides a vital service to humanity as nature's night-soil disposal operative, removing animal excrement that would otherwise accumulate and decompose in fields and pastures and become the breeding ground for pests and disease organisms.

The scarab is part of a large family of beetles whose chosen ecological niche is the excrement of mammalian species, which they eat and use in their reproductive cycle. While some dung beetles have brightly colored bodies in striking metallic hues of blue and green, the scarab has a dull, compact black body. Its antennae form a crown with six short spikelike projections, which have sensitive olfactory receptors that enable it to locate animal dung. The front pair of its six legs is specially shortened and adapted to collect and roll dung into a ball. Found all around the Mediterranean basin, the scarab beetle's preferred habitats are sand dunes and coastal marshlands.

In addition to eating dung, the scarab uses a ball of rolled excrement as an incubation chamber for its eggs. In preparation for mating, the male will roll a dung ball, either assisted by the female, or alone with the female tagging along behind. When the pair finds a suitably soft patch of soil, they bury the ball, and retire underground to mate. The female then lays her fertilized eggs inside the ball, which will serve as a nursery and larder for the hatching larvae. The scarab larvae go through a similar metamorphosis as other insects, from egg to larva, and pupa to adult, and the process takes place entirely within the relative safety of the dung ball.

Like earthworms that recycle organic material as they eat and burrow through the ground, scarab beetles improve the fertility of the soil by burying and eating animal droppings. A second benefit from their activities is a reduction in disease organisms and insect pests that would otherwise breed in the exposed excrement. Australia and New Zealand, which do not have native dung beetles, have conducted successful controlled introductions of several beetle species that have resulted in a marked improvement in soil quality and decrease in insect pest numbers, as well as a reduction in greenhouse gas emissions.

RECYCLER
By burying animal excrement, the dung beetle plays a crucial role in maintaining soil fertility.

TRANSFORMERS

The scarab beetle's lifecycle has attracted the attention of several ancient cultures, which saw in its birth from a ball of inanimate matter a symbol of death and resurrection. The ancient Egyptians had the most complex religious relationship with the scarab, which intertwined their beliefs about the daily death and rebirth of the sun, the process of mummifica-

REBIRTH
To the ancient Egyptians, the scarab was a symbol of rebirth and also a form of the sun god Ra.

TRANSFORMER
In ancient Egyptian writing,
the scarab hieroglyph can be
translated into English as the
verb "to transform."

tion and rebirth in the afterlife, and the divine nature of the pharaohs as incarnations of the sun god Ra. Representations of scarabs were found everywhere in ancient Egypt, as temple statues, grave goods associated with mummies, personal name seals, amulets, gifts, commemorative objects, and personal ornaments. The scarab was also used as a hieroglyphic sign within the Egyptian writing system, and featured in the names of many pharaohs.

The Egyptians believed that there was no female scarab and that the male reproduced asexually by injecting its seed into its dung ball. This led them to associate the scarab with the god Khepri, "he who has come into being," who created himself out of the void, and was one of the incarnations of the sun god Ra. In tomb frescos and temple bas-reliefs, Khepri is represented as a scarab or as a man with a scarab instead of a head. In the shape of the giant sky scarab, Khepri rolled the Sun on its daily course across the sky, exactly like a beetle rolling its dung ball. At dusk, the Sun was swallowed by the sky goddess Nut, and reemerged from her womb at dawn in the form of the newborn Khepri. There are no temples dedicated to Khepri in Egypt, but large scarab statues can be seen in many temples. Visitors to the great temple complex of Karnak troop around a statue of Khepri in the mistaken belief, fostered by their guides, that it will bring them good luck.

The scarab's relationship with the death and rebirth of the sun god gave it an important role in Egypt's complex funerary customs. The body of the pharaoh, who was an incarnation of Ra, was preserved by mummification, during which the internal organs were removed and stored separately from the body in containers known as canopic jars, and the flesh, pickled in a soup of natron and spices, was wrapped in bandages. Scarab-shaped amulets were placed within the mummy wrappings and were also placed in the tomb as grave goods.

A "heart scarab" was placed on the chest of the mummy to replace the absent real heart. According to Egyptian beliefs, the heart was the seat of the human

PHARAOH FAVORS

+

The pharaoh Amenhotep III (c. 1388–c. 1351 BCE) issued hundreds of carved stone scarabs to commemorate important events during his reign. Measuring 1.6–4.3 in (4.5–11 cm) long, the scarabs were painted either green or blue and pierced so that they could be worn as pendants. Like commemorative coins and medals today, they would have been given to local and foreign dignitaries. The events celebrated include two of the pharaoh's marriages (one to his chief queen and one to a foreign princess), two ritual hunts, and the building of a large artificial lake.

soul. After death, the jackal-headed god Anubis weighed the heart of the deceased against the Feather of Truth to see if the person merited eternal life, or should be condemned to eternal death and have their heart devoured by the monster Ammit. The heart scarab was inscribed with magical formulae taken from *The Book of the Dead*, to ensure that the deceased's soul would survive Anubis' judgment. The unplundered tomb of Tutankhamun (1341–23 BCE) contained a richly ornamented heart scarab carved from a single piece of desert glass.

The scarab was one of the hieroglyphic signs used by the ancient Egyptians to write down their spoken language. A hieroglyph could stand for a whole word or name, or it could have a purely phonetic value depending on its context. The scarab hieroglyph is transliterated into the Roman alphabet as (kh)pr, and translates as the verbs "to become," "to come into being," and "to transform." Because of its sacred associations with Ra, the scarab hieroglyph appears in the names of many pharaohs, such as Men-(Kh)eper-Re, which was the given name of Thutmose III (d. 1425 BCE), which can be rendered into English as "The Transforming Strength of Ra."

ROLLERBALL
The scarab has specially modified forelegs designed to hold and roll animal dung into balls.

SCARABAEUS, n. The sacred beetle of the ancient Egyptians, allied to our familiar "tumble-bug." It was supposed to symbolize immortality, the fact that God knew why giving it its peculiar sanctity. Its habit of incubating its eggs in a ball of ordure may also have commended it to the favor of the priesthood, and may some day assure it an equal reverence among ourselves.

Ambrose Bierce

SEAL OF APPROVAL
The Egyptians carved scarab-shaped name seals in a variety of materials.

Desert Locust

Schistocerca gregaria

Native range: North Africa and western Asia

Class: Insect

Size: 3 in (7.5 cm) long

+ EDIBLE
+ MEDICINAL
+ **COMMERCIAL**
+ PRACTICAL

Humans are often accused of despoiling the natural environment with little thought for the future, using up resources as if they were inexhaustible, but even their worst depredations are nothing compared to the damage caused by the arrival of a swarm of hungry locusts.

THE GREGARIOUS GRASSHOPPER

In Aesop's fable "The Ant and the Grasshopper," the ant labors all summer long to store provisions, while the grasshopper kicks back and enjoys itself. As winter sets in, the grasshopper starves and the smug, morally superior ant survives. There you have it kids, work hard or starve! But nature, unlike ancient Greek poetry, is far from being moral or fair, and the harmless-looking grasshopper may not be all that he seems. The word "grasshopper" conjures up images of lazy summer afternoons in the country, the chirping of crickets in the long grass, and childhood chases after hoppers, which though weirdly insectoid, do not sting or buzz annoyingly around the picnic table trying to eat your food. Say "locust," on the other hand, and the image is of trees and fields stripped bare. The two names, however, can be used interchangeably because given the right set of conditions, the solitary desert grasshopper will become the very gregarious desert locust.

Nature makes the locust with an appetite for crops; man would have made him with an appetite for sand.

Mark Twain (1835–1910)

Plagues of locusts have been the terror of humanity since the dawn of farming. Given favorable climatic conditions, the desert locust will breed in huge numbers and gather into swarms many billions strong. Carried by the winds, the swarms can travel thousands of miles to bring desolation to the provident, hard-working ants of neighboring regions. Featured in the Bible as one of the ten plagues sent by God to afflict Egypt, locust swarms are still very much with us, with the last major outbreak occurring in West Africa between 2003 and 2005.

The usual range of the desert locust extends from Mauritania in western Africa, across the Sahara Desert, East Africa, and the Arabian Peninsula, to the arid regions of northwest India. Although this is a huge geographic area, it is sparsely populated with little agricultural activity.

The low rainfall in these areas means that vegetation remains sparse, and locust populations are controlled. The periods of relative locust inactivity are called "recessions." However, with sufficient rainfall in the spring and the resulting increase in the available food supply, large numbers of eggs will hatch into the immature flightless nymph form of the locust, known as "hoppers."

As the hoppers gather to feed, they naturally come into close physical contact. Scientists have worked out that it is when their hind legs bump into one another that the solitary desert grasshopper is transformed into the gregarious desert locust. The changes are both physical and behavioral. The hoppers change color—from green to yellow and black, and adults, from brown to red or yellow depending on their age—and their bodies shorten. They release pheromones that attract them to one another, encouraging the formation of both hopper and adult swarms. The insects become hungrier and breed faster. If optimal climatic conditions persist, the swarms can reach staggering proportions, covering an area of up to 460 square miles (1,200 km²), with a density of between 120 to 240 million insects per square mile.

A swarm of adult locusts can cover between 60 and 120 miles (100–200 km) a day, depending on the prevailing wind, at altitudes of up to 6,500 ft (2,000 m). This means that they cannot cross high mountain ranges such as the Himalayas or the Atlas Mountains. However, locusts will fly across seas. They regularly cross the Red Sea between Arabia and North Africa, and one swarm crossed the Atlantic Ocean from Africa to the West Indies in ten days during the 1987–89 plague. The latest outbreak started in West Africa and lasted from October 2003 to May 2005. The plague began with two days of heavy rain in the fall of 2003, after which the locust population grew rapidly. At its peak in 2004, swarms had reached parts of North and Central Africa, the Near East, the Canary and Cape Verde Islands, and Southern Europe. Despite aggressive measures taken across 20 countries, the outbreak was estimated to have cost US$2.5 billion and led to widespread food shortages.

LA CIGALE ET LA FOURMI. FAB. I.

FABLED
In classical fable, the grasshopper was held up as an exemplar of easy living.

HIGH FLYERS
The fully mature locusts congregate in vast flying swarms billions strong.

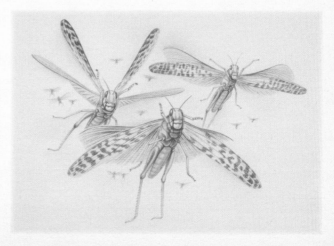

...istosome

Schistosoma mansoni

Native range: Worldwide

Class: Trematode

Size: 0.2–0.3 in
(0.6–1 cm) long

+ EDIBLE
+ *MEDICINAL*
+ COMMERCIAL
+ PRACTICAL

BODYSNATCHER
The schistosome parasite
burrows through the skin of
its host to reach the
bloodstream.

Although schistosomiasis affects over 200 million people in the developing world and kills 200,000 victims annually, it is a largely unreported epidemic. Few have even heard of the *Schistosoma* parasite whose complex lifecycle triggers the disease in humans.

THE HIDDEN EPIDEMIC

Mention the words "schistosoma trematode" and "schistosomiasis," and most people will look at you with a puzzled expression. Although it does not have the notoriety of malaria or HIV–AIDS, or thankfully their death tolls, schistosomiasis is an epidemic of truly global proportions, with 207 million victims in the poorest countries of the world. According to the World Health Organization (WHO), 700 million people, or one-tenth of the Earth's human population, is currently at risk from the disease. Although the disease does not kill many of its victims, its debilitating effects have a serious economic impact on the areas in which it is endemic. Like malaria, schistosomiasis is an avoidable disease spread by contaminated water supplies, and it is only poverty that condemns millions to suffer.

Schistosomes are long trematode worms, or "flukes," with flattened bodies, hence their alternative name, "flatworms." While many trematodes are hermaphrodites, being both male and female, the schistosomes have two distinct sexes. The smaller male is white with a mouth sucker at one end and foot sucker at the other. The female is thinner, and more tubular in shape, with a darker pigmented body. The schistosome has a complex lifecycle that includes an egg-stage spent in freshwater bodies such as lakes and rivers, a developmental phase in an intermediate invertebrate host, and a final reproductive stage in humans.

There are five schistosome species that infect humans. In this article, we shall deal two representative species, *S. mansoni* and *S. haematobium*, which produce different forms of the disease in humans: intestinal and urinary schistosomiasis. Endemic to Africa, South America, and the West Indies, where the disease is known as "Manson's blood fluke" or "swamp fever," *S. mansoni*'s intermediate host is the *Biomphalaria* genus of freshwater snails, and its final hosts, in addition to humans, include baboons, rodents, and raccoons. *S. haematobium*, also known as the "bladder fluke," which is native to Africa, the Near East, and the Mediterranean basin, was introduced accidentally to India during World War Two. Its intermediate host is the *Bulinus* freshwater snail, and in addition to humans, it is occasionally found in monkeys.

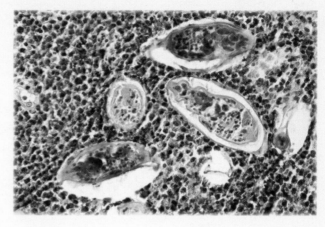

The lifecycles of both schistosomes are similar, but they will ultimately lodge in different parts of the human body. Infected humans excrete the schistosome eggs in their urine and feces. They will hatch into the free-swimming "miracidia" form of the parasite when they reach freshwater. In countries that lack proper sanitation, this means rivers, lakes, and ponds that are also used for bathing and washing. The miracidia first seek out their intermediate host, a freshwater snail, and enter its body through its exposed foot. Inside the snail's body the miracidium turns into a primary "sporocyst," which quickly multiplies. The sporocysts undergo a further transformation in the snail and become "cercariae"—the equivalent of an insect's larval stage. The cercariae are released into the water, where they wait for a mammalian host. They are attracted by water turbulence, changes of light in the water, and the chemicals found on human skin.

When the cercaria locates a host, who may be bathing or washing clothes in the water, it attaches itself to its prey's skin. The head of the cercaria burrows into the upper layers of the skin, discarding the rest of its now useless body. The head then changes into a "schistosomulum," which can remain lodged in the dermis for two days before finding a blood vessel that will enable it to travel into the body. The schistosomulum first goes to the lungs where it continues its metamorphosis, and then migrates to the liver. It takes eight days for *S. mansoni* to complete the journey from skin to liver. The parasite develops its oral sucker in the liver and begins to feed on the host's red blood cells.

DOUBLE WHAMMY

✦

Schistosomiasis has been endemic in Egypt since antiquity. However, the construction of major dam and irrigation works along the Nile during the postwar period exacerbated the epidemic by creating large breeding grounds for the parasite's snail host. Between the 1950s and 1980s victims of the disease were treated with injections. Unfortunately, the campaign unintentionally contributed to the spread of hepatitis C via infected needles.

Chronic schistosomiasis may affect people's ability to work and in some cases can result in death. In sub-Saharan Africa, more than 200,000 deaths per year are due to schistosomiasis.

From the World Health Organization's "Schistosomiasis Factsheet"

At this point the schistosomes mate and pair off, with the male enclosing the female within its own body. The adult pairs then move to their final destinations in the host: *S. mansoni* to the blood vessels of the intestinal wall, and *S. haematobium*, to the blood vessels of the bladder, urethra, and kidneys. After six to eight weeks in the body, the breeding schistosomes begin to produce eggs. *S. mansoni* can produce about 300 eggs a day. Many of its eggs will pass into the intestines to be excreted with the feces, but others will remain trapped in the intestinal blood vessels and in the liver. The eggs of *S. haematobium* are released in the urine, but many remain lodged within the body. Schistosomes live for an average of four to five years, but may survive for as long as 20 years.

SWIMMER'S ITCH

The causes of schistosomiasis were identified in the mid-nineteenth century, and the parasite's full lifecycle was understood in the early twentieth. Examination of mummies by medical archaeologists has shown that schistosomiasis was present in the ancient world, and was a major cause of death among the ancient Egyptians. Today the disease remains a major threat to human health, infecting 207 million people, almost half of whom live in Africa. Many of the victims are children under 14 years of age, who suffer from learning disabilities as a result of the infection.

The damage caused to the human body by chronic schistosoma infections is not from the parasites themselves, but is caused by the body's immune response to the eggs lodged in the body's tissues. The initial symptoms of infection can be an irritation of the skin and a light rash known as "swimmer's itch," which is caused by the penetration of the skin by the head of the cercariae when swimming in infected water. Within two to 12 weeks, the victim may then experience fever (known as "Katayama fever"), fatigue, abdominal pain, cough, and diarrhea, although the infection may also be asymptomatic. The immune response to intestinal schistosomiasis can lead

INFECTED
The parasite's intermediary host, the water snail, is endemic in many of the world's poorer areas.

WATER'S EDGE
Communities located near
infected bodies of water
are at most risk from
schistosomiasis.

to an obstruction of the intestines and blood loss. The individual may
develop an enlarged abdomen, and the swollen intestinal tract can tear
and bleed. Eggs lodged in the liver tissues can lead to a swelling of the
liver and spleen and an impairment of liver function. Genital schistosomiasis can cause genital sores that increase the victim's vulnerability to
that other major killer in sub-Saharan Africa, HIV. Genital cystisis and
urethritis can lead to bladder cancer. In rare cases, victims may suffer
damage to the central nervous system.

Unlike HIV, which is relatively difficult to test for, schistosomiasis
infections are readily identified by the presence of eggs in the feces or
urine of infected persons. Once diagnosed, the infection can be treated
with the administration of an annual dose of the drug praziquantel,
which is inexpensive when compared to treatments for malaria and HIV.
The WHO has established protocols for treating affected communities:
When a village reports that half of its children have blood in their urine,
the entire village is treated; when 20 to 50 percent of children show
symptoms, all school-aged children are treated; and when
the figure drops below 20 percent, mass treatment is not
implemented. In addition to treatment, the other
method used to control schistosomiasis is the elimination of the snails that act as the parasite's intermediate host. This can be achieved through the use of
chemical agents to eliminate the snails; they can also be
controlled through the introduction of predatory species,
such as crayfish.

Pig

Sus domesticus

Native range: Europe, North Africa, and Asia

Class: Mammal

Size: 4–6 ft (1.2–1.8 m) long

+ *EDIBLE*
+ MEDICINAL
+ *COMMERCIAL*
+ *PRACTICAL*

With the pig, we reach the third of the triad of large mammalian species to be harvested for their meat by humans. One of the most widespread mammals of the Old World, the ancestor of the domestic pig, the wild boar, was domesticated independently at least seven times. Although it remains one of the most important food animals in many cultures, the pig is unique in being subject to some of the strictest religious restrictions against the consumption of its flesh.

THE SEVEN TAMINGS OF THE WILD BOAR

In the modern world of agribusiness, three animals are subject to the most intensive farming methods: cattle, chickens, and pigs. As a result, these species have undergone the greatest manipulation by humans to encourage desirable characteristics, historically by selective breeding, and now through genetic engineering. While pork is consumed in huge quantities across the world, as fresh meat, or as processed ham and bacon, it is unique among the major meat animals in that the consumption of its meat is banned by two of the world's leading religious faiths: Judaism and Islam.

The many modern breeds of domestic pig are all descended from the wild hog or boar, which was once one of the most common of mammalian species on earth, with a native range covering Europe, North Africa, the Near East, and Central, South, and East Asia. Unlike horses, cattle, and sheep, whose domestication is thought to have occurred once or twice and then been disseminated throughout the human population, archaeologists believe that the wild boar may have been domesticated independently on seven occasions in different parts of its native range.

The wild boar is a compact animal with a large head and relatively short legs. It is covered in a topcoat of stiff guard hairs over a finer undercoat that varies in color from black or dark brown to gray or almost white. Wild boar piglets have a striped coat for the first six months of their lives. Males (boars) and females (sows) are similar in appearance

WALKING LARDER
The pig has been bred specifically to provide large quantities of meat.

FOREST PIG
Historically, the wild boar
was one of the most
widespread mammal species
in the world.

apart from their teeth. In males, the upper and lower canine teeth grow
into tusks that measure about 2.5 in (6 cm), which they use as weapons
and to dig for food, while in females the canines do not protrude from the
mouth. Adult males are solitary, but sows and their immature offspring
live in groups of 20 to 30 animals known as "sounders," which are led by
a dominant sow. Wild boars are omnivorous, feeding on both vegetable
and animal matter, including carrion and occasional live prey.

Man has hunted wild boar for its meat since prehistoric times, and the
animal's importance is highlighted by its appearance in the legends and
myths of cultures from Scandinavia to China. The boar was a dangerous
adversary for a hunter armed only with a
spear or bow and arrow. A cornered animal
will charge and can injure or kill a human
by goring him with his tusks. In ancient
Greek mythology, several monstrous wild
boars rampaged through Greece, destroying
crops and terrifying the population. The
goddess of the hunt, Artemis (Diana) sent

**And the swine, though he divide the hoof,
and be clovenfooted, yet he cheweth not the
cud; he [is] unclean to you. Of their flesh
shall ye not eat, and their carcase shall ye
not touch; they [are] unclean to you.**
Leviticus 11:7–8

the giant Erymanthian boar to punish the people of Arcadia. Its capture
was one of the 12 labors of Hercules (Herakles). The rather touchy
goddess, displeased that she had not been sufficiently honored by the
king of Aetolia, also sent the Calydonian boar to ravage his kingdom.
This boar was hunted by a band of heroes, including several of the Argonauts, but unusually for a macho Greek myth, it was a heroine, Atalanta,
who drew first blood and was awarded the hide as her prize.

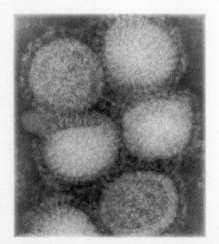

HUNTERS
Several ancient Greek myths feature monstrous boars that killed humans and ravaged crops.

MUTANT
The H1N1 flu virus contains genetic material from human, bird, and swine flu strains.

Archaeologists used to believe that the wild boar was domesticated in two locations: China and Eastern Turkey between 13,000 and 12,000 years BP, and that the practice gradually spread from there to neighboring regions. However, recent studies of the DNA of domesticated pigs present a completely different and unexpected picture that has put into the question all existing theories about animal domestication. When researchers analyzed the DNA of modern pig breeds in different regions, they discovered that they were related to local populations of wild boars. Archaeologists had once believed that Neolithic farmers from Turkey had brought domesticated pigs with them to Europe, but this proved not to be the case as European pigs are most closely related to European wild boars. Therefore, instead of two areas for the initial domestication of the wild boar, the team based at Durham University in the UK have added a further five: Central Europe, Italy, northern India, Southeast Asia, and the islands of Southeast Asia.

THIS SICK LITTLE PIGGY

As with other animals that were domesticated and farmed in the earliest period of the human transition from hunter-gathering to settled agriculture, it has been theorized that wild boars may have played a part in their own domestication. Boars that were less frightened of humans and less aggressive would have been attracted to the waste heaps produced by human settlements, and would have gradually been integrated into human communities in the same way as dogs and cats. The first domesticated pigs were kept for their meat as they are today and also for their hides, for shields, shoes, and containers; bones, for tools and weapons; and bristles for brushes. Before the invention of plastics, pig bristle was the preferred material to make toothbrushes. Domesticated pig breeds have been bred for size and hairlessness, and have lost the tusks of their wild ancestors.

Traditionally, pigs have been farmed by the free-range method, in which they were allowed to roam free under the supervision of swineherds to eat whatever they came across, acting as natural recyclers of human refuse and carrion. But in the modern period they have been farmed intensively in industrialized units, raising both animal welfare issues and health concerns because of the use of antibiotics and growth hormones. Intensively farmed pigs have been identified as reservoirs for the hospital superbug MRSA, and in 2009 the World Health Organization (WHO) declared that the H1N1 strain of swine flu had become a global pandemic. H1N1 is a recombinant virus that includes genetic material from four different flu strains: North American swine flu, North American bird flu, human flu, and Eurasian swine flu. The first outbreak of the disease occurred in Mexico in April 2009, and spread rapidly to the U.S. By October, President Obama had declared H1N1 to be a national emergency. As of May 2010, the WHO reported that the diseases had been confirmed in 214 countries, and that the outbreak had caused over 18,000 deaths from respiratory complications.

VERSATILE
Pork meat can be eaten fresh or processed in many different ways.

In addition to the health risks to humans posed by pigs, the introduction of pigs and wild boars to regions of the world where they were not native has led to major environment degradation and the extinction of local species. Pigs were introduced to North and South America, Australia, New Zealand, and several island groups, including Hawaii, where they quickly established feral populations. They are now listed as one of the hundred worst invasive species. They have been characterized as "major drivers of extinction and ecosystem change," which alter the habitat and trigger "a change in plant succession and composition and a decrease in native fauna dependent on the original habitat."

SPAM, SPAM, SPAM!

Pork meat can be eaten fresh in roasts and stews, but it is also preserved and processed in a variety of different ways. Before the introduction of refrigeration, humans preserved pork by salting or smoking, to produce different types of ham and bacon. Both remain staples of the Western diet, the former being popular in salads and sandwiches, and the latter as one of the main ingredients of the full English breakfast. In continental Europe, pork is the main

ingredient for charcuterie, processed meats that includes pâtés, rillettes, galantines, terrines, confits, salamis, and chorizos. The less adventurous Anglo-Saxon world has produced several varieties of pork sausage, affectionately known in the UK as "bangers," from their propensity to burst and spit when fried. The hotdog, though often thought to be an American invention, dates back to fifteenth-century Germany. Last but not least, chopped pork meat is the main ingredient of processed canned "Spam," a wartime "delicacy" immortalized by *Monty Python's Flying Circus* in their "Spam, Spam, Spam!" sketch.

Despite its popularity and prominence in the culinary traditions of the world, pork is subject to two of the strictest religious prohibitions in Judaism and Islam. According to Mosaic Law, the only meat that can be eaten must come from an animal that is deemed to be "kosher." In order to make the grade, the animal must have a split hoof and chew the cud. While sheep, goats, and cows are kosher because they have a split hoof and are ruminants, camels, horses, and pigs do not pass the kosher test. The pig has split hooves but it does not chew the cud. The Jewish prohibition of pork was adopted by some Christian churches, in particular the Orthodox tradition of Eastern Christianity, and by Islam. The Holy Qur'an states unequivocally:

DIAMONDS IN THE ROUGH

✦

Truffles are a rare kind of edible underground fungus, much in demand in gourmet cookery circles (and therefore extremely overpriced for something that grows in the dirt), which are used as an ingredient in pasta, salads, and meat dishes. In Europe pigs are trained to hunt for truffles, which are found underground in woodland areas. Pigs have a keen sense of smell and are good diggers, and they can find truffles buried as deep as 3 ft (1 m) underground. One theory suggests that they are attracted to the fungus because its smell is similar to that of their own sex hormones.

He hath only forbidden you dead meat, and blood, and the flesh of swine, and that on which any other name hath been invoked besides that of Allah. But if one is forced by necessity, without willful disobedience, nor transgressing due limits, then is he guiltless. For Allah is Oft-forgiving Most Merciful.

Historians and social scientists have put forward several theories why these two religions originating in the Near East share this common abhorrence for pork. The first argues that pigs are ecologically unsuited to the conditions in the Near East, where they would compete for food and water with humans; the second is that the people of the region did not eat pork, and that the prohibition is merely a religious codification of an existing state of affairs; and the third, more specific to Judaism, is that the pig is associated with the gentile occupation of Palestine by the Greeks and Romans, and the Roman desecration of the Temple of Jerusalem. While possible, these explanation lack plausibility. The great medieval Jewish philosopher and scholar Maimonides (1135–1204) put forward what is to my mind the most likely explanation. He suggested that the meat of animals that were considered nonkosher was indigestible or unhealthy. Although he conceded that pork was far from inedible, he argued that because pigs eat carrion and human waste their meat must be unclean.

Maimonides was certainly correct that eating pork could be injurious to human health, as, in addition to the health concerns listed above, it carries an unusually large number of pathogens and parasites. The microorganisms that are found in un- or undercooked pork include *Listeria monocytogenes*, *E. coli*, Salmonella, *Yersinia enterocolitica*, and *Staphylococcus aureus*. In addition to these bacterial nasties, pork is also a carrier of roundworm, hookworm, pinworm, and tapeworm. The two most dangerous parasitic infections transmitted by pork are Trichinosis, caused by a species of roundworm, and Cysticercosis, caused by the tapeworm *Taenia solium*. After the introduction of strict food hygiene regulations and inspection standards, these diseases have been all but eliminated in the developed world, but they are still relatively common in parts of China, Southeast Asia, India, sub-Saharan Africa, and Latin America.

FAIRYTALE
Like other important edible species, the pig features in many folktales.

Oriental Rat Flea

Xenopsylla cheopis

Native range: Asia

Class: Insect

Size: 0.01 in (2.5 mm) long

+ EDIBLE
+ **MEDICINAL**
+ COMMERCIAL
+ PRACTICAL

The animal that has most changed the course of history (apart from ourselves, of course) is not the cow, the horse, or the sheep, but the flea. In the past 1,200 years, the oriental rat flea has been responsible for three pandemics that have killed hundreds of millions, and each time set human civilization on a new course.

CHAMPION HIGH JUMPER

When people have nightmares about being attacked by animals, it is usually about the larger carnivorous species: bears, wolves, big cats, sharks, and crocodiles. Granted, being torn limb from limb and eaten alive is not a pleasant experience for the individual concerned; however, as a species, the animal we should be really terrified of is not a large mammal, fish, or reptile—it is the diminutive flea. If any animal has ever come close to wiping out the human species, it is the oriental rat flea,

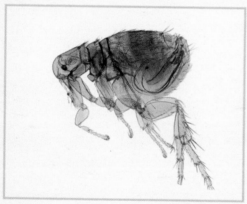

LONG JUMPER
The flightless flea depends on its prodigious jumping ability to find its hosts.

which has been the vector for outbreaks of a disease so terrible that it has gone down in history simply as the "Black Death" or the "Great Plague." Although the medieval Black Death is the best-known outbreak of bubonic plague, it is one of three major pandemics that have swept across the globe between the sixth and twentieth centuries, killing millions and changing the course of human history in the process. The flea, its rodent hosts, and the plague pathogen *Yersinia pestis* have been around millions of years, but what made them into a particularly deadly combination was when humans began to settle and live in villages, towns, and cities around 10,000 years ago.

The flea is a small wingless insect that is grayish-brown in color. It is covered in short spiny hairs directed backward that ease its passage through its host's fur or clothing. The flea's body, as anyone who has tried to kill one will testify, is extremely tough and can resist considerable pressure. One way to kill or, at least, disable a flea, is to squash it between two fingernails. Although the flea cannot fly, it has a prodigious jumping ability. The champion high jumper of the natural world, it uses its powerful hind legs to jump up to 7 in (18 cm) horizontally, and up to 13 in (33 cm) vertically. The flea's mouthparts are a tube through which it sucks blood from its host, and in the process also washes back saliva and undigested blood into the wound, thereby transmitting any pathogens that the flea carries. In addition to the plague bacillus, the flea is also an intermediate host for a species of tapeworm, and like the louse, it is a carrier for epidemic typhus.

The flea, like most other insects, has a four-stage lifecycle of egg, larva, pupa, and adult. The female flea lays her microscopic white eggs in batches of 20 on the host, but these do not attach to the host's skin or fur but fall to the ground. In favorable conditions, the eggs will hatch after two to ten days. The larvae are small blind worms that feed on dead skin cells, flea droppings, and other small parasites. When the larva has matured, it spins a cocoon around itself in order to pupate. The pupa stage of the flea can last for anything from a week to six months depending on the environmental conditions. The ideal temperature for a flea to emerge from pupation is between 68 and 77°F (20–25°C) with 70 percent humidity, but the pupa can survive for up to a year if conditions are not right, which makes infestations particularly difficult to control. The young adult flea needs to find a blood meal within one week in order to survive and breed. It locates a host by smelling the carbon dioxide that it exhales. Once fully mature, however, an adult flea can survive for several months without feeding.

AN EMPIRE DIVIDED

If you say bubonic plague, most people will think of the fourteenth-century outbreak known as the Black Death. But the Black Death was the second pandemic outbreak of bubonic plague to affect the civilized world.

The first, which began in the sixth century and continued until the eighth, is known as the "Plague of Justinian," after the Byzantine emperor Justinian I (483–565 CE), during whose reign the plague struck Constantinople, the capital of the Eastern Roman Empire.

For 500 years, the Roman Empire controlled the Mediterranean basin from Spain to Egypt. As the Empire grew larger, more populous, and more complex, it became ever more difficult to govern from the ancient

VICTIMS
The religious were badly
hit as they provided
medical care to plague
sufferers.

capital, Rome. In the fourth century, Constantine I, the Great (272–337 CE), founded a New Rome in the East, the city of Constantinople, beginning a process that would lead to the division of the empire into two halves. The last emperor to rule both the Eastern and Western empires was Theodosius I (347–395 CE). Soon after his death, the Western Empire went into terminal decline, as barbarians poured across its frontiers to establish their own kingdoms in former Roman provinces, and finally came to an end with the abdication of the last emperor in 476 CE.

Even then, however, the emperors in Constantinople refused to accept that the Western Empire had been lost for good. For the next several centuries, they worked to reconquer the West. Justinian I came closest to restoring the unity of the Roman world when he regained North Africa, parts of Spain, and most of Italy from their barbarian rulers. But then disaster struck. In 541 CE, the plague arrived in Constantinople, transported on grain ships from Egypt infested with rats whose fleas carried the disease. At its height, the plague was killing between 5,000 and 10,000 people a day in Constantinople. Historians estimate that up to 40 percent of the city's population and 25 percent of the population of the eastern Mediterranean perished in the initial outbreak. The first plague pandemic continued until the mid-eighth century, with repeated instances of the disease that further weakened the empire.

Had the plague not struck at this critical juncture, and we imagine that the Eastern and Western empires had been reunited under Byzantine rule, the damaging schism between the Greek Orthodox and Roman Catholic Churches might not have taken place, and a stronger, united Christendom might have been able to better resist the rise of Islam and the Arab invasions of the seventh century. World history might then have followed a very different course, and you might be reading this book in either Latin or Greek.

BRING OUT YOUR DEAD!

While this is a fascinating "what if" scenario, of course, it never happened. Spool forward eight centuries, and the situation in the Mediterranean world was completely different: The eastern Roman Empire was a shadow of its former self—little more than the city of Constantinople—hemmed in to the south and east by rising Turkish states, and to the west and north by expansionist European powers. Europe in the early fourteenth century, however, for all its apparent energy and self-confidence, was a civilization in deep crisis. Overpopulation combined with a sudden cooling in the climate led to widespread famines; society was ossified and dominated by an oppressive feudal nobility and a repressive church that allowed no freedom of thought to a peasantry that was tied to the land by custom, force, and superstition; Europe was embroiled in constant dynastic wars; and in the east, militant Islam was on the rise once more.

How many valiant men, how many fair ladies, breakfast with their kinfolk and the same night supped with their ancestors in the next world! The condition of the people was pitiable to behold. They sickened by the thousands daily, and died unattended and without help.

Giovanni Boccaccio on the Black Death (1313–75)

At this second turning point in European history, the plague struck once more. In 1346, the Mongols laid siege to the Genoese trading port of Caffa on the Black Sea. In the fourteenth century, the Mongols ruled a vast empire that stretched from China to the Near East, allowing free passage to the plague-carrying oriental rat flea and its rodent hosts with the caravans that traveled along the Silk Road from China to the Levant.

OUTBREAKS
Plague outbreaks continued to ravage Europe until the seventeenth century.

When the plague broke out in the besieging army, the Mongols catapulted infected corpses over Caffa's city walls as an early form of biological warfare. The Genoese merchants took to their ships and fled back to Europe, carrying the plague with them, first to Constantinople in 1347, and then to Southern Europe in 1348. The population of Europe, already weakened by decades of war and famine, and without the medical knowledge and technology to protect itself, had no defense against this second bubonic plague pandemic.

The effects of the Black Death were immediate and catastrophic. There are no exact statistics for the death toll from the pandemic, but estimates derived from period sources vary from 75 to 200 million deaths from the outbreaks during the fourteenth century alone. The medievalist Philip Daileader suggested that about half of the European population perished between 1348 and 1351, although mortality rates varied greatly from region to region. He estimated that the death toll might have been as high as 75 to 80 percent in Italy, Spain, and the South of France, while mortality in England and Germany might have been closer to 20 percent. The overcrowded, unsanitary cities of medieval Europe were the worst affected, with half of the population of Paris, Florence, and Hamburg perishing in the initial outbreak, while more sparsely populated rural areas had much lower mortality rates. Priests and members of the monastic orders were hit particularly hard as they provided the only care for plague victims.

To the medieval mind, an epidemic must have either been the work of an angry God or of evil men. Groups of religious fanatics, known as the "flagellants" from the whips they carried to flagellate themselves, attempted to assuage divine anger by shedding their own blood. Others blamed the Jews, accusing them of spreading the plague by poisoning wells, which led to massacres of Jewish communities all over Western Europe. The initial phase of the pandemic burned itself out in 1351, but outbreaks of the disease continued to hit Europe for the next 200 years, with the last major incidence—the "Great Plague of London"— striking the English capital in 1665–66.

The extinction of half of the population might have led to the early demise of Western European civilization, just as the Plague of Justinian had brought an end to the dream of a reunited Roman world. Europe, however, not only survived the Black Death but it emerged reinvigorated. The sudden collapse in population broke the vicious cycle of famine, falling agricultural productivity, and economic stagnation that had afflicted the first half of the fourteenth century. Historians point to the period after the Black Death as the starting point of Western capitalism. Labor was in short supply, and peasants, once tied to the land, were now hired for wages, which led to the monetization of the economy, and improved living standards; the high mortality rates across all classes increased social mobility; and the failure of the Church to avert the disaster put its absolute authority into question. Together these factors would lead to the flowering of art, philosophy, science, and technology known as the European Renaissance.

As for the oriental rat flea, it remains blithely oblivious to the death and destruction it has unwittingly brought down on the human species these past 12 centuries. It caused a third bubonic plague pandemic, which lasted just over a century from 1855 to 1959, and killed millions in China and India. Now introduced to every corner of the globe by humans, the plague flea caused 362 human cases in the western U.S. between 1944 and 1993. Although now dormant, the plague is still with us, and after the discovery of an antibiotic-resistant strain of the disease in Madagascar in 1995, the Black Death could conceivably once again become a major threat to human health.

QUACK

+

The bacterial origin of the Black Death would not be understood until the discovery of germ theory in the nineteenth century. In the Middle Ages, doctors believed that diseases were caused by an imbalance of the four humors (see Leech, pp. 104–109), triggered by environmental factors, and that epidemics were spread by miasma (bad air). To protect himself, the plague doctor, known as a "beak doctor" because of his sinister costume, wore a floor-length coat, leggings, boots, gloves, and hat made of waxed leather. But the oddest part of the outfit was a mask in the shape of a bird's head, complete with a long curved beak. The mask was a kind of primitive respirator, and the beak was packed with dried flowers, herbs, spices, and camphor, that were believed to prevent contagion from the evil smells of the plague.

Human

Homo sapiens

Native range: East Africa

Class: Mammal

Size: 4–7 ft (1.4–2 m) in height

+ EDIBLE
+ MEDICINAL
+ COMMERCIAL
+ PRACTICAL

Humans are the most successful mammals to have evolved on planet Earth—so successful that they may one day exhaust the natural resources that sustain their continued population increase. Humans have colonized every climatic zone from the Equator to the Arctic, not by adapting physiologically to these environments, but by adapting to them culturally and technologically. Since their appearance, humans have changed the natural environment to suit their own needs—creating new landscapes, populated by domesticated plant and animal species. As of the twenty-first century, with the decoding of the human genome, humans are now on the threshold of the next evolutionary step for the species, when they will take full control of their own evolution.

NEW KIDS ON THE BLOCK

At the time of writing there are almost seven billion humans on the planet, with seemingly no limit to the species' exponential growth. Although humans are not the most numerous animals, as invertebrates (insects, worms, etc.) outnumber them many times to one, they are the most successful of the larger animal species—bird, reptile, fish, or mammal—to have ever colonized the earth. With the exception of Antarctica, humans settled every continent and climatic zone of the planet in prehistoric times. And unlike many of the animal species that we have seen in this book that have adapted physiologically to their environments, humans adapted culturally and technologically to new ecological niches.

What is perhaps even more remarkable is that the genus *Homo* to which modern humans belong is barely 2.5 millions years old. Compared to many of the species featured in this book, humans really are the new kids on the block. And if we are to believe the creationist theory of human origins, we are even younger. According to the literal interpretation of Genesis by Bishop James Ussher (1581–1656), God began creating the cosmos at nightfall on the eve of Sunday, October 23, 4004 BCE. He fashioned humanity out of clay "in his own image" on the sixth day. Alternatively, according to paleontology and anthropology, humans and their nearest living relatives, the great apes, began to diverge between eight and four million years BP. The human lineage is usually reckoned to begin with the African australopithecines, which

ASCENT
Modern humans are the result of a 2.5 million-year evolutionary journey.

appeared around 4.1 million years BP. If we met them today, we would acknowledge australopithecines as humanlike, but definitely not as human. They exhibited a strange mixture of human and apelike characteristics; short in stature, with small brain cases, and covered in hair, they were nevertheless bipedal tool users, although their tools were probably very simple objects like the ones made and used by chimps today.

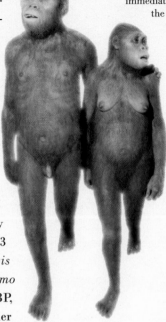

Scroll forward 1.7 million years, and the first member of the genus *Homo* bursts onto the African scene: *Homo habilis*, meaning "handy man," named for his ability to make and use stone tools. Although the human evolutionary tree remains fairly cluttered with proto-humans that may or may not be direct ancestors, including *Homo erectus* (1.8–1.3 million years BP) and *Homo neanderthalensis* (350,000–30,000 years BP), modern humans, *Homo sapiens*, emerged from Africa around 250,000 years BP, colonized the entire planet, and supplanted all other members of the genus. What the fossil record shows is a slow evolution of physiological, morphological, and behavioral changes from the apelike australopithecines to more humanlike hominids, who developed larger brains, smaller teeth, more agile hands, and a voice box capable of modulated speech, and created increasingly sophisticated material culture.

Creationist theory, on the other hand, as an article of faith, does not have to account for the fossil and archaeological record that stretches back several millions of years. However, one website, creationwiki, has a rather simple solution to explain away the four-million-year-old hominid family tree. In a rather short entry on human evolution, it defines all pre-*Homo* hominids as apes, and therefore as no relation to modern humans; and all subsequent *Homo* fossils as modern *Homo sapiens*. Hence the Neanderthals, according to creationism, were rather heavy-set humans who needed to shave three times a day.

And God said, Let us make man in our image, after our likeness: and let them have dominion over the fish of the sea, and over the fowl of the air, and over the cattle, and over all the earth, and over every creeping thing that creepeth upon the earth.

Genesis 1:26

THE NEOLITHIC REVOLUTIONARIES

Whether created on the sixth day in Eden, or evolved over 2.5 million years, modern humans took possession of planet Earth a quarter of a million years ago, and spent the next 240,000 years exploring it as nomadic hunter-gatherers, wandering from place to place, following the herds of large herbivores they predated and harvesting plants as they seeded and fruited. But around 10,000 years ago, a man or woman came up with a revolutionary idea. We can imagine that he or she stood up and said, pointing to a particularly nice piece of scenery, "I'm fed up of moving around all the time! Why don't we just settle down here?" In the opinion of certain social scientists, this is where things started to go wrong for humanity (but then some people believe that the first mistake our ancestors made was to come down from the trees).

Life as a member of a band of Neolithic hunter-gatherers would have been fairly egalitarian, as can be seen from the few surviving hunter-gatherer cultures left on earth today, but settled life entails the development of all kinds of social institutions, such as property rights and the division of labor, and a few thousand years on, you're getting up in the morning to go to work in the fields, not for yourself but for some guy who calls himself the king or high priest. There are several theories to account for why humans decided to settle, including the ever-popular climate change and population growth that could no longer be sustained by the hunter-gathering lifestyle, but as written language would not be invented for thousands of years, we will never find a first-hand account of the event. It could be just as likely that ET landed and told our ancestors, "Settle down, build towns, develop technology, and before you know it, you'll be eating TV dinners and listening to Lady Gaga on your iPods."

Archaeologists have proposed seven sites where the Neolithic farming revolution could have taken place between 11,000 and 3,000 years BP: the Fertile Crescent (now Iraq, Israel, Jordan, Lebanon, Syria, southeast Turkey, and western Iran), central China, highland New Guinea, and sub-Saharan Africa in the Old World, and the eastern U.S., Mexico, and northeast South America in the New World. Humanity's agricultural Garden of Eden is reckoned to be the Fertile Crescent, where humans first grew and harvested the "founder crops" of wheat, barley, peas, lentils, chickpeas, and flax, and also first began to propagate fig trees.

TOOLKIT
Although apes use simple tools, early humans were unique in the amount of elaboration they used in creating their early artefacts.

INNOVATION
Around 10,000 years BP, humans came up with the revolutionary idea of settled agricultural life.

By 10,000–9,000 BP, large-scale agriculture had become established in southern Mesopotamia (now Iraq) and the Nile Valley. At around the same time, the ancient Chinese domesticated rice, millet, and soybeans. Europeans began farming around 9,000 years BP, and the oldest known enclosed fields have been found in Ireland dating back to 7,500 years BP. Farming of wheat, barley, peas, dates, and mangoes began in the Indus Valley civilization (now Pakistan) around 6,000 years BP, and rice and sugar cane cultivation was added around 5,000 years BP. Agriculture in the Americas developed later (5,000–3,000 years BP) and was based on different cropping plants, including the potato, maize, tomato, beans, pepper, and squash.

As humans were establishing settled agricultural communities and domesticating plant species, they were simultaneously domesticating animal species, first for their meat, but later for other products such as milk, leather, and wool, and for their labor as beasts of burden. For millennia, there existed a major division in human lifestyles between settled farmers who planted crops and raised animals, and nomadic pastoralists, who moved from place to place with their herds. The competition between the two lifestyles led to major confrontations from antiquity into historical times, with the conflict between the Native Americans of the Great Plains and European settlers being one of the most recent examples. In the modern world, settled life dependent on agriculture has supplanted hunter-gathering and nomadic pastoralism.

We are the product of 4.5 billion years of fortuitous, slow biological evolution. There is no reason to think that the evolutionary process has stopped. Man is a transitional animal. He is not the climax of creation.

Dr. Carl Sagan (1934–96)

NEOLITHIC NEW YORK

Once humans had decided to settle, they did so in style. One of the earliest known cities—the Neolithic New York—was Çatalhöyük in southern Anatolia, Turkey—established some 9,500 years BP, it remained in constant occupation for the next 1,800 years. Even by today's standards, Çatalhöyük was not just a one-horse town: Archaeologists estimate that it had a population of between 5,000 and 10,000 inhabitants. If we were transported back to Çatalhöyük in its heyday, we would be struck by two major differences with our own cityscapes: there were no obvious public buildings, such as palaces or temples, and there were no streets or footpaths between the buildings.

Downtown Çatal consisted of mud-brick houses that were packed tightly together like the cells in a honeycomb. The rooftops would have served as the city's streets and plazas, and it is probable that in good weather communal life was led on the outside, where remains of communal food ovens have been found. The front "doors" of the houses were, in fact, holes in the ceiling, linked to the floor below by ladders or simple staircases. The opening in the roof also served as a window to let air and light in and as a chimney to let smoke out.

BEEHIVE
The city of Çatalhöyük (top) had no streets or public buildings. The "front doors" of its houses were holes in the roofs accessed by stairs or ladders (bottom).

The typical Çatal house consisted of one main room with several ancillary storerooms. The stairs, hearths, and ovens were located on the south wall—a logical arrangement to let the smoke out. The main living area was furnished in what we'd call minimalist style with raised platforms, which were probably used for sleeping, arts and crafts, and other daily activities. Both the walls and platforms were plastered to a smooth finish. The decorative scheme was completed with vivid murals showing sexually aroused men, hunting scenes, aurochs (wild cattle) and other animals, as well as relief figures carved out of the walls and mounted aurochs heads.

Like us, the people of Çatal were house-proud. Very little refuse was found inside their houses, and waste was taken to garbage heaps outside the settlement. This would have protected the inhabitants from the dangers of disease and also controlled vermin. However, in one respect, they were very different from us: when our nearest and dearest die, we bury or cremate them, and in most cases the remains are left in a cemetery, but the people of Çatal liked to stay close to their ancestors. They buried their dead inside their houses, under the floors, platforms, and hearths. The bodies were not buried immediately, and they were probably left in the open air to decompose, and the bones were then interred inside the houses of their descendants. When the house needed renewing, instead of tearing it down and rebuilding, the people of Çatal filled the old house with rubble and mud bricks and used it as the foundation for their new homes. Considering the close proximity of the dwellings, rebuilding must have been a communal activity. In all, there are 18 successive settlement levels in the city.

The absence of public buildings and of larger houses that could have been the homes of an elite has led archaeologists to conclude that Çatal was an egalitarian society with little or no class distinctions. An analysis of burials and skeletal remains shows that men and women were treated equally, and that the genders in Neolithic Çatal were probably far more equal than they would be in later historical periods. The site has yielded many images and figurines, which suggest that, although the town had no separate places of worship, the citizens had a rich religious life, possibly based around the cult of a Mother Goddess.

The people of Çatal were farmers who grew wheat, barley, and peas, and harvested fruits and nuts from the trees in the surrounding hills. They kept sheep and may have also kept aurochs, the ancestors of our own domestic cattle. However, it is likely that hunting provided them with much of their protein and fat requirements. They used pottery for cooking and eating utensils, storage containers, religious icons, and decoration, and they fashioned tools from the hard black stone obsidian. There is evidence that they engaged in trade with other communities, exchanging their produce and tools for seashells and flints from Syria further south. From the above description, Çatalhöyük might be a lot of people's ideal town—a small, tightly knit, egalitarian community, where people lived, farmed, hunted, prayed, and died in close proximity to one another.

PREHISTORIC HOBBITS

✦

Scientists are discovering that the human family tree has many side branches leading to evolutionary dead ends. In 2004, a possible new species of human was discovered in a cave (shown below) on the island of Flores in Indonesia. The defining characteristic of *Homo floresiensis* is its small stature.

EVOLUTION
The deciphering of the
human genome will allow
humans to take control of
their own evolution.

We shall never know whether the people of Çatalhöyük were less, just as, or more happy than the men and women of twenty-first-century cities like London, New York, Delhi, or Beijing. It would be nice to imagine that they were, and that there was one blissful time in human history when humans lived quite contentedly at peace with one another, only taking from the planet what they needed.

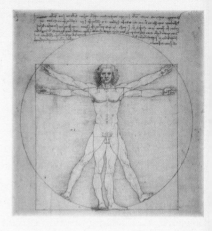

However, as soon as recorded history began a few thousand years later, we get a glimpse of far darker times for humanity. Examine the records of any civilization from ancient China to the super-technological present, and you will find a tragic catalog of wars, genocides, famines, epidemics, and manmade and natural disasters that rival the script of any big-budget disaster movie.

HUMAN BLUEPRINT

✦

Ever since human DNA was first successfully described in 1953, researchers have dreamed of completing the full genetic map, or "genome," of a human being. The task was a formidable one: the human haploid genome consists of just over three billion DNA base pairs that make up the 23,000 protein-coding genes stored on 23 chromosome pairs. The Human Genome Project, an international effort conducted by geneticists based in the U.S., UK, France, Germany, China, and Japan, completed the initial sequence in 2003. The cracking of the human genetic code enables us to under-stand our own biology at the molecular level, which has already led to the first gene therapies, and opens up the possibility of control-ling the evolution of our own and other animal species.

FUTURE SHOCK

According to many futurologists, humans have already reached the point of no return in terms of climate change and the exhaustion of resources such as hydro-carbons and rare metals, putting a serious question mark on the sustainability of technological civiliza-tion. Environmentalists warn that humanity's constant population growth and the resulting expan-sion of agriculture is now the major driver of species' extinctions, reducing the biodiversity of the planet and making it vulnerable to an ecological catastrophe. However, the one thing that we can say with any certainty about the predictions of futurologists is that, based on past experience, they have always been wrong. The natural randomness of the universe, combined with human creativity, has so far allowed humanity to overcome any disaster, and not only survive but thrive.

Looking back at the 49 animal species that are featured in this book, we can see that humans have been transforming animals for the past 20,000 years, reshaping them through selective breeding to suit their own needs. At the same time, directly through the expansion of agriculture or indirectly through such by-products of our its development such as pollution and climate change, humanity has become the major driver of animal evolution, deciding which species survive and which are condemned to extinction. Although the ideal might be to turn back the clock to a stage in human history when civilization had a less damaging effect on the natural environment, this would mean condemning billions either to death or to a much poorer lifestyle than the citizens of the developed world have enjoyed since the advent of industrial civilization.

Realistically, we have only one choice, which is to continue on the path that we have always followed. The secret of humanity's success since the Neolithic Revolution 10,000 years ago is that it has taken control of the natural environment through culture and technology. Humans did not adapt to the environments they colonized, they changed the environments to suit themselves. And now that humanity has deciphered its own genetic code, it is about to embark on the next stage of human evolution that may see the elimination of disease, aging, and perhaps of death itself.

Although the existing races of man differ in many respects, as in colour, hair, shape of skull, proportions of the body, &c., yet if their whole organisation be taken into consideration they are found to resemble each other closely in a multitude of points. Many of these points are of so unimportant or of so singular a nature, that it is extremely improbable that they should have been independently acquired by aboriginally distinct species or races. The same remark holds good with equal or greater force with respect to the numerous points of mental similarity between the most distinct races of man.

Charles Darwin, The Descent of Man *(1871)*

INTERIOR DESIGN
In addition to their stone tools, our distant ancestors left vivid cave paintings of the animals they once hunted.

Further Reading

Attenborough, David (1998)
  The Life of Birds, London: BBC

Attenborough, David (2002)
  The Life of Mammals, London: BBC

Attenborough, David (2010) *Life Stories*,
  London: BBC

Barnett, S. Anthony (2002)
  *The Story of Rats: Their Impact on Us,
  and Our Impact on Them*, London:
  Allen & Unwin

Beckwith, Christopher (2011)
  *Empires of the Silk Road: A History
  of Central Eurasia from the Bronze Age
  to the Present*, Princeton, NJ:
  Princeton University Press

Budiansky, Stephen (1992)
  *The Covenant of the Wild:
  Why Animals Chose Domestication*,
  New York: W. Morrow

Clements, James (2000) *Birds of the World*,
  Vista, CA: Ibis

Cocker, Mark and Mabey, Richard
  (2005) *Birds Britannica*, London:
  Chatto & Windus

Cocker, Mark and Mabey, Richard
  (2010) *Bugs Britannica*, London:
  Chatto & Windus

Coren, Stanley (2003) *The Pawprints of
  History: Dogs and the Course of Human
  Events*, New York: Free Press

Crane, Ethel Eva (1999) *The World History
  of Beekeeping and Honey Hunting*,
  New York: Routledge

Darwin, Charles (2004) *The Descent
  of Man*, London: Penguin

Darwin, Charles (2009) *The Voyage
  of the Beagle*, Washington, DC: National
  Geographic

Darwin, Charles (2009 [1859])
  On the Origin of Species, Cambridge:
  Cambridge University Press

Dolin, Eric (2008) *Leviathan:
  The History of Whaling in America*,
  New York: W.W. Norton

Donkin, R.A. (1998) *Beyond Price: Pearls
  and Pearl-Fishing: Origins to the Age of
  Discoveries*, Philadelphia, PA: Memoirs
  of the American Philosophical Society

Ekarius, Carol (2008) *Storey's Illustrated
  Breed Guide to Sheep, Goats, Cattle and
  Pigs: 163 Breeds from Common to Rare*,
  North Adams, MA: Storey Publishing

Girardet, Herbert (2008) *Cities People
  Planet: Urban Development and Climate
  Change*, Oxford: John Wiley & Sons

Goodall, Jane and Redmond, Ian
  (2010) *Primates of the World*, London:
  New Holland Publishers

Greenberg, Paul (2010) *Four Fish:
  The Future of the Last Wild Food*,
  New York: Penguin

Greenfield, Amy Butler (2005)
  *A Perfect Red: Empire, Espionage
  And The Quest For The Colour Of Desire*,
  New York: Harper Collins

Hamilton, Gary (2010) *Super Species*,
  Richmond Hill, Ontario: Firefly

Hoare, Philip (2011) *The Whale:
  In Search of the Giants of the Sea*,
  New York: Ecco

Hodder, Ian (2006) *Çatalhöyük:
  The Leopard's Tale*, London:
  Thames & Hudson

Hudson, Pat (2002) *The Genesis of
  Industrial Capital: A Study of West
  Riding Wool Textile Industry,
  c.1750–1850*, Cambridge: Cambridge
  University Press

Irwin, Robert (2010) *Camel*, London:
  Reaktion Books

Johns, Catherine (2011) *Cattle:
  History, Myth, Art*, London: British
  Museum Press

Johns, Catherine (2006) *Horses:
  History, Myth, Art*, Cambridge, MA:
  Harvard University Press

Kelekna, Pita (2009) *The Horse in Human
  History*, Cambridge: Cambridge
  University Press

Kistler, John M. (2005) *War Elephants*,
  Westport, CN: Greenwood Press

Lewis-Williams, David and Pearce, David
  (2009) *Inside the Neolithic Mind:
  Consciousness, Cosmos and the Realm of
  the Gods*, London: Thames & Hudson

Liu, Xinru (2010) *The Silk Road in World
  History*, New York: Oxford University
  Press U.S.A.

Lloyd, T.H. (2005) *The English Wool Trade
  in the Middle Ages*, Cambridge:
  Cambridge University Press

Macdonald, David (2009) *The Princeton
  Encyclopedia of Mammals*, Princeton,
  NJ: Princeton University Press

Anton, Mauricio (2000) *The Big Cats
  and Their Fossil Relatives: An Illustrated
  Guide to Their Evolution and Natural
  History*, New York: Columbia
  University Press

McGavin, George (2002) *Smithsonian
Handbooks: Insects*, New York: Dorling
Kindersley

McGhee, Karen and McKay, George (2006)
*National Geographic Encyclopedia of
Animals*, Washington, DC: National
Geographic

Mithen, Steven (2006) *After the Ice:
A Global Human History 20,000–5000
BC*, Cambridge, MA: Harvard
University Press

Mobini, Seyedmehdi (2006) *Goat
Handbook*, Hauppauge, NY: Barron's
Educational

Nickell, Nancy (1999) *Nature's Aphrodisiacs*, Freedom, CA: Crossing Press

Ostling, Brutus (2008) *Kingdom of the
Eagle*, London: A & C Black

Palmer, Douglas and Barrett,
Peter (2009) *Evolution: The Story
of Life*, Berkeley, CA: University of
California Press

Paul, Gregory (2010) *Dinosaurs*, London:
A&C Black

Sturm, C.F., Pearce, T.A., and Valdes, A.
(2006) *The Mollusks: A Guide to Their
Study, Collection, and Preservation*,
Piscataway, NJ: Transaction

Ucko, Peter and Dimbleby, G. (2007)
*The Domestication and Exploitation of
Plants and Animals*, Boca Raton, FL:
Universal Publishers

Zimmer, Carl (2001) *Parasite Rex:
Inside the Bizarre World of Nature's
Most Dangerous Creatures*,
New York: Free Press

Useful websites

American Museum of
Natural History
www.amnh.org

Animal domestication
www.archaeology.about.com

American Society for the
Prevention of Cruelty to
Animals
www.aspca.org

British Museum
www.britishmuseum.org

Conservation International
www.conservation.org

Creationwiki
www.creationwiki.org

Darwin (complete works) online
www.darwin-online.org.uk

Encyclopaedia Britannica online
www.britannica.com

Food and Agriculture
Organization (U.S.)
www.fao.org

Food and Drug
Administration (U.S.)
www.fda.gov

Greenpeace
www.greenpeace.org.uk

Insects and Bugs on the Web
www.insects.org

London Zoological Gardens
www.zsl.org

National Aquarium, Baltimore
www.aqua.org

National Geographic
www.nationalgeographic.com

Natural History Museum
www.nhm.ac.uk

Royal Society for the Prevention
of Cruelty to Animals
www.rspca.org.uk

Royal Society for the
Protection of Birds
www.rspb.org.uk

Smithsonian Institution
www.si.edu

United Nations Environment
Program
www.unep.org

UNESCO
www.unesco.org

United States Department of
Agriculture
www.usda.gov

World Health Organization
www.who.int

World Wildlife Fund
www.wwf.org

Wikipedia
www.en.wikipedia.org

Index

A

Abraham 147

Abulcasis 108

Adams, Richard:
  Watership Down 141

Aesop 192

Agnus Dei 147

Alexander the Great
  79, 122–3

*Alice's Adventures in
  Wonderland* (Carroll) 183

Allen, Woody 171

alpaca 40, 116, 118

Amenhotep III 190

American buffalo 22–5

Andean civilization 118

Angora goat 54

Angora rabbit 140

annelids 104

Anning, Mary 111–12

Anopheles gambiae 8–11

aphrodisiacs 128–9

Apis mellifera 12–17

Aqua Tofana 129

aquila 102–3

Archaeopteryx 90

Aristotle 96

Artemis (deity) 199

Ashurbanipal 155

Atalanta 199

Atlantic cod 88–9

Atlantic herring 60–1

Attenborough, David 125

aurochs 35, 168, 214

Austin, Greg 83

avian flu 95

Avicenna 108

Ayurvedic medicine 106

Aztecs 23, 24, 66, 75,
  80, 101, 131

B

Balaclava, Battle of (1854)
  80

Balaenoptera acutorostrata 18–21

bald eagle 100–3

barber surgeons 109

Bardot, Brigitte 167

Barnum, P. T. 124

Basilosaurus 19

Bast (deity) 86

bat 174–7

Bateson, William 70–1

Batman 177

"beak doctors" 209

beaver, North American 56–9

bee 12–17

beeswax 16

Belloc, Hilaire 119

Bierce, Ambrose
  105, 131, 132, 191

Bivalvia 168–73

Biobreeding Diabetes
  Prone rat 187

Bison bison 22–5

Black Death
  86–7, 204, 205–9

bladder fluke 195

Boccaccio, Giovanni 207

Bolinus brandaris 26–7

Bombyx mori 28–33

Bos taurus 34–9

Botai people 78

Browning, Robert:
  "The Pied Piper" 184

Bryson, Bill 39

bubonic plague *see* Black Death

Buckland, William 111, 112

Buddhism 31, 134, 137, 156

buffalo, American 22–5

Bugs Bunny 141

bullfighting 38

Butler, Samuel 95

Byron, Lord George 176–7

C

Cabot, John 88

Caesar, Julius 122

camel 40–3

camelids 40

Camelus dromedarius 40–3

Canis lupus subsp. 44–7

C. l. familiaris 48–51

Capra hircus 52–5

capybara 59

carp 64–5

Carroll, Lewis:
  *Alice's Adventures in
  Wonderland* 183

cashmere 54

Castor canadensis 56–9

castoreum 58–9

cat 84–7

Çatalhöyük, Anatolia 214–16

cataphracts 79

Chaplin, Henry, 1st Viscount Chaplin
  200

"Charge of the Light Brigade" (1854)
  80

chariots 79

Charlemagne 103

chicken 90–5

Chikungunya 8

chimpanzee 148–51

Chiroptera 174–7

Clodius (Publius Clodius
  Pulcher) 94

cloning 146

Clupea harengus 60–1

cobra 134–7

cochineal 66–7

cockfighting 92, 94

cod, Atlantic 88–9

Cody, "Buffalo Bill" 24, 25

Colony Collapse Disorder 12, 17

Columba spp. 62–3

Columbus, Christopher 72

conquistadors, the
  24, 37, 72–3, 119

IMAGE CREDITS